Rome, Season Two

Screening Antiquity

Series Editors: Monica S. Cyrino and Lloyd Llewellyn-Jones

Screening Antiquity is a cutting-edge and provocative series of academic monographs and edited volumes focusing on new research on the reception of the ancient world in film and television. Screening Antiquity showcases the work of the best-established and up-and-coming specialists in the field. It provides an important synergy of the latest international scholarly ideas about the conception of antiquity in popular culture and is the only series that focuses exclusively on screened representations of the ancient world.

Titles available in the series:

Rome *Season Two: Trial and Triumph*
Edited by Monica S. Cyrino

Forthcoming Titles:

Ben-Hur*: The Original Blockbuster*
By Jon Solomon

Cowboy Classics: The Roots of the American Western in the Epic Tradition
By Kirsten Day

STARZ Spartacus*: Reimagining an Icon on Screen*
Edited by Antony Augoustakis and Monica S. Cyrino

Rome, Season Two

Trial and Triumph

Edited by Monica S. Cyrino

EDINBURGH
University Press

Edinburgh University Press Ltd
13 Infirmary Street, Edinburgh, EH1 1LT

www.euppublishing.com

Typeset in 11/13 Sabon by

Servis Filmsetting Ltd, Stockport, Cheshire
and printed and bound in Great Britain by
CPI Group (UK) Ltd, Croydon CR0 4YY

A CIP record for this book is available from the British Library

ISBN 978 1 4744 0027 5 (hardback)
ISBN 978 1 3995 7174 6 (paperback)
ISBN 978 1 4744 0028 2 (webready PDF)
ISBN 978 1 4744 0445 7 (epub)

Contents

PART II SEX AND STATUS

Series Editors' Preface

Screening Antiquity is a new series of cutting-edge academic monographs and edited volumes that present exciting and original research on the reception of the ancient world in film and television. It provides an important synergy of the latest international scholarly ideas about the onscreen conception of antiquity in popular culture and is the only book series to focus exclusively on screened representations of the ancient world.

The interaction between cinema, television, and historical representation is a growing field of scholarship and student engagement; many Classics and Ancient History departments in universities worldwide teach cinematic representations of the past as part of their programmes in Reception Studies. Scholars are now questioning how historical films and television series reflect the societies in which they are made, and speculate on how attitudes towards the past have been moulded in the popular imagination by their depiction in the movies. Screening Antiquity explores how these constructions came about and offers scope to analyse how and why the ancient past is filtered through onscreen representations in specific ways. The series highlights exciting and original publications that explore the representation of antiquity onscreen, and that employ modern theoretical and cultural perspectives to examine screened antiquity, including stars and star text, directors and *auteurs*, cinematography, design and art direction, marketing, fans, and the online presence of the ancient world.

The series aims to present original research focused exclusively on the reception of the ancient world in film and television. In itself this is an exciting and original approach. There is no other book series that engages head-on with both big screen and small screen recreations of the past, yet their integral interactivity is clear to see: film popularity has a major impact on television productions and, for its part, television regularly influences cinema (including film spin-offs of popular television series). This is the first academic series to identify and encourage the holistic interactivity of these two major media institutions, and the first to promote interdisciplinary research in all the fields of Cinema Studies, Media Studies, Classics, and Ancient History.

Screening Antiquity explores the various facets of onscreen creations of the past, exploring the theme from multiple angles. Some volumes will foreground a Classics 'reading' of the subject, analysing the nuances of film and television productions against a background of ancient literature, art, history, or culture; others will focus more on Media 'readings' by privileging the onscreen creation of the past or positioning the film or television representation within the context of modern popular culture. A third 'reading' will allow for a more fluid interaction between both the Classics and Media approaches. All three methods are valuable, since Reception Studies demands a flexible approach whereby individual scholars, or groups of researchers, foster a reading of an onscreen 'text' particular to their angle of viewing.

Screening Antiquity represents a major turning point in that it signals a better appreciation and understanding of the rich and complex interaction between the past and contemporary culture, and also of the lasting significance of antiquity in today's world.

Monica S. Cyrino and Lloyd Llewellyn-Jones
Series Editors

Editor's Acknowledgments

As the editor of this volume, I offer my heartfelt appreciation and admiration to the seventeen cooperative and inspiring contributors who collaborated with me on this project. True to the title of this volume, they stuck with me through both the trials and triumphs of doing the work. Special thanks and recognition are owed to my friend Antony Augoustakis for his exceptional aesthetic sense and technical help with the images used in this volume. My gratitude also goes out to Jonathan Stamp, historical consultant and co-producer of *Rome*, for indulging my many questions about the show and the details of its production. At Edinburgh University Press, I am indebted to Carol MacDonald for her support of this project from the beginning, and to her professional staff, Dhara Patel, Kate Robertson, and James Dale, for their assistance in the production process; I also appreciate the work of the two reviewers of the volume whose comments and suggestions improved it immensely. I am deeply grateful to my friend and co-editor, Lloyd Llewellyn-Jones, for his generous partnership in creating our series, Screening Antiquity. As always, I want to thank my students and colleagues who make the study of classics and popular culture such an entertaining and worthwhile enterprise.

For Chloe

'*amata nobis quantum amabitur nulla*'

Contributors

Monica S. Cyrino is Professor of Classics at the University of New Mexico, USA. Her academic research centers on the reception of the ancient world on screen, and the erotic in ancient Greek poetry. She is the author of *Aphrodite* (Routledge, 2010), *A Journey through Greek Mythology* (Kendall-Hunt, 2008), *Big Screen Rome* (Blackwell, 2005), *In Pandora's Jar: Lovesickness in Early Greek Poetry* (Rowman & Littlefield, 1995); she is the editor of *Screening Love and Sex in the Ancient World* (Palgrave Macmillan, 2013), Rome, *Season One: History Makes Television* (Blackwell, 2008), and co-editor of *Classical Myth on Screen* (Palgrave Macmillan, 2015). She has published numerous articles and book chapters and gives lectures around the world on the representation of classical antiquity on film and television. She has served as an academic consultant on several recent film and television productions.

****

Eran Almagor is Lecturer in General History at Ben Gurion University of the Negev, Israel. His research interests are ancient ethnography and historiography, the image of ancient Persia in Greek literature, ancient biography, and the reception of antiquity in popular culture. He is the co-editor of *Ancient Ethnography: New Approaches* (Bloomsbury, 2013). He has published extensively on Greek imperial authors (Strabo, Josephus, Plutarch) and the reception of the ancient world in modern media (especially comics). His book *Plutarch and the Persica* is forthcoming from Edinburgh University Press.

Antony Augoustakis is Associate Professor of Classics at the University of Illinois, Urbana-Champaign, USA. His research interests include Roman comedy and historiography, Latin imperial epic, women in antiquity, classical reception, and gender theory. He is the author of *Motherhood and the Other: Fashioning Female Power in Flavian*

Epic (Oxford, 2010), and he is the editor of the *Brill Companion to Silius Italicus* (2010), *Ritual and Religion in Flavian Epic* (Oxford, 2013), *Flavian Poetry and its Greek Past* (Brill, 2014), and co-editor of the *Blackwell Companion to Terence* (2013). His current project is a volume on the STARZ *Spartacus* series.

Barbara Weiden Boyd is the Henry Winkley Professor of Latin and Greek at Bowdoin College in Brunswick, Maine, USA. She is the author of *Ovid's Literary Loves: Influence and Innovation in the Amores* (Michigan, 1997), editor of *Brill's Companion to Ovid* (2002), and co-editor of *Approaches to Teaching the Works of Ovid and the Ovidian Tradition* (MLA, 2010). She has written several textbooks on Vergil's *Aeneid*, and her current project is a book on Ovid's reception of the Homeric poems. She is also the Latin editor for the series of Oxford Greek and Latin College Commentaries.

Lee L. Brice is Associate Professor of Ancient History at Western Illinois University, USA, and the President of the Association of Ancient Historians. His research focuses on military unrest in the ancient world and on Corinthian numismatics. He has published three edited volumes on ancient warfare as well as articles and book chapters on military unrest, pedagogy, and experimental history, the Athenian expedition to Sicily, and the coins of Corinth. He serves as the series editor for Brill's *Warfare in the Ancient Mediterranean*. He is completing a monograph on the Roman frontier mutinies of AD 14.

Angeline C. Chiu is Associate Professor of Classics at the University of Vermont, USA. Her research interests include ancient Greek and Roman drama, Latin epic, Ovid in particular, and classical reception in the plays of Shakespeare. She has published articles on Euripides, Lucan, Silius Italicus, Plautus, and the depiction of Hercules on children's television. Her current book project focuses on the representation of women, genre, and Roman identity in Ovid's *Fasti*.

Gregory N. Daugherty is the Shelton H. Short III Professor in the Liberal Arts and Chair of the Department of Classics at Randolph-Macon College in Ashland, Virginia, USA. His research focuses on the reception of classics in American popular culture, especially representations of Cleopatra. He is the co-author of *To Be A Roman: Topics in Roman Culture* (Bolchazy-Carducci, 2007). He has been president of the Classical Association of the Middle West and South, and the Classical Association of Virginia.

Kirsten Day is Associate Professor of Classics at Augustana College in Rock Island, Illinois, USA. Her interest in classical receptions has led to the publication of articles on epics and Western cinema, the portrayal of Olympias in films on Alexander, and the depiction of female possession in the horror genre. She is the editor of *Celluloid Classics: New Perspectives on Classical Antiquity in Modern Cinema* (*Arethusa* 41.1, 2008). Her book *Cowboy Classics: The Roots of the American Western in the Epic Tradition* is forthcoming from Edinburgh University Press.

Juliette Harrisson is Lecturer in Ancient and Classical History at Newman University in Birmingham, UK. Her research interests include the reception of the classical world in popular culture, and myth and religion in ancient Rome. She is the author of *Dreams and Dreaming in the Roman Empire: Cultural Memory and Imagination* (Bloomsbury, 2013), and co-editor of *Memory and Urban Religion in the Ancient World* (Bloomsbury, 2012). Her current projects include a co-authored book on screen representations of Roman Britain and a textbook on religion in ancient Rome.

John J. Johnston is Vice-Chair of the Egypt Exploration Society and a postgraduate research student at the Institute of Archaeology, University College London, UK. He sits on the Editorial Board of *Egyptian Archaeology*, and is co-editor of *Narratives of Egypt and the Ancient Near East* (Peeters, 2011) and *Unearthed* (Jurassic London, 2013), his introductory essay for which was a finalist for a British Science Fiction Association Award. He has published extensively and gives frequent lectures on mortuary archaeology, sexuality in the ancient world, and the reception of ancient Egypt in film, television, and literature.

Rachael Kelly is a graduate of the University of Ulster, Northern Ireland, where she was awarded a PhD in Film and Gender Studies. Her research explores the cultural function of Mark Antony in screen texts and screen portrayals of Cleopatra in light of recent debates in feminist film theory. She is the author of *Mark Antony and Popular Culture: Masculinity and the Construction of an Icon* (I. B. Tauris, 2014), and she has published several articles on gender anxieties in the screen constructions of Antony and Cleopatra.

Lisa Maurice is Senior Lecturer of Classical Studies at Bar-Ilan University in Israel. Her research interests center on Roman comedy and the reception of antiquity in popular culture. She is the author of *The Teacher in Ancient Rome: the Magister and his World* (Lexington, 2013), and the editor of *The Reception of Ancient Greece and Rome in Children's Literature: Heroes and Eagles* (Brill, 2015). She has published articles on Plautus and the reception of the ancient world on stage and screen. Her current work explores the connections between ancient Roman and early Jewish pedagogical practice.

Alex McAuley is a doctoral student in Classical Studies at McGill University in Montreal, Canada. His principal research centers on local culture and pluralism in Hellenistic Greece, and he has several current and forthcoming articles on Hellenistic dynastic practice and ideology, royal women, and Greek federalism. His interest in classical receptions focuses primarily on film and television series, particularly on the impact of 9/11 on depictions of the ancient world.

Anna McCullough is Assistant Professor of Classics at Ohio State University, USA. Her research interests focus on gender in the ancient world and the reception of classical culture in modern America. She has published articles on female gladiators, gender ideals in imperial Latin literature (particularly Statius), and the reception of ancient athletics in modern American culture. Current projects include a monograph on masculinity in the Flavian and Trajanic eras and the use of Greco-Roman heritage in Ohio history, art, and architecture.

Arthur J. Pomeroy is Professor of Classics at Victoria University of Wellington, New Zealand. His research interests include Roman social history, Flavian epic, and the reception of the ancient world on screen. He is the author of *The Appropriate Comment: Death Notices in the Graeco-Roman Historians* (Peter Lang, 1991), *Roman Social History: A Sourcebook* (with T. G. Parkin, Routledge, 2007), and *Then it Was Destroyed by the Volcano: The Ancient World in Film and on Television* (Duckworth, 2008). He is presently editing the *Companion to Ancient Greece and Rome on Screen* (Wiley Blackwell).

Amanda Potter is a Research Fellow in Classical Studies with the Open University, UK, where she completed her PhD on viewer reception of classical myth in *Xena: Warrior Princess* and *Charmed*. Her research interests include the classical world in film and television, and classics and gender, and she has published on Greek myth in the television shows *Xena: Warrior Princess*, *Charmed*, and *Torchwood*.

She is currently working on Greek myth in *Doctor Who* and fan engagement with STARZ *Spartacus*.

Stacie Raucci is Associate Professor of Classics at Union College in Schenectady, New York, USA, where she teaches an undergraduate course on the ancient world in the cinema. Her academic research focuses primarily on Roman love elegy and the reception of the ancient world in popular culture. She is the author of *Elegiac Eyes: Vision in Roman Love Elegy* (Peter Lang, 2011). She has published articles and delivered papers on the popularization of antiquity, Medusa Barbie, Roman orgies in film, and the Roman poet Propertius.

Margaret M. Toscano is Associate Professor of Classics and Comparative Literary and Cultural Studies at the University of Utah, USA. Her scholarly publications on classics and film stem from her fascination with how the past is incorporated into popular culture. Her interest in gender and myth has led to articles on female desire on Attic Greek vases, and the Cupid and Psyche myth. She is the co-editor of the volume *Hell and its Afterlife: Historical and Contemporary Perspectives* (Ashgate, 2010). She has also published extensively on Mormon feminism.

Illustrations

Rome, *Season Two Episode Listing*

Episode 13, "Passover," written by Bruno Heller, directed by Tim van Patten

Episode 14, "Son of Hades," written by Bruno Heller, directed by Allen Coulter

Episode 15, "These Being the Words of Marcus Tullius Cicero," written by Scott Buck, directed by Alan Poul

Episode 16, "Testudo et Lepus (The Tortoise and the Hare)," written by Todd Ellis Kessler, directed by Adam Davidson

Episode 17, "Heroes of the Republic," written by Mere Smith, directed by Alik Sakharov

Episode 18, "Philippi," written by Eoghan Mahony, directed by Roger Young

Episode 19, "Death Mask," written by Scott Buck, directed by John Maybury

Episode 20, "A Necessary Fiction," written by Todd Ellis Kessler, directed by Carl Franklin

Episode 21, "Deus Impeditio Esuritori Nullus (No God Can Stop a Hungry Man)," written by Mere Smith, directed by Steve Shill

Episode 22, "De Patre Vostro (About Your Father)," written by Bruno Heller, directed by John Maybury

Rome, *Season Two Cast List*

Lucius Vorenus	Kevin McKidd
Titus Pullo	Ray Stevenson
Atia of the Julii	Polly Walker
Octavia of the Julii	Kerry Condon
Servilia of the Junii	Lindsay Duncan
Mark Antony	James Purefoy
Octavian	Max Pirkis (episodes 13 and 14) and Simon Woods
Brutus	Tobias Menzies
Cassius	Guy Henry
Cleopatra	Lyndsey Marshal
Charmian	Kathryn Hunter
Timon	Lee Boardman
Levi	Nigel Lindsay
Eirene	Chiara Mastalli
Gaia	Zuleikha Robinson
Vorena the Elder	Coral Amiga
Cicero	David Bamber
Posca	Nicholas Woodeson
Livia	Alice Henley
Agrippa	Allen Leech
Maecenas	Alex Wyndham
Mascius	Michael Nardone
Newsreader	Ian McNeice
Erastes Fulmen	Lorcan Cranitch
Jocasta	Camilla Rutherford
Duro	Rafi Gavron
Caesarion	Max Baldry
Ptolemy XIII	Scott Chisolm
Julius Caesar	Ciarán Hinds
Niobe	Indira Varma

Introduction: The Trials and Triumphs of Rome, *Season Two*

Monica S. Cyrino

The plan was simple: the second season of HBO–BBC's *Rome*, scheduled to premiere in January of 2007, was going to build on the huge popular success of the critically acclaimed first season, weaving together "real" Roman historical events and people with compelling fictional subplots and characters into another set of powerful, pleasurable episodes.[1] Critics were conspicuously excited by the narrative and dramatic prospects of the new season, with its combination of "sex, violence, and fancy book learnin' – everybody wins."[2] Lisa Schwarzbaum of *Entertainment Weekly* declared: "Everything ... is still reliably rotten, wantonly carnal, and spectacularly costumed as HBO and the BBC resume their dramatic collaboration on the world's largest standing film set at Italy's Cinecittà Studios."[3] Tad Friend of *The New Yorker* praised the series' continued focus on character-driven storylines, especially its female protagonists: "*Rome*, in its new season ... showcases its brusquest and most soldierly characters: its highborn women. The show's pitiless gorgons campaign ceaselessly to have their men crowned or killed, whichever."[4] And Gary Kamiya of *Salon.com* confessed he was "addicted" to the way the series shocked the past back to life and startled him out of his comfortable nest of modernity: "*Rome* is based on solid historical research. But what makes it draw imaginative blood is the fact that it's uncensored scholarship, audacious history. *Rome* is incredibly entertaining, while also being incredibly shocking. It's history porn."[5]

All this breathless anticipation was clearly due to the sensational achievement of the series' first season, which aired in the autumn of 2005.[6] The first season of *Rome* chronicled the trajectory of Julius Caesar's later career, as it followed the events that took place between Caesar's return to Rome after his conquest of Gaul in 52 BC and his assassination by senatorial conspirators in 44 BC. As the series begins, Caesar is planning to return to Rome after eight years of warfare to seek his political fortune, and the first season brilliantly narrates his conflict with Pompey, his dalliance with Cleopatra, and his ultimate betrayal by Brutus. The second season, which would open dramatically with Caesar dead on the Senate floor, was to chart the beginnings of the violent power struggle between Antony, Caesar's most trusted general and ally, and Octavian, his great-nephew and legal heir. As series creator Bruno Heller has noted, the intention was for the second season to cover the period immediately after Caesar's assassination in March 44 BC to the defeat and death of the tyrannicides, Brutus and Cassius, at Philippi in October 42 BC.[7] In presenting events covering a span of only two-and-a-half years – and resonating with the closing mirror-image scenes of Caesar and Brutus each stabbed to death by mobs of assailants in their respective season finales – the second season would have been free to develop in a sequence of rich, unhurried, meticulously detailed episodes. In fact, Heller has explained that he envisioned the series continuing for a few more rounds: the third and fourth seasons would have taken place in Egypt and ended with the deaths of Antony and Cleopatra, and a possible fifth season would have followed the rise of the Messiah in Palestine, thereby taking the series into entirely new dramatic (and geographical) territory.[8]

But then the cold hand of Fortune – or the television industry equivalent – moved to intervene. In September of 2006, the suits at HBO decided to cancel *Rome* before shooting even began on the second season, and announced that the ten episodes of Season Two would be the last ones ever.[9] Their executive reasoning was less than mysterious: critical acclaim and a substantial audience of nearly eight million viewers were not enough to justify the nearly $120 million price tag of the first season alone.[10] With its high production values, sumptuous sets and costumes, and generous array of international talent, *Rome* was simply too expensive, and the cost was deemed unsustainable over the course of subsequent seasons. So when Heller discovered, "halfway through writing the second season," that the series had been cancelled, he decided to collapse the narratives outlined for the third and fourth seasons into the second one, and scuttled plans for the fifth altogether.[11] Curiously, the decision to telescope the narrative into a single condensed second/final season seemed to liberate the creative impulses of those involved in the show, as Heller claimed: "We poured everything into these episodes . . . We knew we weren't going to get another crack at this." But Heller's intent was always to preserve *Rome*'s distinctively brisk tempo and balanced approach to storytelling: "Our aim was to make people feel like it could go for another season." Actor Kevin McKidd, who played centurion-turned-mob-boss Lucius Vorenus, also put a positive spin on the news of the abridged series run: "It gave us license to really go for it with the stories . . . We could get to the heart of stuff. It's quite visceral."[12]

Yet the cancellation of *Rome* and resulting compression of several storylines into the second/final season did indeed have a profound impact on the pace and composition of the narrative. The first season comprised twelve episodes covering approximately eight years of Roman history (52 to 44 BC), and so moved ahead no more than a few months in time from episode to episode, allowing for a successful balance between the stories of the elite and plebeian characters, their personal lives, and the broader political context;[13] the second season had only ten episodes to recount events over a period of fifteen years, from Caesar's death in 44 BC, all the way to Antony and Cleopatra's defeat at the battle of Actium in 31 BC, their suicides shortly thereafter, and Octavian's triumph of 29 BC celebrated in the final episode. However, this fifteen-year time span does not adequately describe the narrative structure and episodic rhythm of the second season, since the sudden termination of the series resulted in a second season with two separate and radically asymmetrical sections.

The first and longer section of Season Two of *Rome* runs from episode 13 ("Passover") to episode 18 ("Philippi"), and covers the originally planned second season – the two-and-a-half years from the death of Caesar to the death of Brutus – which was already mostly written at the time of the series' cancellation. These six episodes effectively follow the narrative technique of *Rome*'s first season, unfolding with a measured tempo of precise storytelling that linked together the boundaries between the historical events and fictional subplots, and between the elite and lower-class characters. One evocative example is the portrayal in episode 13 of the high political intrigue and shifting alliances surrounding the public funeral of Julius Caesar, while the camera cuts back and forth to the humble private funeral of Niobe, Vorenus' wife, with its quiet pulse of personal emotions exposing the devastating impact of her death upon their immediate family. Note, too, how in episode 18 Heller intentionally chose to subvert the historical tradition in order to highlight the dramatic parallelism of two major characters by having the death of Brutus visually echo that of Caesar: instead of falling on his own sword, Brutus martyrs himself on the battlefield as he is assailed by armed foes who stab him multiple times.

The second part of the final season of *Rome* runs from episode 19 ("Death Mask") to episode 22 ("De Patre Vostro") and reflects the condensed narrative of the Alexandrian story that was planned for the third and fourth seasons, from the volatile (and temporary) alliance of Antony and Octavian in the second triumvirate, to the brutal aftermath of their military conflict at the battle of Actium. With the challenge of covering a period of more than a decade in only four episodes came an obvious acceleration in the pace of the storytelling, alongside a marked shift in the narrative style and some unexpected twists to various plots and characters. "Everything we did in Egypt," noted co-producer Jonathan Stamp, "was impossible to defend on historical grounds ... We were up against a myth."[14] Most significantly, the (in)famous love affair of Antony and Cleopatra is compressed into the last two episodes, and the role of Cleopatra, perhaps the most well-known queen and *femme fatale* in human history, is thus diminished by temporal necessity.[15] An announcement for the series finale teased: "This is the part you think you know – all that Antony and Cleopatra doomed-love stuff, settled with snakes and suicide."[16] Indeed, it is apparent that the final two episodes relied heavily on the familiarity of the Antony/Cleopatra plotline in the popular imagination, from Shakespeare to Elizabeth Taylor and beyond, to fill in the unintended gaps of the lovers' tragic story for *Rome*'s audience.

Over the ten-episode arc of the second season, taken as a whole, several creative choices were brought into sharper relief by the effect of the drama's compacted narrative. A few plots and characters that were launched are later abandoned, while others that enjoyed positive critical or audience reception during the first season are emphasized and given greater screen time. An example of a discarded storyline is the Jewish subplot, which was introduced early on as an expansion on the character of Timon, the horse trader, but then eliminated midway through the second season, as he and his family are seen literally walking out of the city of Rome in the transitional episode 18;[17] the cancellation of the series no doubt mitigated the need to establish a Jewish backstory that would be picked up later in a fifth season set in Palestine. In contrast, the ongoing vigorous portrayal of the miraculously un-aging Pullo and Vorenus, who were particular audience favorites from the first season, maintained a powerful and persistent influence on the narrative of the second season, as the brothers in arms continued to perform the dyadic Everyman/"Forrest Gump" roles that had made them so popular from the outset.[18]

Finally, consider the effects of the creative decision to keep the

Figure 1 Atia (Polly Walker) gazes at the spoils paraded at her son Octavian's triumph in episode 22 ("De Patre Vostro") of *Rome* (2007). HBO BBC.

"love to hate her" character of Atia (played by Polly Walker), mother of Octavian and lover of Antony (in *Rome*), alive to the end of the series and thus well past the historically attested date of her death in 43 BC.[19] As one critic described her popularity as the central female figure in *Rome*'s second season: "Sweeping battlefield showdowns offer high drama, but the soap-operatic subplots – orchestrated by the cunning, stunning, emerald-eyed Atia (Walker) – are where the real action is."[20] Throughout the course of the second season, the character of Atia continues to control everything and everyone around her, although she is defied at first by her bitterest rival, Servilia, and later briefly by Octavian's young wife, Livia.[21] Moreover, Atia must remain on the main stage of the series so that she can be present as a witness at her son Octavian's great triumph (Figure 1): her remorseful, knowing gaze during that extended final sequence as she observes her son's parade of spoils perfectly encapsulates her agency over the series' twenty-two episodes, and her ambitious yet deadly machinations to elevate her son at all costs. The audience watches with Atia's sense of foreboding, as the Republic becomes an Empire; with her haunted look, she seems to ask: "Was it all worth it?"

ABOUT THIS VOLUME

Rome, *Season Two: Trial and Triumph* is a collection of original research that responds to both the successes and the challenges of the second season of the series. By exploring, for the first time, the visual, narrative, and thematic aesthetics of the show's second season, this volume opens up new avenues of scholarly discussion. The chapters in this volume reflect upon the proposition that the producers of *Rome*'s second season, even within the limitations of its condensed narrative, still had a great deal of creative freedom to develop individual plots and characters, and the dramatic imagery associated with them, without losing any ground in terms of the show's much-praised commitment to historical authenticity. All chapters draw attention to the interconnections between the series and the ancient historical and literary sources, as well as *Rome*'s place among other modern cinematic and televisual productions, and its reception among critics, audiences, and fans.

The chapters in this volume investigate the ways in which *Rome* nods to earlier receptions of ancient Rome as well as to more recent popular onscreen recreations of antiquity, while at the same time the series applies new techniques of interrogation to current social issues and concerns. The contributors are all leading authorities in their various subfields of ancient history, literature, and culture, as well as film and gender studies, whose academic work also engages enthusiastically and expertly with popular culture and modern media appropriations and adaptations of antiquity. Individual chapters address questions of politics, war, and social history, while examining the representation of gender and sexuality, race and class, spectacle and violence, all within the setting of late Republican Rome. As the chapters of this volume demonstrate, the second season of *Rome* stands as a testament to the effects of studio decisions and audience reception upon the creative, artistic, and narrative choices of the show's writers and producers. Altogether this volume considers the second season of *Rome* to be a provocative contribution to our understanding of how specific threads of reception are constantly being reinvented to suit contemporary tastes, aspirations, and anxieties.

The chapters of the first section of this volume, "Power and Politics," explore various aspects of the representation of power and authority in *Rome*, and how characters in the drama negotiate tricky politics at both the elite and lower levels of society. In the opening chapter, "A Touch Too Cerebral: Eulogizing Caesar in *Rome*," Angeline C. Chiu analyzes the decision to undermine audience expectations in episode 13 by not directly depicting the iconic public speeches of Brutus and Antony over the fallen Caesar, but rather staging a series of scenes that emphasize the power of literary reception, interpretation, and dramatic re-enactment. In the second chapter, "Discharging Pullo and Vorenus: Veterans in *Rome*," Lee L. Brice assesses the second season's historically authentic and pervasive portrayal of veterans, especially the protagonists, Pullo and Vorenus, by observing the way they are shown dealing with demobilization, and how their loyalty to their former military commanders defines their later careers. In the third chapter, "Gangsterism in *Rome*," Arthur J. Pomeroy examines the show's depiction of organized violence to set up a parallelism of criminality between the upper and lower strata of society: while Antony and Octavian use the triumvirate to cover their abuses of power, Vorenus and Pullo try to make the gangs of the Aventine *collegium* more legitimate. The fourth chapter, "Class, Chaos, and Control in *Rome*," continues to illuminate the series' high/low narrative technique, as Margaret M. Toscano describes the chiasmus of intimate bonds formed between Octavian and Pullo, and Antony and Vorenus, which criss-cross boundaries of class and focus instead on issues of personal temperament and compromise.

In the fifth chapter, "Earning Immortality: Cicero's Death Scene in *Rome*," Eran Almagor details the presentation of the much-anticipated murder of the famous orator during the proscriptions, as the series deftly interweaves historical fact with dramatic invention using the themes of fatherhood and immortality, as well as Pullo's status as incidental agent of history. In the sixth chapter, "The Triumvirate of the Ring in *Rome*," Barbara Weiden Boyd elucidates the significance of the show's visual use of Octavian's sphinx seal and ring to affirm his authority as the man chosen by destiny to rule Rome, and how the ring motif is also brought into play to symbolize the shifting Roman identities of Brutus and Antony. The seventh chapter, "Jews and Judaism in *Rome*," explores the implications of the second season's Jewish subplot as an exercise in modern reception, as Lisa Maurice reviews the traditional portrayal of Jews and Judaism in recent cinema and television as well as the influence of contemporary Middle East politics on the creation of this storyline.

In the second section of the volume, "Sex and Status," chapters investigate a wide range of issues arising from the show's explicit portrayal of sexuality and the representation of gender, which were crucially important elements of the first season and are further developed in the second through the delineation of the sex, gender, and power hierarchies of several pairs of lovers and rivals, both historical and fictional.[22] The eighth chapter, "Revenge and Rivalry in *Rome*," looks at the gendered dynamics of vengeance as a dominant theme of the second season, as Stacie Raucci employs the tools of feminist film theory to evaluate *Rome*'s depiction of both female and male vengeance within the context of recent cinema. In the ninth chapter, "Effigies of Atia and Servilia: Effacing the Female Body in *Rome*," Antony Augoustakis unravels the nexus of female sexuality in the series' portrayal of the bitter feud between the two main female protagonists, and how their bodies are abused and ultimately controlled to underscore their de-sexualization and loss of power. In the tenth chapter, "Livia, Sadomasochism, and the Anti-Augustan Tradition in *Rome*," Anna McCullough demonstrates how the second season deftly echoes the ancient sources critical of Octavian by exhibiting graphic scenes of his wife Livia as sexually dominant and aggressive in bed to signal her unconventional authority over him in their marriage. The eleventh chapter, "Windows and Mirrors: Illuminating the Invisible Women of *Rome*," turns to the lower-class fictional women of the second season, as Kirsten Day reveals how characters such as Eirene and Gaia use their limited resources to establish their social/sexual status and thereby provide an instructive complement to the more famous historical women in the series.

The twelfth chapter, "Antony and Atia: Tragic Romance in *Rome*," traces the second season's development of this key relationship as an echo of Octavian's propaganda against Antony, as Juliette Harrisson explains that Atia (rather than Octavia) assumes the role of the Julian woman shamefully wronged and abandoned for the foreign temptress, Cleopatra. In the next chapter, "Problematic Masculinity: Antony and the Political Sphere in *Rome*," Rachael Kelly examines Antony's failure to perform the paradigm of the political, hegemonic male against the series' creative decision to subordinate his doomed love affair with Cleopatra to the wider story of the end of the Roman Republic. Chapter 14, "*Rome*, Shakespeare, and the Dynamics of the Cleopatra Reception," explores the show's bold, innovative portrayal of the Egyptian queen, as Gregory N. Daugherty describes its visual and narrative resonances to Plutarch, Shakespeare, and numerous other cinematic versions, resulting in a greater dramatic focus on the tragic couple. In chapter 15, "The Rattle of the Sistrum: 'Othering' Cleopatra and Egypt in *Rome*," John J. Johnston appraises the set and costume design of the court in Alexandria and its exotic denizens, exposing the designers' intention to heighten the sense of alien-ness and decadence as epitomizing the queen herself, while in contradiction to any historical authenticity of Hellenistic Egypt.

Chapter 16, "Gateways to Vice: Drugs and Sex in *Rome*," delves into the drama's depiction of narcotics consumption, often associated with sexual impropriety and juvenile deliquency, as Alex McAuley investigates the retrojection of this modern vice on to ancient onscreen elites to uncover its origins and connotations within the world of the series. In the final chapter of the volume, "Slashing *Rome*: Season Two Rewritten in Online Fanfiction," Amanda Potter analyzes the extensive level of fan engagement with the second season in the creation of fanfiction, where the primary focus is on sexual relationships between characters, and demonstrates how fanfiction based on historically themed series initiates a new category that merges with existing categories such as slash and crossover. Like fan internet activity, scholarly interest in the series *Rome* remains equally enthusiastic, as the following chapters richly demonstrate.

NOTES

1 On the first season of *Rome*, see Cyrino (2008a).
2 "What To Watch" headline for *Rome*'s new season, *Entertainment Weekly* (January 12, 2007).
3 Schwarzbaum (2007: 63).
4 Friend (2007).
5 Kamiya (2007).
6 Cyrino (2008b: 3–4).
7 Hibberd (2008).
8 The concept for a fifth season focused on Palestine would also have been a canny foreshadowing of the recent surge in popularity of Bible-themed films: for example, Darren Aronofsky's *Noah* (2014), Christopher Spencer's *Son of God* (2014), and Ridley Scott's *Exodus* (2014).
9 Rice (2007).
10 *Rome* still ranks as the most expensive television series ever made, averaging over $10 million per episode. Compare this to HBO's current fantasy series *Game of Thrones* (2011–), the second most expensive series, with a per-episode budget of $6 million: the pilot cost over $10 million, and the first season budget reached $60 million; see Garofalo (2014).
11 Hibberd (2008).
12 Heller and McKidd quoted in Rice (2007).
13 On *Rome*'s first season narrative technique of cutting between "high" and "low" worlds, see Cyrino (2008b: 6–7).
14 Personal interview with Stamp (June 12, 2014).
15 See the chapters by Harrisson, Kelly, Daugherty, and Johnston in this volume.
16 "What To Watch" headline for *Rome*'s series finale, *Entertainment Weekly* (March 23, 2007).
17 See the chapter by Maurice in this volume.
18 On the friendship of Pullo and Vorenus in the first season, see Cooke (2008); on the "Forrest Gump" comparison, see Cyrino (2008b: 5),

and Daugherty (2008: 141, 151). On Pullo and Vorenus in the second season, see the chapters by Brice and Pomeroy in this volume.

19 See Cyrino (2008c: 139) on the possible influence of the historical Fulvia, one of Antony's wives, on the portrayal of Atia in *Rome*.

20 Stransky (2007).

21 On Atia's rivalry with Servilia, see the chapters by Raucci and Augoustakis in this volume; on the challenge posed by Livia, see the chapter by McCullough in this volume.

22 See Cyrino (2014: 623–5) for *Rome*'s escalation in the depiction of graphic sexuality compared to earlier screen texts.

PART I

Power and Politics

1 *A Touch Too Cerebral: Eulogizing Caesar in* Rome

Angeline C. Chiu

The second season of the series *Rome* opens with the frantic moments immediately following Julius Caesar's assassination on the Ides of March 44 BC. The natural crux of the aftermath is the rivalry of Brutus and Mark Antony, for their speeches at Caesar's funeral are pivotal in their competing attempts to shape public opinion and rally support for their respective causes. The season premiere episode, "Passover" (episode 13), presents a narrative of these adversaries that can stand on its own terms, but a closer look reveals the writing as a complex tissue of elements engaging the audience's expectations of action, Shakespeare's culturally iconic play *Julius Caesar*, and Plutarch's biographies that were Shakespeare's chief sources for his play. Antony's jibe to Brutus in *Rome* – that his speech was "a touch too cerebral for that audience" – becomes a most metaliterary meditation on adaptation. With this in mind, let us consider the chain of reception from Plutarch to Shakespeare to twenty-first-century television as it culminates in the dramatic effect of screenwriter Bruno Heller's creative choices.[1]

PLUTARCH

Our discussion begins with Plutarch's account of the speeches of Brutus and Antony in his *Life of Brutus* and *Life of Mark Antony*. A prolific Greek writer living under imperial Rome, Plutarch (ca. AD 46–120) composed his *Parallel Lives* as pairs of biographies intended to be read as comparative diptychs.[2] In Plutarch's work, Brutus' speech takes place immediately after the death of Caesar, and it is a reflection of the speaker's own public standing and personal *dignitas* (*Life of Brutus* 18.5–6):[3]

> When the multitude was assembled there, Brutus made a speech calculated to win the people and befitting the occasion. The audience applauding his words and crying down to him to come down from the Capitol, the conspirators took heart and went down into the forum. The rest of them followed along in one another's company, but Brutus was surrounded by many eminent citizens, escorted with great honour down from the citadel, and placed on the rostra. At sight of him the multitude, although it was a mixed rabble and prepared to raise a disturbance, was struck with awe, and awaited the issue in decorous silence. Also when he came forward to speak, all paid quiet attention to his words.

In Plutarch's account, Brutus' speech in the Forum is unequivocally well received by the crowd in spite of the fact that it was a motley, volatile mob on the verge of rioting. The Roman noble, by dint of his virtuous reputation, captures the crowd's attention and indeed commands its respect even from its first view of him. The precise content of the speech is unspecified, though Plutarch asserts that it was chosen to fit the moment and therefore the product of skill and strategy. The core of the passage is Brutus' effect on the crowd: he calms the turbulent masses first with his personal moral authority and then with his carefully crafted words. His appearance defuses the perilously fraught atmosphere, bringing calm and order not unlike the honorable statesman at the opening of Vergil's *Aeneid*.[4]

According to the *Life of Brutus*, Mark Antony addresses the crowd on a different occasion from Brutus' speech. Antony is slated to deliver the eulogy at the funeral of Julius Caesar, though the act takes on a life of its own when Antony exploits his opportunity (20.2–4):

> And now, in allowing Caesar's funeral rites to be conducted as Antony demanded, he [Brutus] committed a fatal error. For, in the first place, when it was found that the will of Caesar gave to every Roman seventy-five drachmas, and left to the people his gardens beyond the Tiber, where now stands a temple of Fortune, an astonishing kindliness and yearning for Caesar seized the citizens; and in the second place, after Caesar's body had been brought to the forum, Antony pronounced the customary eulogy, and when he saw that the multitude were moved by his words, changed his tone to one of compassion, and taking the robe of Caesar, all bloody as it was, unfolded it to view, pointing out the many places in which it had been pierced and Caesar wounded. All further orderly procedure was at an end, of course; some cried out to kill the murderers, and others, as formerly in the case of Clodius the demagogue dragged from the shops the benches and tables, piled them upon one another, and thus erected a huge pyre; on this they placed Caesar's body, and in the midst of many sanctuaries, asylums, and holy places, burned it. Moreover, when the fire blazed up, people rushed up from all sides, snatched up half-burnt brands, and ran round to the houses of Caesar's slayers to set them on fire.

In his separate biography of Antony, Plutarch also describes the funeral oration and the mayhem it inspired, albeit in slightly different terms (*Life of Antony* 14.3–4):

> Now, it happened that when Caesar's body was carried forth for burial, Antony pronounced the customary eulogy over it in the forum. And when he saw that the people were mightily swayed and charmed by his words, he mingled with his praises sorrow and indignation over the dreadful deed, and at the close of his speech shook on high the garments of the dead, all bloody and tattered by the swords as they were, called those who had wrought such work villains and murderers, and inspired his hearers with such rage that they heaped together benches and tables and burned Caesar's body in the forum, and then, snatching the blazing faggots from the pyre, ran to the houses of the assassins and assaulted them.

In both of Plutarch's accounts, Antony's incendiary speech is the product as much of nimble opportunism and extemporaneous speaking as it is of calculating premeditation. Both the *Life of Brutus* and the *Life of Antony* include the crucial detail of Antony dramatically displaying Caesar's bloody robes as a tactic to incite the crowd into frenzy against Brutus and the other assassins. Nevertheless, Antony's speech is not portrayed particularly as a direct riposte to that of Brutus. It is a separate act that sways the Roman masses to Antony. The speeches are delivered separately at two different times and in two different contexts.

SHAKESPEARE

Plutarch in turn became the main source that William Shakespeare (1564–1616) employed in writing his tragedy *Julius Caesar* (1599), one of the first plays performed at the newly built Globe Theatre.[5] Shakespeare's familiarity with the classics has been well documented, and his thorough-going engagement with Plutarch via the renowned English translation of 1579 by Sir Thomas North gave rise not only to *Julius Caesar* but also to the other Roman plays *Antony and Cleopatra* (ca. 1606/7) and *Coriolanus* (ca. 1608/9).[6] In the creation of *Julius Caesar*, Shakespeare both drew upon and adapted his Plutarchan source with a professional playwright's eye for creating a work of dramatic theater. One should keep in mind that *Julius Caesar*, though now so often studied as a text, was written specifically for the stage and meant to be experienced aurally and visually.[7] Accordingly, the play's pivotal third act presents Brutus and Antony giving their speeches in quick succession at Caesar's funeral in the Forum. This unhistorical choice sets up an unmistakable, explicit contrast between them; the scene becomes a showpiece of dueling rhetoric and personal animus. Where Plutarch does not specify the content of either Brutus' speech or Antony's, Shakespeare places two vastly different but meticulously crafted orations on the stage and sets them on a collision course.[8]

Brutus addresses the crowd first, and the beginning of his speech is carefully calculated to establish his authority and engage the audience's intellect. The ultimate goal is to justify his participation in the assassination of Caesar, who had enjoyed much popular support (*Julius Caesar* 3.2.13–30):[9]

> Be patient till the last.
> Romans, countrymen, and lovers! hear me for my
> cause and be silent that you may hear. Believe me for
> mine honour and have respect to mine honour, that you
> may believe. Censure me in your wisdom and awake
> your senses that you may the better judge. If there be
> any in this assembly, any dear friend of Caesar's, to him
> I say that Brutus' love to Caesar was no less than his.
> If then that friend demand why Brutus rose
> against Caesar, this is my answer: not that I loved Caesar less,
> but that I loved Rome more. Had you rather Caesar
> were living, and die all slaves, than that Caesar were
> dead, to live all free men? As Caesar loved me, I weep
> for him; as he was fortunate, I rejoice at it; as he was
> valiant, I honour him; but as he was ambitious, I slew
> him. There is tears, for his love; joy, for his fortune;
> honour, for his valour; and death, for his ambition.

The speech is a work of cool clarity hinging on Brutus' personal integrity ("mine honour") and the public deployment of such authority. Indeed, this oration depends almost entirely on the force of Brutus' own *ethos* and presence. The words "I," "me," and "mine" underpin the speech and present Brutus' connection with Caesar as something to which the audience are third-party spectators. Additionally, this prose speech, occurring in a play that is mostly comprised of poetry, has been often (mis)characterized as an artless utterance and therefore evidence of Brutus' honesty and guilelessness, particularly as it is destined to be spectacularly outmaneuvered by the wily Mark Antony. On the contrary, Brutus' words form a highly crafted piece of art and artifice. One critic has identified no fewer than thirty rhetorical figures and devices in this short thirty-four line speech.[10] Note, for example, the piquant rhetorical question (complete with false dichotomy) and the careful paralleling of numerous phrases to create a complex interlocking set of balances. The response of the

Roman multitude is indisputably positive, even to the point of shouting for Brutus to be the new Caesar (3.2.53). As Plutarch had stated that Brutus gave a speech calculated to win public favor and be fitting for the circumstances, so Shakespeare has crafted words to match.[11]

Antony's subsequent speech is a rhetorical showpiece that has achieved iconic cultural status. Its opening gambit is a *captatio benevolentiae* – an attempt to gain the audience's goodwill – that contains some of the most recognizable lines in English literature, and thereafter the speech seemingly grants Brutus' points both about his own honor and Caesar's ambition (3.2.82–93):

> Friends, Romans, countrymen, lend me your ears:[12]
> I come to bury Caesar, not to praise him.
> The evil that men do lives after them:
> The good is oft interred with their bones.
> So let it be with Caesar. The noble Brutus
> Hath told you Caesar was ambitious:
> If it were so, it was a grievous fault,
> And grievously hath Caesar answer'd it.
> Here, under leave of Brutus and the rest—
> For Brutus is an honourable man;
> So are they all, all honourable men—
> Come I to speak in Caesar's funeral.

Antony delivers a masterfully subtle speech that gradually presents tactics that reinforce each other: questioning Brutus' declaration of Caesar's ambition, indirectly casting doubt on Brutus' integrity, establishing Antony's own *ethos*, and engaging the crowd through its personal emotional investment in Antony's words. The turning point of the speech, capitalizing on the growing swell of the audience's passions, is as much *coup de théâtre* as crafted rhetoric; Mark Antony definitively wins the crowd's favor when he displays Caesar's bloody robe. Plutarch had stated that this happened, but Shakespeare gives Antony the opportunity to dramatize the moment (3.2.181–95):

> If you have tears, prepare to shed them now.
> You all do know this mantle. I remember
> The first time ever Caesar put it on.
> 'Twas on a summer's evening in his tent,
> That day he overcame the Nervii.
> Look, in this place ran Cassius' dagger through.
> See what a rent the envious Casca made.
> Through this the well-beloved Brutus stabbed,
> And as he plucked his cursed steel away,
> Mark how the blood of Caesar follow'd it,
> As rushing out of doors to be resolved
> If Brutus so unkindly knocked or no;

For Brutus, as you know, was Caesar's angel.
Judge, O ye gods, how dearly Caesar loved him!
This was the most unkindest cut of all.

Antony makes this moment deeply personal for the audience ("You all do know this mantle"), for himself ("I remember the first time ever Caesar put it on"), and for Brutus and the assassins themselves, individually identified with bloody holes in the fabric. Given that Antony himself had not been present at the assassination, since conspirators had detained him outside, he could not possibly know which assassin had made which stab wound, least of all Brutus. Factuality is not the point, however, for the goal is the persuasion of the listener. The impact of the cloak is explosive, for Antony elicits pity from the crowd and then deftly depicts the fall of Caesar as the fall of all Romans to treachery (3.2.199–209):

And in his mantle muffling up his face,
Even at the base of Pompey's statue,
Which all the while ran blood, great Caesar fell.
O, what a fall was there, my countrymen!
Then I and you and all of us fell down,
Whilst bloody treason flourished over us.
O, now you weep, and, I perceive you feel
The dint of pity. These are gracious drops.
Kind souls, what weep you when you but behold
Our Caesar's vesture wounded? Look you here,
Here is himself, marred as you see with traitors!

When Antony unveils the corpse of Caesar, the effect on the crowd is galvanizing: the agitated plebeians begin to shout: "Revenge! About! Seek! Burn! Fire! Kill! Slay! / Let not a traitor live!" (3.2.216–17). Antony's visual and visceral appeal transforms the audience's emotions organically from pity to grief to, finally, rage. Brutus' previous elegant, coolly intellectual speech is swiftly forgotten in the mob violence that erupts in the Forum. Although Antony claims that he has no talent at public speaking "to stir men's blood" (3.2.235) and even insists, "I am no orator as Brutus is" (3.2.229), the actual effect of his speech belies his disingenuous demurral.

As the riot begins in earnest, Antony says to himself with grim satisfaction: "Now let it work. Mischief, thou art afoot, / Take thou what course thou wilt!" (3.2.275–6). He has won both the duel of rhetoric and the gamble for control of the city; he now has the upper hand as Brutus is on the back foot. The two men will not meet again until the battle of Philippi in Act 5, and even there they will not meet as individuals or exchange words. They do not need to do so. The dueling orations in Act 3 are the true focus and climax of their personal rivalry in the play.

ROME

The season premiere, "Passover," depicts several narratives unfolding simultaneously, of which one is the struggle between Mark Antony and Brutus. The portrayal of their rivalry capitalizes on the audience's anticipation of their competing public speeches and then subverts it. In the aftermath of Caesar's assassination, Antony contrives a meeting with the assassins in order to propose a reconciliation. Though Brutus is as distrustful of Antony as the other conspirators are, he agrees to an alliance as a matter of political expedience. He does, however, add the stipulation that he and Antony will both preside over Caesar's public funeral. This condition departs from Plutarch and adheres to Shakespeare's arrangement; it also indicates the wary Brutus' desire to keep careful watch over his rival. Furthermore, for an audience familiar with Shakespeare, this sets up the expectation of Antony's and Brutus' dueling orations. This is an expectation that becomes explicit in the subsequent scene when the Newsreader makes a public announcement in the Forum that Brutus and Antony will be delivering eulogies at the funeral of Caesar.

The weight of expectation increases as we see both Antony and Brutus preparing for the occasion. On the morning of Caesar's funeral, both men are depicted grim-faced and being dressed by servants in a montage without dialogue. The visual elements evoke the classic trope of warriors arming for battle; Brutus even appears to be practicing his gestures in front of a round mirror. At the prelude to the funeral, the two men assemble with other nobles around the corpse of Caesar, and the camera lingers on the faces of Antony and Brutus as they silently exchange hostile glances. Antony's expression is almost a smirk, a tantalizing hint of his intentions. When the doors open for Caesar's funeral to begin – one that we know will include the speeches of Brutus and Antony – we are primed for a public rhetorical showdown between the two rivals.

This, however, does not happen. Bruno Heller's script takes a different tack entirely. The next thing that appears on screen is Caesar's massive funeral pyre burning in the Forum. This scene contains no dialogue at all; it focuses on the fire and the Roman crowd in a riotous frenzy around it, shouting and hurling objects on to the pyre as a cordon of soldiers struggles to hold back the mob. The image is disorienting until we as spectators realize that we are watching the aftermath of Brutus' and Antony's public appearances. The visual narrative has leapt over their speeches entirely, but the final result is clear: public order fallen into chaos.

The educated audience knows that this is the handiwork of Antony's speech, and the scene concludes with the camera pulling up and away to reveal the full scale of the disturbance. That visual image communicates the narrative thrust of the incident with great economy – how Antony outflanked Brutus and outmaneuvered the conspirators, who now face Rome rioting against them. Heller has chosen to convey the effect of the speeches without including the speeches themselves, thus both conserving time and avoiding a direct confrontation with the culturally iconic Shakespearean orations, the tone and tenor of which would be incompatible with the personality of the series and of Antony and Brutus as Heller has written them.[13]

As the episode continues, however, the "missing" speeches appear in two specific instances of recall and retelling where *Rome*'s radical innovation is the prioritization of the reaction over the actual delivery. The first instance occurs in the aftermath of the funeral as Antony and Brutus, along with Cassius and Servilia, gather in the house of the Junii. Before any dialogue takes place, the scale of the disaster is immediately apparent in the body language of the characters: Brutus and Cassius sit slumped on a bench as Servilia hovers grimly in the background. The triumphant Antony, on the other hand, wears an impudent grin as he stands leaning carelessly against a column. Indeed, Antony twists the knife by offering an insincere apology to Servilia: "I'm sorry about all this. I got a bit carried away." He then says to Brutus with sardonically syrupy *faux*-sympathy: "You gave an excellent speech, incidentally. Perhaps a touch too cerebral for that audience." In this scene, the importance of the speeches becomes clear without the audience ever needing to hear the speeches themselves. Antony notes the contrast in the nature of the two orations, obliquely characterizing his own as emotionally provocative and overtly tagging Brutus' as (too) coolly dispassionate. From this dialogue, it is clear that Antony's false apologies refer to the mob violence in the previous scene.

Furthermore, the adaptation makes possible a personal confrontation between Brutus and Antony that does not occur in Plutarch or Shakespeare. As a private argument behind closed doors, the face-to-face exchange possesses an uninhibited authenticity that would be difficult to convey with carefully polished words meant for public consumption. Heller has taken the drama of expected public rhetoric and transmuted it into another kind of theatrics, the private quarrel of bitterly impassioned individuals. Eventually the dispute will end on the battlefield with armies on both sides (episode 18, "Philippi"), but this vicious exchange between the two principals intensifies the drama as the playing out of personal animosities with vast political ramifications. Brutus can declare that he has patricians on his side, but as Antony snarls in reply: "And I have an angry mob that will roast and eat all your men of quality in the ashes of the Senate House!" The practical effect of his speech is laid out in stark terms both for the outmaneuvered Brutus and the viewing audience. The balance of power has shifted in the aftermath of the funeral.

The second and arguably more striking treatment of the speeches takes place in a seedy tavern belonging to the gangster Erastes Fulmen. There, surrounded by rowdy plebeians, the barfly Troilus recounts what he had seen earlier in the Forum. This narrative tack is notable for first taking the common crowd's perspective and then presenting recollection and retelling as interpretation. Troilus' account is reductive, but he is also delivering an oration of his own – an energetic and degraded version of both Brutus' and Antony's official eulogies. This in itself is in keeping with one of the themes of the series as a whole – the ignoble face of Rome alongside the glorious, the dirt beside the marble, the personal troubles of Vorenus and Pullo juxtaposed with the dynastic struggles of great men. This incident in the tavern, however, has a far more important role: it establishes the perniciously infectious effect of Antony's speech on its intended audience, the volatile urban mob.

For the tavern storyteller and his audience of Roman inebriates, his re-enactment is interpretation and analysis: this is what they see as memorable and therefore important in those orations. Troilus begins with Brutus, but in his account Brutus is not the dignified noble and accomplished orator of Plutarch and Shakespeare: instead he is a pompously gesturing popinjay boring his audience: "And he goes blah blah blah, the law this, and the Republic that, and Twelve bloody Tables. I couldn't understand 'alf of it. I thought I'd be off for a bevvy." This Brutus, at least in the selective memory of the narrator, is an emotionally detached speaker who droned on about abstractions and utterly failed to forge a personal, visceral connection with his audience.[14] Suddenly Antony's jibe of "a touch too cerebral for that audience" hits home, even as it harks back to the Shakespearean Brutus' elegantly wrought speech that focused on the abstraction of honor.

The highlight and crux of the retelling, however, is the speaker's re-enactment of Antony's emotionally manipulative display of

Figure 2 Erastes Fulmen (Lorcan Cranitch) observes Troilus (Jay Simpson) re-enact Antony's eulogy in episode 13 ("Passover") of *Rome* (2007). HBO BBC.

Caesar's bloody robes (Figure 2). This tactic and its spectacular effect form the core of Shakespeare's treatment, and the plebeian narrator gives an oversimplified version that nevertheless communicates its own debased sense of the dramatic: "He's crying, saying how much he loved Caesar . . . Then he pulls out Caesar's toga, all covered in blood . . . Everyone goes 'whoa' . . . And the crowd, 'alf of them are crying, sobbing like babies!" The storyteller throws his own cloak into the audience, imitating Antony and gleefully noting the result: "Whoosh! The whole place goes up like a tar barrel! The whole crowd goes mad!" For a moment, Troilus has become a surrogate for Antony himself, reiterating that strategic eulogy to its intended audience and magnifying its effects. The actual content of this reductive speech has its Plutarchan and Shakespearean credentials, and it also has an affinity with Greek tragedy's messenger speech in its refusal to depict outright a scene of great violence and significance; it insists instead on reporting the event at second hand and engaging the audience's own febrile imagination.

The effect is immediate. Even as Erastes Fulmen complains that Antony's speech showed "No respect! No fucking respect! It's a consular fucking funeral!" the audience experiences a raw, unvarnished interpretation of Antony's speech in contrast to that of Brutus. Seeing the tavern audience's rowdily appreciative response to Antony's eulogy as told by a fellow plebeian may ultimately pack more of a dramatic punch than hearing that speech itself, for the next scenes depict Brutus and Cassius fleeing to the countryside as Antony takes up his ascendancy in the city – a turn of events that is possible because of plebeian support for him.

Eulogizing Caesar has resulted in far wider ramifications for power politics and deadly factional rivalry. As Plutarch and then Shakespeare did, so *Rome* makes sweepingly creative, adaptive choices in depicting Caesar's funeral and its fallout through the now-infamous pair of eulogies. Although these choices initially appear to frustrate audience expectations, the absence of the actual speeches – coupled with their double appearance via recollection and retelling – becomes an asset in the dramatic contemporary construction of how Antony employed the appeal of visceral emotion and outmaneuvered Brutus in spectacular fashion. The oratory may have been intentionally "a touch too cerebral for that audience" within the show, but the narrative depends on its modern viewer to be cerebral indeed to appreciate its full effects.

NOTES

1 In this chapter I am not so much focused on historicity, historical accuracy, or source criticism as on the dramatic narratives presented by Plutarch, Shakespeare, and Bruno Heller, all of whom took creative liberties for their own artistic purposes.

2 Furthermore, Plutarch states that his purpose is not so much to record history, as it is to consider how character and personality affect the lives of great men. For Plutarch and his intellectual context, see Mossman (1997). For Plutarch and history, see Pelling (1997) and (2002).

3 All quotations of Plutarch are taken from the translation of Perrin (1918).

4 Vergil, *Aeneid* 1.148–56.

5 Drawn from the 1559 French translation of Jacques Amyot, the first edition of Sir Thomas North's translation of Plutarch was published in 1579. A second edition (1595) and a third (1603) followed, containing additional *Lives*.

6 For Shakespeare and the classics, see Baldwin (1944); Riehle (1990); Bate (1993); Martindale and Martindale (1994); Taylor (2000); Martindale and Taylor (2004); and Burrow (2013). For Shakespeare's Roman plays, Miola (1983); Miles (1989); Holderness *et al.* (1996); Kahn (1997); and Del Sapio Garbero (2009). For Shakespeare and Plutarch, see most recently Cook (1996); Braden (2004); and Roe (2004).

7 Several American film adaptations of this play exist: a rather obscure 1950 version directed by David Bradley and starring Charlton Heston, the landmark 1953 production directed by Joseph Mankiewicz and starring Marlon Brando, and the 1970 film directed by Stuart Burge and

starring Heston again. For a general history of Shakespeare on screen, see Rothwell (2004).

8 The secondary literature on rhetoric in *Julius Caesar* is vast, but see Wills (2011) for a useful overview of major considerations.

9 Line numbers are taken from the Folger Shakespeare Library edition of *Julius Caesar*, Mowat and Werstine (1992).

10 Fuzier (1974). See also Wills (2011: 37–61).

11 The historical Brutus was known for his rhetorical skills. Note Cicero's works on oratory, *Brutus* and *Orator*, which were both addressed to Brutus himself.

12 For an example of a modern filmmaker's subversive engagement of audience familiarity with this line, see the 1993 comedy *Robin Hood: Men in Tights*, in which Robin Hood (Cary Elwes) addresses a number of peasants by declaiming: "Good people, who have traveled from villages near and far, lend me your ears!" The listeners proceed to detach their ears and throw them as a sight gag at Robin, who recoils, complaining: "That's disgusting!"

13 In particular, the Brutus of the show is depicted as a nervous, slight figure who is deeply shaken by the assassination of Caesar and whose resolve must be bolstered by his formidable mother, Servilia; this is a characterization fundamentally at odds with the Brutus of both Plutarch and Shakespeare.

14 The mention of the Twelve Tables, the first official codification and publication of Roman law that dates from the mid-500s BC, nearly half a millennium before the time of the scene, also carries a distinct whiff of esoteric pedantry and pretension.

2 *Discharging Pullo and Vorenus: Veterans in* Rome

Lee L. Brice

Readers' interest in the Roman army and battles often does not extend to considering veterans, yet they were a significant part of Roman military life.[1] Every man not killed during service became a veteran. Since two of the primary characters in the series *Rome* start out as soldiers, and the military is present in every episode, it should not be surprising that veterans figure prominently. As with its treatment of active military life, the treatment of veterans in *Rome* is similarly successful. Once we disregard those production choices made for the dramatic and narrative requirements of a historical television series, what emerges is a useful treatment of some issues veterans faced in ancient Rome. Examining two specific aspects of veterans' experience in the series and in the historical record – their reintegration into society and relationships with political leaders of the period – highlights some ways in which the treatment of veterans in *Rome* is useful for an audience seeking to understand veterans better, whether Roman or other.

ROMAN VETERANS IN FILM

Whereas one can write about a tradition of the Roman army in film, there is much less to be reported about Roman veterans on film. In the last forty years there are only four feature films in which Roman veterans appear: *Gladiator* (2000), *King Arthur* (2004), *The Last Legion* (2007), and *The Eagle* (2011).[2] Admittedly, the protagonist in *Gladiator* was not a veteran for long on screen, but even so brief a veteran status justifies inclusion. It is no coincidence that in all four films the veterans play similar roles – after being abused, abandoned, or forgotten (or some combination) by flawed leaders and/or policies, the veterans are eventually provoked into picking up weapons and armor to restore freedom and order, if not also Rome itself. The success of *Gladiator* spawned many imitators, and the plot of a redeemed hero restoring order and getting revenge is a standard one.[3] While it may be surprising that Roman veterans do not appear more often in feature films, it is more astonishing that this "revenge plot" has been the only one for Roman veterans in film, especially given that the military veteran has been a staple character in film history.

The film industry has included veterans among film characters for almost as long as there has been an industry, from their first appearance in *The Birth of a Nation* (1915). Like the literature on which they often draw, films portray veterans of many wars, and show them in a variety of "types" across a wide spectrum of complexity. Veterans as film characters are not necessarily present as a means for society to grapple with recent military conflict and demobilization, but films that employ veterans as protagonists in that way are not uncommon.[4] Given the diversity of roles veterans have played in film, it is obviously surprising that films devoted to ancient Rome are so monolithic in their treatment of veterans. Fortunately, the series *Rome* did not follow that pattern.

The veterans in *Rome* fit into this film industry standard in a variety of ways. They demonstrate the same variety that such characters portray in most film genres; beyond the dramatic requirements of the series, veterans have a variety of roles – positive, negative, and neutral. The graphic violence in the series is consistent with contemporary filmmaking as well. Regardless of whether it reflects increased historical accuracy, film audiences have come to expect it in films punctuated with combat.[5] The violence in *Rome* is part of the setting, but much of it is actually committed by the two characters Lucius Vorenus and Titus Pullo while they are veterans.

The violence committed by Roman veterans is, in a way, reflective of another trend in film. Particularly in American films made since 1965, such as *Born Losers* (1967), *The Outlaw Josey Wales* (1976), *First Blood* (1982), and *Stop Loss* (2008), veterans are portrayed as troubled and prone to anti-social and violent acts. Whether this presentation reflects society's fears or recognition (or perhaps both) of the stress that war inflicts on some veterans, it is important to remember that cinematic treatment of veterans and the issues they face is more complicated than space permits here.[6] Some audience members will see the violence by veterans in *Rome* and perceive it as connected to the effects of the actual wars in the Middle East that were ongoing during production. Others will see it and recall that this personal violence is one of the ways films have often presented veterans. From a cinematic perspective, the varied presentation of veterans in *Rome* is consistent with the film industry's history.

HISTORICAL VETERANS

Regardless of how long they serve, upon discharge soldiers enter another realm of military life, that of the veteran. This aspect of military service is as true of the Roman legionary as it is of modern members of the military. Like their modern counterparts, Roman veterans encountered and grappled with a variety of complex issues arising from their new status. Many probably had minimal troubles making the transition, while others had more difficulty and some eventually re-enlisted. Each veteran's story was different, but there were certain similarities to which we can point.

The return home to family and community was for many veterans the first issue. We have precious little information from the Republican era about veterans returning to the towns from which they were recruited. Families were generally glad to have family members return even with the disruption to home life. For example, the Roman historian Livy reports that following the battle of Lake Trasimene in 217 BC, families were desperate for news from the front and in two cases mothers died when their sons, who had been reported dead, returned home; similar reports convey the sense that families paid attention to any news and official intelligence.[7] This reliance on news about the fate of veterans is well illustrated in the first season of *Rome* (episode 2, "How Titus Pullo Brought Down the Republic") when Lucius Vorenus returns home from long duty. His wife tells him he was reported as dead and that she had no other news of him. At the end of episode 2 and also in episode 3 ("An Owl in a Thornbush"), Niobe again has informal news of the army's movements and reacts to it. Then at the end of the second season (in episode 22, "De Patre Vostro"), Vorenus' children receive news of Mark Antony's defeat at Actium, where their father was serving; it is the only information they have about his potential fate until he returns wounded to Rome at the end of the episode. This lack of information reflects an ancient reality in our sources.

Often veterans would return home with no warning, thus causing immense disruption. As already noted, Livy writes (*History of Rome* 22.7.13–14) that two mothers died when their sons returned home unexpectedly. One can imagine all the different kinds of situations returning veterans might have found. Vorenus' return home in episode 2 provides a sense of how disruptive an unexpected return could be for all concerned in the Roman community. Vorenus has difficulty getting along with his wife and children and *vice versa*. Pullo, his associate who comes to live with him, proves to be an additional disruption. The house is made topsy-turvy for some time until everyone adjusts to the new state of affairs.

The community with which veterans were most familiar during service was their army unit. In the Roman military of the Republic, men might be called for service several times over the course of their life and serve in various units, so that most men were not as loyal to a particular legion as they would become during the Empire. However, they would still have had close ties to the military as a whole.[8] Throughout the series veterans are shown clinging to that community in a variety of ways. Veterans in *Rome* greet and address each other as "brother." No ancient source suggests that this greeting was necessarily standard for all veterans, but a variety of letters and inscriptions record that it was a cultural norm for soldiers to address other soldiers with whom they were familiar as "brother" or "tent-mate."[9] Similarly, in *Rome* the issue of loyalty is constantly a theme between all veterans who remind each other of combat rescues. Pullo's disappointment at not being permitted to march in Caesar's triumph with his former unit (episode 10, "Triumph") communicates how some veterans could retain a strong connection with the military community they knew, especially soon after discharge. The military community was not the family, however, for men who had one to which they could return.[10]

Once home, the Roman veteran had to find a way of making a living if he was not already a farmer, as most would have been during the Republic. Vorenus tries his hand at various occupations, as does Pullo. Some but not all of their attempts involve drawing on the violent skills learned as soldiers, including serving as bodyguards. The point is not that these were the kinds of jobs to which veterans resorted, but that both men had difficulty adjusting to the new demands of life.

The veterans in *Rome* respond to the stress of readjustment differently not just for dramatic reasons, but as we would expect of historical Roman veterans. As we know from studies of modern veterans, the stress of combat affects every participant, but not in the same ways or to the same degrees, so they respond differently. These responses to combat may be manifested in various ways or perhaps not appear at all. There is no reason to think ancient veterans would have been so different in their physiological responses to combat stress given that their physiology was the same as that of twenty-first-century veterans. True, the impact of gunpowder warfare is different as is culture, but the physiology is the same, even if we do not yet entirely understand all aspects of physiological stress responses.[11]

As a veteran, Pullo tends in the first season to lose himself in drinking until he finds more stability. He does, occasionally, demonstrate extraordinary and violent anger. Vorenus' character seems to avoid excessive consumption, but as a veteran he demonstrates a hair-trigger temper and often loses control. His behavior in episode 13 ("Passover") is indicative of the trouble he has adjusting. Of course even non-veterans may have a bad temper and suffer from depression, so we should not assume his temper is a function of his military service. These expressions of his personality seem to subside when Vorenus is back in the army. Regardless of whether either character's behavior rises to the level of actual PTSD (post-traumatic stress disorder), the outbursts are a reminder that some ancient veterans did suffer from the stress of combat.[12] We have no accounts from ancient Rome about this aspect of veterans' activities, but *Rome* again provides viewers a sense of the difficulties some veterans may have faced.

Some veterans simply re-enlisted despite having fulfilled their required six years in service. Men who re-enlisted did so for a variety of reasons. Some re-enlisted because they were invited by former commanders and lacked any alternative. Such men were called *evocati* (singular, *evocatus*) because they were "called back." Most of our evidence for them comes from the late Republic and Empire, but they are attested during the Second Punic War.[13] Some became centurions and other lower ranking officers or were asked to take roles in legionary administration, but most seem to have remained in the ranks, possibly organized as separate units within the legion under their own lower rank officers. In several cases during the civil wars at the end of the Republic we know of entire legions made up mostly or entirely from veterans (as will be discussed further below).[14]

Other reasons men re-enlisted voluntarily are reported in sources and are not difficult to imagine. A few veterans may have returned to the ranks because they found the adjustment after discharge too disruptive or troublesome for them and their community. Some veterans returned for the status and rewards, or because they liked military life.[15] One such case might be that of Spurius Ligustinus who served twenty-two years during the early second century BC and was promoted repeatedly.[16] Other veterans found it difficult to prosper or survive without the regular military pay and special bonuses. In general, soldiers were better off than many poorer Romans because they had a guaranteed wage and opportunities for enrichment. Cassius Dio reports an incident when a large group of men originally discharged for indiscipline appealed to Octavian in 33 BC to be permitted to re-enlist because they lacked the financial means to get by. This case was unlikely to have been isolated. We also know that sometimes veterans returned to the ranks out of loyalty to their commander or his memory.[17] Reasons for re-enlisting were varied, but it was common enough that there was no loss of status in doing so.

The series *Rome* provides viewers with examples of why some men re-enlist. Vorenus counts himself discharged first in episode 3 after returning to Rome. Pullo's status is less certain until episode 9 ("Utica") when both men return from the war. Antony even predicts in episode 4 ("Stealing from Saturn") that Vorenus will not succeed in any endeavor outside of soldiering and offers him a chance to enroll as a prefect of the *evocati*. Vorenus re-enlists soon thereafter when all his efforts at finding an occupation outside the military fail. After both men return to Rome in episode 9, they are tempted at various points to re-enlist. Vorenus again re-enlists when all else falls apart in the second season (episode 20, "A Necessary Fiction"). Pullo provides viewers a sense of the temptation of re-enlistment. He considers it during Caesar's triumph (episode 10) when he realizes he is sundered from the military community; he considers it again in episode 18 ("Philippi") when he looks at his soldier kit in a box under the bed, and even pulls out his old helmet for a good polishing (Figure 3). He re-enlists finally only when he has lost his family in Rome and is called upon by Octavian in episode 21 ("Deus Impeditio Esuritori Nullus"). Mascius, their colleague in Season Two, provides a good example of a veteran who would not re-enlist, even after losing his farm and running out of most options. These episodes of re-enlistment may follow the dramatic requirements of the series, but they are also true to some of the reasons men might have re-enlisted. Of course as Antony's offer to Vorenus in episode 4 suggests, there is another side of re-enlistment – the relationship between soldiers and politicians.

VETERANS AND GENERALS

Just as soldiers were extremely important to the success of Caesar, Pompey, Antony, and other political figures, so too were the veterans, as it turned out. We may be inclined to dismiss the central importance of Lucius Vorenus and Titus Pullo to the political leaders in Rome as

Figure 3 Pullo (Ray Stevenson) polishes his old helmet and considers re-enlisting in episode 18 ("Philippi") of *Rome* (2007). HBO BBC.

dramatic license, but we must also recognize that these two characters serve as symbols for the relationship between political leaders and soldiers and veterans. Because Rome's legions were originally citizen militias, veterans were important politically too. During the late Republic and especially the period covered by the series *Rome*, veterans acquired even greater significance. This historical importance is reflected in the series in several ways.

Both Caesar and Pompey were charismatic leaders who created strong personal bonds with their soldiers. When Pompey says in episode 3 that he summoned his armies to assemble, he is referring to his veterans, who had been discharged in and since 62 BC. These men had been critical to Pompey's political success and he relied on these *evocati* to fill out his ranks with capable men. Caesar's actions in January of 49 BC may have been disturbing to some men in ways similar to that portrayed by Vorenus in episodes 2 and 3, but Caesar was able to rely on his experienced legions, most of whom knew only his leadership and followed him in terms similar to those expressed in the series by Pullo. Caesar and Pompey both had *evocati* in their army ranks at Pharsalus, but it was Caesar's veterans who turned the tide. Even after Pompey's death, other generals fighting against Caesar continued to rely on Pompeian veterans.[18] The plot point of Vorenus' re-enlistment in episode 5 ("The Ram Has Touched the Wall") is a reminder that Caesar did indeed rely on re-enlisting veterans.

When needed, the veterans were available rapidly because they lived in colonies and holdings set up by their former generals. By the time Caesar crossed the Rubicon, it had become a common tactic for powerful generals to try to secure land for their veterans. Pompey had, with Caesar's help in 59 BC, secured land for his veterans. Before the civil war ended in 45 BC, Caesar had to begin settling the veterans who had served longest. *Rome* illustrates the land issue through secondary veteran characters such as Mascius who appears in episode 11 ("The Spoils") asking Vorenus for assistance. In the series Caesar offers land for Mascius and his fellow veterans, just as in the historical period he made great efforts to settle his veterans without disrupting Italy. Caesar's plans took time to enact because he tried to purchase the land for his veterans instead of seizing land and causing unrest among the dispossessed as had occurred when earlier generals settled their soldiers. The delay in purchasing land had created a situation where there were veterans who had still not received land years after discharge.[19] The land that Mascius received in episode 11 was part of this enormous settlement plan. In a way, Vorenus' grant of land in episode 12 ("Kalends of February") is symbolic of the same settlement program. Mascius' belief that he could get something from Caesar suggests the hope and expectation Roman veterans may have clung to that a successful general could help his men even after discharge. The triumvirs also settled veterans, but only their own.[20] These grants of land were something that powerful generals could try to secure, but not all veterans were so lucky as the men of Pompey, Caesar, and the triumvirs.

The land settlement plan was a success and it distributed Caesar's veterans all over Italy without causing the unrest earlier settlements had; but not all the men who received land succeeded at being farmers.[21] The series illustrates this fact when Mascius reappears in the second season in episode 14 ("Son of Hades"). By then, he has failed as a farmer and lost the land. Mascius may not have re-enlisted, but it is not hard to imagine that many other failed farmers would have done so. The series thus carries through a historical reality of the period in that some veterans did not succeed and many of these failed farmers were available for the powerful leaders to recruit into their armies during the next civil war.

When the sparring between Antony and Octavian became more serious in October of 44 BC, Octavian left Rome to start recruiting veterans among Caesar's colonies in Campania. In the series, the recruitment is handled as hearsay in Cicero's letters in episode 15 ("These Being the Words of Marcus Tullius Cicero"), no doubt a cost-effective way to present historical exposition. The reality, which was suggested in *Rome*, was that both Antony and Octavian recruited veterans in large numbers among Caesar's veteran colonies, who signed on for reasons as varied as the veterans in the series. Each of the generals of the period after 44 BC relied militarily on Caesar's and Pompey's veterans as the core of their forces, just as Antony and Octavian do in the series.

The manner in which Caesar, Antony, and Octavian each treat Pullo and Vorenus with remarkable public favor and seek their support in various instances is not just drama, it is true to the political climate in which Roman veterans were important to all leaders in the period covered by *Rome*. These leaders were not just generals, they were politicians who needed the favor of the people to secure their political ambitions. Caesar was dictator in 48 BC and continuously from 46 BC, but if the veterans had turned against him politically he would have had great difficulty leading. Similarly, if a portion of the people were against a law sought by a political figure he was able to call on his veterans to turn out for the vote or canvass support and help sway the assembly. Antony's political popularity in Rome during the triumvirate (from 43 to 33 BC) was genuine and it was founded in no small part on his winning and keeping the support of Caesar's and his own veterans, even when he was in Egypt.[22] Thus, while we recognize the importance of legions in the late Republic, these men did not become politically inconsequential once they became veterans.

The series effectively provides viewers with ways of visualizing this political role for veterans. An example of how the series illustrates Caesar's sensitivity to veterans and politics occurs in episode 11. Caesar cannot intervene on Pullo's behalf, nor have his adherents do so, and at the close of the episode the slave Posca finally tells the crime boss Erastes Fulmen not to use veterans in the future. Vorenus' rise to magistrate (episodes 11 and 12) and his later dominance of the criminal gangs in the second season of *Rome* may be dramatic license, but these themes are also illustrative of the political importance of veterans to Caesar and the triumvirs. Support of veterans for Antony is illustrated by Vorenus' unwavering loyalty to him; and in episode 21 when Pullo has to tell Octavian about his friend's loyalty to Antony, he is asked to try to sway Vorenus with a promise of safety under Octavian. Thus, Pullo's and Vorenus' relationship with Caesar and the triumvirs, indeed their role in the narrative, symbolizes the political as well as the military relationship between veterans and leaders and their importance in the tense politics of this period.

CONCLUSION

Several years ago in the process of evaluating the treatment of the military in *Rome*, I suggested that "although its very nature as filmed entertainment makes it a fictionalization of history, in its treatment of major issues *Rome* remains true to the atmosphere of the period with which it is concerned – the Civil Wars at the end of the Republic."[23] That verdict applies equally to the ways in which the series presents Roman veterans.

As long as we accept *Rome* for what it is, a cinematic work of historical fiction, we can enjoy the spectacle while also using many of its details to illuminate aspects of Republican Rome that remain incompletely presented in our sources. Roman veterans, despite their obvious political and military importance, are lost to us historically in many respects. They are not lost in a fog, but to some extent are historically invisible. Our sources seldom discuss them and when they do, it is without many of the details we would like to know. Using the themes of readjustment and political importance, the series *Rome* can be seen as effective in its various depictions of the trials and tribulations of veteran characters dealing with or failing to readjust to life outside the military. *Rome*'s narrative handling of Roman veterans is both valuable and historically reasonable, and it functions as a strong, identifiable feature of the entire series, especially in the second season, as Pullo and Vorenus grapple with their status as veterans.

NOTES

1 I am grateful for the comments of Larry Tritle and Georgia Tsouvala on this essay. Any errors that remain are mine.
2 Note, too, that the protagonist of the STARZ cable television series *Spartacus: Blood and Sand* (2010) was supposed to be a veteran of the *auxilia*, the non-citizen corps of the Roman army.
3 On the history of the plotline, see Hark (1993: 152). On *Gladiator*, see Winkler (2004).
4 See Tritle (2000: 161–3); Tritle (2015). Both Tritle's works are critical to our understanding of ancient veterans; much he suggests about Greek veterans should also apply to Romans.
5 Brice (2008: 61–3).
6 Clark (1986); Tritle (2000: 161–3) with references; Tritle (2015).
7 Livy, *History of Rome* 22.7.6–14; Cicero, *Philippics* 14.11.31, 13.35.
8 Livy, *History of Rome* 42.34; MacMullen (1990); Rankov (2007: 32–5).
9 "Brother" (*frater*), see *Tabulae Vindolandenses* 2.311; 2.343; Tacitus,

Annales 1.61–2. "Tent-mates" (*commilitones*), see Cicero, *Letters to Friends* 11.7; Caesar, *The Civil War* 3.71; Appian, *The Civil Wars* 2.72; 3.65; 4.90, 117; 5.39; Plutarch, *Life of Marius* 7.4–5.

10 Bowman (1998: 90–3); Hope (2003).

11 Tritle (2000); Shay (2002); Tritle (2015); Heidenreich and Roth (2015).

12 Tritle (2015).

13 Livy, *History of Rome* 42.34; Keppie (1983: 35–8).

14 Cicero, *Letters to Friends* 3.6; 10.24; 15.4.3; Caesar, *The Gallic War* 7.57; *The Civil War* 1.3; 1.17; 3.88; 3.91.

15 Tritle (2015).

16 Livy, *History of Rome* 42.34.

17 On the events of 33 BC, see Cassius Dio, *Roman History* 49.34.3–35; Brice (2011: 49–51). On loyalty, see Cicero, *Letters to Atticus* 16.8 and 11; Caesar, *The Civil War* 1.3; Appian, *The Civil Wars* 3.40–2.

18 Keaveney (2007: 42–6).

19 Cicero, *Letters to Friends* 9.17; Plutarch, *Life of Julius Caesar* 51; Cassius Dio, *Roman History* 42.54; Keppie (1983: 49–58).

20 Keppie (1983: 58–82); Brice (2011: 49–51).

21 Appian, *The Civil Wars* 3.42; Keppie (1983: 122 n.7); Brunt (1988: 270–1); Keaveney (2007: 54–6, 62–5).

22 Livy, *History of Rome* 31.6.3–4; Cicero, *Letters to Atticus* 4.16; Appian, *The Civil Wars* 5.17; Cassius Dio, *Roman History* 45.12. See also Keppie (1983: 101–12); Keaveney (2007: 42–56); Brice (2011: 41–51).

23 Brice (2008: 61).

3 *Gangsterism in* Rome

Arthur J. Pomeroy

Illegal activities and the violence that underpins them form a large part of the storyline of *Rome*. Up to now, however, little attention has been paid to the depiction of criminality in the series, perhaps because the sexual politics are so prominent in their own right.[1] Still, like love and marriage, sex and violence are a natural combination for a modern audience and the second component deserves closer attention. If the sex cannot be viewed as simply gratuitous, so the violence contributes to one of the most important motifs of the series: the will to succeed and gain one's desires by whatever means might be necessary and the human cost of such behavior. As with much of *Rome*, the narrative presentation is modern, but draws on themes already present in the Roman world. During the breakdown of order in the late Republic and the triumviral period after the assassination of Julius Caesar, aristocratic politicians act like leaders of criminal gangs, while in the face of ineffective government the general populace is subject to local forces that maintain a tenuous order by both exploiting their fellows and preventing others from doing the same. This gangster theme is well worth exploring both for what it reveals about ancient Rome and the modern viewers' expectations.

CALLING OUT THE BAD GUYS

The accusation of criminality and the consequent assumption that the speaker making this claim is defending the peaceful and lawful privileges of all society is deeply embedded in Roman political discourse. These are, of course, the words of the wealthy and powerful, since the plebs in general had no voice in government.[2] Following the death of Augustus, two bronze plaques were set up at the entrance to his tomb to memorialize his services to the Roman state. Amid various, often tendentious claims in this summary of imperial services that he had arranged to be distributed throughout the Empire, the emperor declared that he had brought peace to the seas, freeing them from the ravages of "bandits."[3] He meant by this his defeat in the 30s BC of Sextus Pompey, whose control of the shipping lanes around Italy had threatened Octavian's power in the west. The people of Rome thus had their food supplies restored by the efforts of Octavian and his general, Agrippa. Yet on his coinage Sextus had portrayed himself as the successor of his father, Pompey the Great, who thirty years before had cleared the Mediterranean shipping routes from the crippling attacks of pirates. Whether one ended up as pirate or savior depended on the history that was written by the victors.

Indeed, the abuse of the Latin language shown in this case was nothing new. In the late Republic, the orator Cicero's rhetoric was replete with the term "brigand."[4] This could refer to the Sicilian governor Verres, whom he was prosecuting for corruption and whom he described not merely as a brigand but as the brigand chief. Cicero uses the same term to describe the supporters of Catiline, accused of plotting to destroy the city of Rome itself. He does not limit his use of brigand to describing his enemy, the tribune Clodius, but includes those he saw as the latter's accomplices, the scoundrelly consuls of 58 BC who colluded with his enemy to bring about his exile. In short, any criminal – for to oppose Cicero was, in his mind, to oppose the lawful business of the Roman state – was a brigand. As one might expect the rhetoric is ratcheted up further when referring to his nemesis, Mark Antony, who is in addition an assassin and a Spartacus to boot.[5] During the reign of Tiberius, the historian Cremutius Cordus was accused of treason for having spoken respectfully about the assassins of Julius Caesar, Brutus and Cassius, famously not calling them brigands and parricides.[6] Cremutius' offense was implicitly to reject the official version of *The Deeds of the Divine Augustus* 3, according to which Octavian was forced to take up weapons against those who had murdered his "father," thus reducing the civil war that culminated in the battle of Philippi to an unproblematic police action. Just as modern political opponents may be labeled terrorists or freedom fighters, the Liberators, as Brutus and Cassius styled themselves, could equally be referred to as assassins and parricides.[7] All this is stock invective, typical of Roman politics. Such accusations of violent behavior and criminality were as much designed to suggest that one's opponents had far overstepped the limits of the socially acceptable and to defame them as to describe actual behavior. Of course, similar accusations of illegality can be found in the heat of modern politics worldwide. Sometimes they may actually indicate hidden or even public violent and criminal behavior, but often they should be taken with more than a grain of salt.[8]

Rome is certainly full of henchmen (*operae*) and assassins (*sicarii*) and even the occasional poisoner (*veneficius*: the slave boy Duro in episodes 14, "Son of Hades," and 15, "These Being the Words of Marcus Tullius Cicero"). For instance, Timon is regularly called in to do the dirty work for Atia, whether it be disposing of Octavia's first husband, Glabius (episode 3, "An Owl in a Thornbush"), or staging a highly public assault to humiliate Servilia (episode 9, "Utica"). Quintus Pompey, who attempts to kill Antony, performs a similar function for Servilia (episodes 12, "Kalends of February," and 13, "Passover"). Erastes Fulmen is introduced as the gang leader of the Aventine, who demands a public apology from Vorenus for beating up one of his men. After a long build-up, the showdown between Fulmen's gang and Pullo and Vorenus is thwarted at the last moment by the arrival of Caesar's troops (episode 9). When Vorenus is given responsibility for keeping the Aventine settled and acting as Caesar's personal bodyguard, the connection between criminal activity at the highest level (Caesar's overthrowing of the Republic) and on the street becomes clear. Indeed it is one of the basic themes of *Rome* that the behavior of the small folk echoes and comments on the actions of the great. Julius Caesar is revealed as a successful gangster beneath an aristocratic façade when he uses Vorenus to make an offer to Mascius that cannot be refused and thus persuade the Thirteenth Legion to accept settlement in Pannonia (episode 11, "The Spoils"). At the same time, he is indirectly using Pullo – by a chain of deniability that runs through Posca and Fulmen (episodes 10, "Triumph," and 11) – as his hitman to eliminate political rivals in the capital. In brief, Rome is portrayed as a society permeated by brutality, whether it be the official power of the army against foreign peoples (represented in the series by the Gauls and Vercingetorix), the males and females of aristocratic families competing with one another, or the men of the lower classes displaying their masculine hegemony by protecting their females and ruthlessly seeing off male rivals. Caesar may appear to have achieved dominance, but a series of incidents involving those beneath him – Atia's quarrel with Servilia, and Vorenus' murderous rage when he discovers in episode 12 that his wife had borne a child during his absence and the rest of his family had covered this up – leave him exposed to the "hit" that occurs on the Ides of March.

In Season Two of *Rome*, the anarchy the follows Caesar's murder is reflected in the disappearance and presumed rape and murder of

Vorenus' children. Erastes, who has resumed his dominance of the Aventine, displays a lumpenproletarian disdain for Antony's histrionics at Caesar's funeral. While he desires to increase his standing with the upper classes as the guarantor of law and order (he commands his men not to participate in the riots with the commoners – "Show some respect"), his career comes to a sudden halt when Vorenus decapitates him (episode 13). Like Antony at a higher level, Vorenus proceeds to take advantage of the power vacuum and in a terrifying display of disregard for any social or religious scruples forces the local gang leaders to agree to his control of the *collegium*, the headquarters of the criminal groups on the Aventine (episode 14). The parallelism with political events – Antony and Octavian first at war with one another, then allies – seems extended with Vorenus first proving himself in conflict with the other gangs (episode 15), then arranging a truce, apparently from weakness but intended to give himself time to regroup and, if necessary, strike later (episode 17, "Heroes of the Republic"). This "Syndicate" quickly turns into Murder Incorporated when the triumvirs, the new coalition of aristocratic warlords, make use of their skills to eliminate the proscribed. This depiction of corruption in government and on the streets, Chicago-style, actually has classical precedents: Pliny the Elder, writing safely in the middle of the first century AD, can describe the triumvirate of Octavian, Antony, and Lepidus as a *collegium.*[9] While the word chosen could refer to an upper-class "board of administrators," it equally associates the unconstitutional behavior of the new rulers of Rome with that of the street-level gangs.

Wealth and quasi-respectability flow from the gangs' connection with political power, and under Vorenus' guidance the *collegia* advance from simply extorting money from their neighborhoods to become a form of "friendly societies," providing security and assistance to the locals and even organizing the grain supply in times of dearth (episodes 18, "Philippi," and 21, "Deus Impeditio Esuritori Nullus"). However, the divisions between the gang leaders remain and come to the fore when Memmio steals a shipment of gold that was under Vorenus' protection, one that had been already earmarked by Maecenas and Posca for their own peculation. The upshot of this confused larceny is a major confrontation between Pullo and Memmio at the *collegium* (episode 20, "A Necessary Fiction") that in its bloody resolution foreshadows the conflict to follow between Octavian and Antony (Figure 4). Only one gangster can prevail to become *capo di tutti capi*, the Godfather, just as only one of the triumvirs will achieve control over the Roman world as *princeps*, Number

Figure 4 Pullo (Ray Stevenson) and Memmio (Daniel Cerqueira) face off at the Aventine *collegium* in episode 20 ("A Necessary Fiction") of *Rome* (2007). HBO BBC.

One.[10] The *collegium* last appears in the series when Pullo brings home the critically wounded Vorenus from Egypt for a final reconciliation with his children (episode 22, "De Patre Vostro"). Apparently business is now "legit" and Rome, after the defeat of Antony and Cleopatra, enjoys at least the semblance of law and order.

THE HISTORICAL *COLLEGIA*

Historically, *collegia* were distrusted by the Roman authorities, and as organized groups they offered the possibility of fostering violence. So Clodius used the *collegia* to support his political campaigns against the triumvirate and against Cicero.[11] Julius Caesar and Augustus both sought to restore order in Rome by banning non-traditional clubs, as it was easy to use these for disruptive or even criminal activities.[12] Long-established groups associated with trades, for instance butchers' or leather-workers' guilds, were exempt.[13] Augustus turned the ad hoc bodies of firefighters that had been used by Marcus Licinius Crassus and especially Egnatius Rufus into the state-controlled *vigiles* in order to remove the possibility that others might in future exploit such organized groups for their own purposes.[14] The concern that associations might turn into gangs can still be seen in Trajan's reluctance to permit Pliny to form a fire brigade in Nicomedia.[15] In *Rome*, the *collegia* are amalgamated with the local associations that existed in the approximately 250 neighborhoods (*vici*) of Rome and had shrines at major crossroads (*compita*) within the districts.[16] These compital shrines were particularly important for the celebration of the festival of the *Compitalia* in late December or early January that was organized by the *vici magistri*, local officials of lower-class status who assumed the robes of office (the purple-striped toga) for this event. The *vici* certainly once had individual tutelary divinities: so Mercurius Sobrius looks out for the Vicus Sobrius and Vortumnus guarded the Vicus Tuscus.[17] In *Rome*, the custom of having a localized divinity is represented by the goddess Concordia who protects the Aventine *collegium*.[18] Such local deities were later replaced by the Lares Augusti that were handed over to the appointed officials of the districts in 7 BC.[19] These were most likely guardian divinities donated by the emperor rather than guardians *of* the emperor, but the change shows Augustus extending his public patronage of the plebs throughout the city.

In the late Republic the confusion between *collegia* and *vicus* associations seems to have been common among the Romans themselves. Perhaps particular craft associations dominated certain neighborhoods, or *collegia* and neighborhood associations shared meeting quarters. It may even be that both groups were seen by the upper classes of Rome as similarly illegitimate aspirants to positions of authority within the state. Cicero deliberately seems to regard all lower-class individuals as equivalent when he speaks of Clodius going around the neighborhoods (*vicatim*) and offering freedom to the slaves[20] – a distortion of Clodius' more likely approach to the neighborhood associations in defense of popular rights encapsulated in *Libertas*, the catch-cry of his anti-Ciceronian campaign. In 64 BC a senatorial resolution banned *collegia* that were harmful to the public interest – probably any that seemed likely to offer political support to populist politicians – and the magistrates were entrusted with ensuring that they did not organize public entertainments (*ludi*).[21] This suggests that the Roman Senate thought that the *collegia* leaders were acting as "friendly neighborhood gangsters" in supporting the Crossroad Games in their districts. When Sextus Cloelius, acting for Clodius, put on (presumably spectacular) *ludi Compitalicii* on January 1, 58 BC, Cicero claimed that it was the duty of the incoming consuls once more to suppress these games. Again, Cicero elides the differences between clubs and residents' associations as part of his political attack on his enemy Piso, who had been one of the consuls in 58.[22] That the local associations – but not the *collegia* – in some way became involved in the distribution of food handouts seems likely since Caesar's list of eligible residents was arranged by neighborhoods.[23] Popular support, perhaps also involving the *collegia* in the form of workmen (*cheirotechnai*), for the aedile M. Oppius in the triumviral period[24] might suggest that provision of services such as food supplies, which came under considerable pressure due to Sextus Pompey's blockade of the delivery of grain to Rome, was delegated down from traditional magistrates (the *aediles*) to local delivery.

In brief, *Rome*'s suggestion that autonomous lower-class groups were mainly responsible for the welfare of much of the populace of Rome in the late Republic generally corresponds with what we know about urban society in this period. But there is no evidence that the *collegia* followed the traditions of Italian and American gangs in moving via stand-over tactics and protection rackets to rival state power in their neighborhoods or even play an appreciable role in politics. That portrayal may have its kernel in Cicero's alarmist rhetoric, but it is ultimately derived from the cinematic tradition of gangster films, particularly involving the Mafia or other forms of organized crime.

ROME AND THE HOLLYWOOD GANGSTER

In essential form, the Hollywood gangster is the perverted embodiment of the American dream. He rises to the top through his entrepreneurial skills (such as in bootlegging or racketeering), but although he obtains the symbols of success (a beautiful woman, fine clothes and housing), he does not find happiness. In the end, because of the way he has sought the good life – what in ancient times would have been described as *eudaimonia* – by vice and not by virtue, his world collapses around him and he perishes. So goes the story of *Scarface* – whether Paul Muni in Hawks' 1932 version or Al Pacino in De Palma's 1983 film – Edward G. Robinson in *Little Caesar* (1930), and James Cagney in *Public Enemy* (1931). The most spectacular application of this form to a classical context is in Ernest B. Schoedsack's version of *The Last Days of Pompeii* (1935), which makes barely a nod to Bulwer Lytton's novel. The hero Marcus is a blacksmith who goes off the rails after tragedy befalls his family. Beginning his ascent as a ruthless gladiatorial star, he moves on to provide muscle for slavers and enters a horse-stealing racket in Judea with a corrupt Roman official, none other than Pontius Pilate. Established as a wealthy pillar of the community in Pompeii, Marcus' world disintegrates when his son turns out to be a Christian convert. A mass execution in the arena is only just forestalled by the famous eruption. This gives

Marcus a chance to lay down his life so that others may live – rather than dying in a hail of bullets, he meets a heavenly choir of angels in the final scene.

There are various commonplaces from such films in *Rome*. For instance, when Erastes Fulmen finds himself alone in his tavern, his sudden isolation announces to the viewer that he has not long to live, a point reinforced by the black humor of Vorenus' reply to Erastes' desperate call for his henchman. "Flavio!" "Flavio's not coming." Furthermore, Vorenus' unhinged performance at the *collegium* when he destroys the image of the goddess Concordia is perhaps modeled on the erratic behavior of Al Capone, whether as portrayed by Lee J. Cobb in *Party Girl* (1959) or Robert De Niro in *The Untouchables* (1987). One might also add that the tragic ethos that Robert Warshow famously identified with the American gangster film[25] is particularly obvious in the figure of Vorenus, whose jealousy leads to his wife's death, and whose curse on his children ends in their enslavement and his elder daughter's prostitution. That Vorena engages in an affair with one of Memmio's men and betrays her father is a scenario that could come from a gangster movie, from Jacobean revenge drama, or even Greek tragedy. Even the childlike violence of Pullo has its counterpart in the pre-Code American gangster films of the 1930s.[26] In addition, the brutal treatment of women by the characters in *Rome* has many similarities with the gangster genre, although misogyny was clearly rife in historical Rome as well.

Still, the gangster film has developed a good deal since the morality tales made within the constraints of the Production Code of the 1930s. The form has become international. Lorcan Cranitch's portrayal of Erastes Fulmen as Irish hard man and racist is perhaps descended from the Hollywood Irish characters played by James Cagney in the 1930s. But his characterization probably owes more to the English form, perhaps Bob Hoskins in *The Long Good Friday* (1980) with a hint of Guy Ritchie's *Lock, Stock, and Two Smoking Barrels* (1998). But perhaps most influential has been Francis Ford Coppola's *The Godfather* trilogy (1972, 1974, 1990) which shows crime developing from the actions of individuals into a corporatist enterprise. The juxtaposition of the jolly family picnic in the countryside with Pullo's elimination of Cicero ("Not such a bad bloke") seems almost a parody of Coppola's style, recalling the intercutting of family ritual and assassination at the end of *Godfather* I. Just as Michael Corleone was, in Coppola's opinion, a loose metaphor for America,[27] the concomitant corruption of the major institutions of society has been a strong theme of the modern gangster film. Church and state are equally tainted in *The Godfather*, while Sergio Leone's *Once Upon a Time in America* (1984) chronicles the corruption of the ordinary decent criminal when organized crime and political institutions move in. All these depictions thus show the criminal not as the outsider in society but as a particularly strong image of its failed ideals.

The influence of one particular modern film may be detected in the second season of *Rome*. This is Martin Scorsese's *Gangs of New York* (2002), which was actually filmed in the same Roman studio, Cinecittà, as was *Rome* in 2004–7. Indeed, before the 2007 fire that destroyed many of the sets at Cinecittà, including many of those for *Rome*, passage to the set for the series was through the *Gangs* set. It can hardly be accidental, then, that the confrontation between Pullo and his men and Memmio's gang in *Rome* (episode 20) echoes the battle scenes of Scorsese's film: for instance, the axe-wielding Pullo recalls Daniel Day-Lewis' Bill the Butcher.[28] The Aventine has considerable similarities to the Five Points of New York, as a barely controlled area housing the urban poor and new immigrants, and Tammany Hall rule was as much a perversion of democracy as Roman government is of Republican ideals in *Rome*. But more significantly, *Gangs of New York* is set in a city "born of blood and tribulation" whose actual creators will be ignored by history ("It would be like no one ever knew he was here"). Scorsese's film shows the harnessing of the physical aggression of the impoverished by the wealthy to create and protect their property and (by the civil war motif) parallels state and private violence.[29] Rome, too, was founded by criminals when Romulus opened up his asylum,[30] and *Rome* seems to suggest that their genetic traits were passed down to their descendants, as soldiers channel their brutality into actions against external foes or internally against one another. What seems like a modern analysis of the collapse of the Roman Republic is, however, the traditional explanation given by Roman writers themselves, including Sallust, Horace, and Livy, who lived during this period.

Not that the representatives of order, the Roman police force, are entirely absent in *Rome*: soldiers turn up promptly enough when Timon and his brother Levi provoke a riot in the synagogue (episode 19, "Death Mask"). But that is the violence of the state directed at outsiders within Roman society. As with many depictions of gangster life, the state delegates its power to the organized criminal fraternity in Rome and no legionaries appear on the Aventine. In brief, in the second season of *Rome*, the use of violence in pursuit of one's aims, be they political or personal, is no longer disguised under the triumvirs as it was under Caesar's dictatorship. We might expect that the re-establishment of a traditional government under Octavian, soon to be Augustus, would be reflected at a lower level in society. Would the new emperor's "rotten soul," to use Cleopatra's words (episode 22), be mirrored elsewhere or would violence now be sublimated to a personal level as it is in the sadomasochistic bedroom games of the first family? Unhappily, financial exigencies and mischance prevented such depictions from ever being realized. In the final episode, Vorenus' death after a reconciliation with his children following his self-sacrifice to save Pullo's son provides a sadly redemptive ending, but one that is out of line with *Rome*'s ethos. If *Rome: the Movie* is ever made (reviving Vorenus, like Holmes from the Reichenbach Falls) it will be interesting to see how a veneer of respectability comes to be placed over all the layers of Roman society.

CONCLUSION

Rome succeeds, then, not as a "historically accurate" depiction of the events of the late Republic. In many ways the RAI-Lux Vide television production *Imperium: Augustus* (2003), starring Peter O'Toole and Charlotte Rampling, was closer to the traditional account of events. Yet, unfortunately, that mini-series was a generally dull depiction of the first emperor sacrificing all for Rome and achieving peace at the cost of happiness for himself and his family. The Roman poet Lucan in the first century AD had already discovered that "facts" should take second place to dramatics in his epic, *The Civil War*. The influence of that poem, which described Julius Caesar's rise to power according to the sensibility of the Neronian Age, can be observed in the first season of *Rome* – in particular, in the sympathetic depiction of Pompey the Great in defeat. Similarly, the scriptwriters of *Rome*, while utilizing the archaeological background of first century BC Rome, have translated the storyline into a modern idiom, using the tropes of a particular film genre that would be familiar to their audience. If *I, Claudius* (1976) appealed to audiences worldwide because it portrayed the lives of the Julian and Claudian families as an upper-class domestic drama, *Rome* makes its protagonists closer to the Corleones, the Tony Camontes and Tony Montanas, and other "Little Caesars" familiar to modern viewers.

NOTES

1 For instance, there is no entry for "gangs" or "gangsters" or even "Erastes Fulmen" in the index to Cyrino (2008a).

2 For the dominance of the Roman elite in defining banditry, see Reiss (2011: 696).

3 *praedones*: *Deeds of the Divine Augustus* 25.1.

4 *latro*. Varro, *Latin Language* 7.52, derives an etymology for *latro* from *latus* ("side"), hence "sidekicks" or "henchmen."

5 Verres as brigand chief: *Against Verres* 2.4.1; Catiline's men: *Against Catiline* 1.33; Clodius: *Against Piso* 11, *For Sestius* 39; Piso and Gabinius: *Against Piso* 24; Antony: *Phillipics* 4.15.

6 Tacitus, *Annals* 4.34.3.

7 *sicarii, parricidae*: Cicero, *Letters to Friends* 12.3; *Philippics* 2.31.

8 Opelt (1965: 131–7) provides a long list of parallels from Roman orators and writers of the late Republic and early Empire for such political insults.

9 Pliny the Elder, *Natural Histories* 7.147.

10 While *princeps* is regularly translated "First Man," I here use a term popular in Hong Kong gangster films.

11 Cassius Dio, *History of Rome* 38.13.2. Historical consultant Jonathan Stamp's occasional comments in the "All Roads Lead to Rome" feature (especially on episodes 14 and 20) indicate that Clodius and his use of gangs is the model for the portrayal in *Rome*.

12 Suetonius, *Life of Julius Caesar* 42.3; *Life of Augustus* 32.1.

13 For a summary of scholarship on *collegia*, especially the clubs of the empire, see Perry (2011). Our evidence about such groups stems almost entirely from the "respectable" *collegia*, which often had upper-class patrons and might serve to consolidate social distinctions while permitting some distinction to members of the group. The prominence of the emperor as "super-patron" marks the difference between imperial Rome and the acute social competition of the late Republic.

14 Crassus: Plutarch, *Life of Crassus* 2.4; Rufus: Cassius Dio, *History of Rome* 53.24.4–6; Cassius Dio, *History of Rome* 55.26.4–5. In nineteenth-century New York the voluntary fire brigades were likewise sometimes indistinguishable from hooligan gangs: Anbinder (2001: 183–5).

15 Pliny the Younger, *Letters* 10.34.

16 For the *vici*, see in particular the detailed study by J. Bert Lott (2004); also Tarpin (2002: 111–35).

17 Mercurius: Festus, *The Meaning of Words* 382 (Lindsay); Vortumnus: Propertius, *Elegies* 4.2; Ovid, *Metamorphoses* 14.642.

18 Vorenus' destruction of Concord's statue indicates his readiness to take on all comers at this point in the drama. Later "Augustan Harmony" (*Concordia Augusta*) and "Duty to the Family" (*Pietas*) become watch-

words of the Augustan era, as can be seen on Eumachia's dedication of her building for public use at Pompeii: Dessau (1892–1916: no. 3785).

19 Suetonius, *Life of Augustus* 30.2.

20 Cicero, *Letters to Atticus* 4.3.2.

21 Asconius, *Commentary on* Cicero, *Against Piso* 6–7.

22 For a detailed discussion of the evidence and the various arguments associated with this material, see Lott (2004: 45–55).

23 Cassius Dio, *History of Rome* 43.21.1.

24 Cassius Dio, *History of Rome* 53.38.4.

25 Warshow (1948).

26 Wood (2007 [1968]).

27 Leitch (2002: 122); Fordham (2004).

28 The audio commentary on *Rome* episode 20 by John Melfi and Carl Franklin indicates the parallel: "Typical street fight. Our *Gangs of New York, West Side Story* moment."

29 For discussions of the historical accuracy of Scorsese's depiction of the Five Points, which had been strongly influenced by Sante (1991), and in particular the conflating of events and chronological shifts for dramatic reasons, see Walkowitz (2003); Gallman (2003); and Henkin (2003).

30 Livy, *History of Rome* 1.8.5–6.

4 *Class, Chaos, and Control in* Rome

Margaret M. Toscano

The tension and interplay between social classes was a major appeal of the first season of the series *Rome*.[1] By juxtaposing the stories of the fictional lower-class characters Pullo and Vorenus with that of historical aristocrats, such as Caesar, Octavian, and Antony, *Rome*'s filmmakers show both the complexity of life in the ancient city and the difficulty of wielding power and getting and maintaining control.[2] The comparison and contrast between the plebs and aristocrats continues in the second season of *Rome*, as does the desire for power and revenge in each segment of society. But another factor enters the picture that changes the relationships among the characters and classes: the extreme chaos of civil war. It is true that the civil war between Julius Caesar and Pompey Magnus disrupts the lives of all Romans in the first season. However, the strong hand of Caesar keeps the capital from disintegrating into complete lawlessness. At the beginning of the second season, however, neither the soldier Antony, nor the senatorial conspirators, nor the young Octavian has sufficient support, resources, or leadership to keep the Republic intact. The situation on the Aventine mirrors the problems among the upper-class people. Without a strong leader to keep order in the city's commercial districts, anarchy reigns among the lower classes; thugs and gangsters terrorize the neighborhoods, making normal, everyday life almost unbearable.[3]

This chapter focuses on two relationships between a plebeian and an aristocrat that epitomize the importance of allegiances across class boundaries in *Rome*: the relationship between Titus Pullo and Octavian Caesar, and that between Lucius Vorenus and Mark Antony. At first glance this appears to be an odd pairing because Antony and Pullo seem more alike, as do Octavian and Vorenus. The first two are both soldiers given to excess with women, drinking, and gambling;

while Octavian and Vorenus are both stoical by nature, dedicated to traditional republican values and prone to acting on their principles more than their emotions. The fact that Vorenus ends up serving Antony while Pullo remains Octavian's man is more a matter of circumstance than political or personal leaning. However, in the end it is the commonalities between Pullo and Octavian that enable them to survive, just as it is the commonalities between Vorenus and Antony that doom them to their tragic deaths.

CLASS AND FRIENDSHIP

Octavian and Pullo are the only main characters whose lives do not end in tragedy or thwarted frustration in the second season of *Rome* – unless we count the freed slave Posca and his wife Jocasta. Posca is astute, clever, and an adept survivor. Although he loved Julius Caesar deeply, he does not follow his master in death. This Greek man always sees himself as equal to the upper-class Romans, even when he is a slave; after all, everyone depends on his knowledge, and can therefore be manipulated by him. His wife Jocasta, who represents the upwardly mobile merchant class, seems equally adaptable to new circumstances, whether in Egypt or Rome.[4] But none of the other women's lives end particularly well.[5]

The ability of Pullo and Octavian not only to survive but also to move forward into a new Rome is rooted in the individual character of each, as shown by the nature of their friendship. Neither man is fixed in the class structures of the past, although both men are decidedly influenced by their class positions and backgrounds. Both men are flexible and able to adjust to new circumstances. Both see outside the parameters of the rigid categories of the past, and can therefore negotiate and manipulate people and situations to create a new order. Their friendship and ability to cooperate reflects the larger social reality: without cooperation between the aristocrats and plebs, the Roman nation cannot survive. Putting an end to civil conflict is not simply a matter of a strong leader putting down his enemies (Caesar vs. Pompey, Octavian vs. Antony). It is also about creating the proper relationship among the classes. This does not mean ending class divisions, which are inherent to the Roman social order,[6] but it does mean making the classes aware of their interdependence.

In the DVD Bonus Feature, "A Tale of Two Romes," co-producers Bruno Heller and Jonathan Stamp explain how the class structures laid out in the series are drawn from Roman history itself. They illustrate how the legendary story of the brothers Romulus and Remus builds a rivalry between the Palatine district, where the aristocracy live and rule, and the Aventine, where the plebeian working class live and ply their trades. While, as the producers claim, there is "a vast divide between the rich and the poor" and the poor have to treat the rich with respect, nevertheless the rich depend on the poor working classes for the proper functioning of the infrastructure – the flow of goods and services that maintains the city's vitality.

ANTONY AND VORENUS: CHAOS

This interrelationship between the rich and poor districts of Rome is highlighted in episode 14 ("Son of Hades") in a sequence of scenes. Various people come to Antony to complain about the chaotic situation on the Aventine, where gang warfare is destroying "commerce, the root of civic virtue," according to one rich merchant. The whole city is in danger of collapse because, as Cicero points out, "whoever controls the Aventine" controls trade and the distribution of food in Rome, and thus the welfare of the whole city. It is for this reason that Antony visits the despondent Vorenus, whose vengeful killing of Erastes Fulmen has thrown the Aventine into complete disorder. Though Vorenus obeys Antony's command to take over the leadership of the *collegium*, the order Vorenus establishes on the Aventine is tenuous, as is the order Antony barely manages to maintain for the entire city and state. The civil strife that is exhausting Rome is rooted in the internal conflicts among the classes, as well as in the power struggles among demagogues. What happens on the Aventine mirrors what is happening on the Palatine; the problems Antony faces reflect what Vorenus faces. Their fates are intertwined, even though they are unaware of this until they both meet their end.

Antony seems at first simply a brutish soldier, a man ruled by degenerate appetites, which is Octavian's opinion of him. But eventually both Octavian and the viewer see Antony as a more complex man. When the food crisis intensifies in episode 21 ("Deus Impeditio Esuritori Nullus"), Octavian tells Maecenas that Antony will not give in if they offer a higher price for the Egyptian grain because he is not motivated by money. Though Octavian still sees Antony as weak, he nevertheless realizes that Antony is not simply stupid or a traitor. Loyalty is part of Antony's character, which he shows to Caesar when he desires to avenge his death and to Atia when he refuses to kill her, although Cleopatra requests it. And Antony is ultimately loyal to Rome too; he will not simply attack the city. He tells Cleopatra: "Make war on my own people? I will return as a savior not as a conqueror." Antony refuses to run away and hide after his defeat at Actium because he does not see himself as a criminal. He sees himself as a Roman and dies as a Roman by taking his own life. Thus, Antony shows his sense of honor, the old-fashioned variety belonging to a soldier of Rome. Antony's primary motivation is finally revealed as he sails away in a little boat after the battle of Actium. He tells Vorenus: "All my life I've been fearful of defeat. But now that it has come, it's not near as terrible as I'd expected."

Both Vorenus and Antony end tragically, and ironically as compatriots. Though they are both brave soldiers, they are opposites in character, or so it appears. Antony is a hedonist, while Vorenus is a stoic. Yet, at the end, Antony takes a stoical approach to his own downfall. In episode 21, when Vorenus reports to Antony that he has sent Atia and Octavia away, though they have just arrived in Egypt, Vorenus has no compunction about telling Antony that Octavia says her husband is "cowardly scum." When Antony insists that Vorenus give his opinion, he responds that Antony is no coward but he has a "strong disease" of the soul that is killing him. What is it? Antony asks. Vorenus says he does not know, but he recognizes it because "I have the same symptoms myself."

The connection between the two men's characters is shown in two other scenes that reflect each other visually and thematically.[7] The first is the scene where Antony goes to Vorenus' house to rouse him from his grief and despair and to get his help with the situation on the Aventine (episode 14). When Vorenus mumbles that he is beyond redemption, Antony moves close to Vorenus and whispers in his ear: "No man is beyond redemption, Lucius, not even you" (Figure 5). Antony's surprising comment is one of the first hints that there is more to him than a man of appetites. He is no doubt speaking of himself, as well as of Vorenus. Much later, as Antony dies, the two men face each other in the same pose they took in the earlier scene, but this time Vorenus is holding his sword for Antony to fall upon. "It has been an honor to serve you, sir," Vorenus says. Antony answers, a little surprised: "Good, I hope so. Tell the people I died well. I died Roman." When Vorenus wipes the Egyptian make-up off the dead body of his commander and dresses him in his Roman uniform, he restores Antony's outward appearance to his Roman identity. Loyalty and courage bind Antony and Vorenus together, but neither of them can compromise to fit in with the new order of things. Neither man even seems to understand that a new order of things is emerging in Rome.

Vorenus joins up twice as a soldier under Antony's command when

Figure 5 Vorenus (Kevin McKidd) is redeemed from his grief by the intervention of Antony (James Purefoy) in episode 14 ("Son of Hades") of *Rome* (2007). HBO BBC.

all is in ruin in his personal life: the first time when the Aventine falls apart, and the second time when he learns that his daughter Vorena the Elder has betrayed him. In both cases the chaos in Vorenus' life reflects the chaos of the Roman state, among both the aristocrats and the plebs. Vorenus joins Antony in Gaul when the conflict breaks out between Antony and Octavian. Vorenus again joins Antony when the general is forced by Octavian to go to Egypt in episode 20 ("A Necessary Fiction"). Vorenus remains loyal to Antony to the end, in spite of the fact that he does not like Egyptians or agree with Antony's political position or personal lifestyle. "The man turns loyalty into a vice," says Octavian when he finds out that Vorenus has escaped with Caesarion after the deaths of Antony and Cleopatra. At the end of the final episode, when Pullo meets with Octavian to report (falsely) that he has killed Caesarion but Vorenus did not survive, the new *imperator* muses that it is a shame because he was "a good man." Octavian recognizes the value of the old Roman virtues that Vorenus epitomizes.

Vorenus demonstrates these virtues when he tells the leaders of the *collegia* they should use their "blood money" from killing prominent men to establish peace and order in Rome by distributing bread and fish among the people (episode 18, "Philippi"). He tells these gang leaders they must change and follow the ancient pattern when leaders provided advice and justice. While he is right that such changes are necessary for the *collegia* to prosper, still Vorenus can only conceive of answers that relate to old ways of doing things. It is true that Vorenus is capable of showing mercy when he spares young Lucius, though strict old-fashioned honor demands that he kill the boy since he is the son of Evander. Still, it is Vorenus' sense of honor and unfailing honesty that will not let him hide the fact that his daughter was forced into prostitution as a slave. When Lyde tells him that he could still find Vorena a good husband, Vorenus sees this as impossible because he is tied to the old order of things. His inability to see that the world around him has changed is a central cause of his eventual tragedy: he cannot reconcile with his daughter, who then betrays him.

VORENUS AND PULLO: IMPASSE

Vorenus remains rigidly bound to the system of the old Republic throughout the chaotic events in *Rome*, in contrast to Pullo, who understands that compromises must be made to survive in this new world. In a sequence of four scenes in episode 15 ("These Being the Words of Marcus Tullius Cicero"), the two men disagree about how to handle the growing problems on the Aventine. Their personal conflict, which escalates from one scene to the next, reflects the disintegration of order in Rome among all classes. In the first scene, while Vorenus is negotiating with Memmio and Carbo, Pullo interrupts to make a suggestion. "Silence," commands Vorenus. Later, when Pullo suggests that his friend "didn't have to insult me," Vorenus answers emphatically: "Do not question my authority under any circumstances." In the second scene, when Pullo tells Vorenus that his methods are starting a gang war, Vorenus says: "It is your fault for showing me disrespect." Pullo retorts: "Everyone is in the wrong here. I take orders from no man." When Vorenus replies that Pullo does not know his place, Pullo answers: "I am your friend. I am trying to help you." In the intensity of the exchange, Pullo lets slip that he "took care of the snake Evander." Rather than accept Pullo's obvious loyalty, Vorenus explodes with jealousy, accuses Pullo of cuckolding him, and refuses to believe his friend's oath that he did no wrong.

In the third scene, Pullo comes to Vorenus to apologize again and to deny any misconduct with Niobe. Vorenus is reasonable now and acknowledges their friendship: "I forgive you. You are all I've got left in life." But in the fourth scene, Pullo is upset because gang war has exploded on the Aventine, just as he predicted. Vorenus blames Pullo again and accuses him of "fucking my wife." Pullo says: "I am your friend. I would never betray you." When Vorenus will not listen, Pullo reacts in anger, which leads to physical blows that end with Pullo walking away from the Aventine with Eirene. The conflict between the two men centers around their different views about status and order. Vorenus does not believe Pullo has the right to question his authority, while Pullo sees himself as Vorenus' "brother" and equal. For Pullo the important question is finding a way to stop gang warfare and senseless violence; for Vorenus the situation can be controlled if he maintains his authority. Vorenus thinks order comes from a respect for authority, while Pullo believes order comes from compromise within a larger sense of what is right.

PULLO AND OCTAVIAN: CONTROL

Of all of the characters in *Rome*, Pullo is the least concerned about class status. He is a son of a slave woman and an unknown father, but he feels no shame about his origins. He is also the least influenced by a sense of family or class honor, yet at the same time he has a solid sense of his self-worth and what is honorable and just before the gods. In fact, Pullo is arguably the most religious of any character in the show. Though Vorenus believes in the gods and the afterlife, for him religion is a matter of following the correct forms. For Pullo, it is about the right order of things. Pullo has heart and a strong sense of loyalty; he is honorable, but not honor-bound. He does not need noble ancestors, money, or power to feel worthwhile. In the scene where he kills Cicero (episode 18), the statesman tells him that his killer will live on throughout history. "Your name will be known," says Cicero. "Oh my name," says Pullo. "I thought you meant me." He is more than his name, his family, his status. But he does struggle with his identity, and he deteriorates when he cannot fight as a soldier and is left without respectable work. Still, Pullo has street smarts and is a keen observer of character and situation. Alhough Pullo is grief stricken by the death of his beloved Eirene, he is able to go on after this personal tragedy. Vorenus, on the other hand, can never move past Niobe's death; nor can he form another close relationship. Pullo connects easily with others, as he does with Octavian, though he has to remind himself to stay in his place so as not to give offense.

Octavian has a strong sense of his noble class and status as a member of the Julii clan and the "son" of Caesar. When he will not consider marrying his sister to Agrippa, it is likely not because his friend is from a lower class, but because Octavian is a brilliant strategist and has other plans. Octavian is concerned with honor and virtue from a philosophical point of view, but he can act coldly to do what is expedient. He has the rare ability to combine idealism and practicality; he realizes that cunning and intelligence are his greatest weapons in his struggle to gain control of the Roman state. He sees his own abilities to end civil strife and rule Rome better than any other man because he is governed by a sense of what is best for Rome, not just for himself, though he sees the two as intertwined. In episode 16 ("Testudo et Lepus"), when Maecenas says of Antony, "You taught the bully a lesson," Octavian replies, "It was not a personal issue." Still, Octavian is concerned about his personal power. He asks Cicero for a triumph, which Cicero refuses to facilitate. But later Octavian outmaneuvers Cicero by getting the Senate to vote Brutus and Cassius as enemies of Rome for having killed his "father." First Octavian makes a speech to the Senate saying he will institute an "era of moral virtue and dignity" and that "chaos and degeneracy" will end under his leadership. But then his armed soldiers enter the Senate House, and he asks: "Who will speak against the motion?" Octavian is prepared to use force to impose what he thinks is best.

After Octavian gives a speech to the leading women in the city about restoring the old-fashioned Roman virtues (episode 20), Maecenas congratulates him for being politically astute. Octavian replies without irony: "I meant every word." Still, Octavian is not merely a moralist; he understands the necessity of compromise, not only with those who are powerful, but with those of other classes. It was the young Octavian (in the first season of *Rome*) who gave his uncle Julius Caesar the idea to pack the Senate with his own men from other classes and locations to disrupt the power of the old aristocracy. In the second season, Octavian insists on giving the Roman people the money Caesar promised them in his will, even though he must borrow to do so. He explains to his sister that he can provide the leadership Rome needs. Since he wants to lead the Caesarian party, he knows getting the people on his side is the way to do it. While Octavian is not a strong general who can lead men into battle, he is a great leader because he understands what motivates the soldiers. He tells the troops (episode 16): "We have saved the Republic, and we are owed a great deal of money. It is time to tell the Senate to pay up." Octavian knows he needs an army to establish his control in Rome.

Octavian's physical weakness stands in stark contrast with Pullo's physical prowess. But both men have the ability to make an honest assessment of their own weaknesses and strengths, which gives each the ability to negotiate his circumstances to his own advantage. Both Pullo and Octavian maintain control by cunning and an awareness of human behavior and motive. Both can be ruthless, but both also see the limits of raw power and cruelty. Antony and Vorenus only know how to maintain control by force. They expect others to yield to their authority and status because it is the way things have always been. The sickness that both Vorenus and Antony have is a fear of defeat and humiliation, leading them to an obsessive concern about their personal honor that in the end leads to their self-destruction. Each fears he is inadequate in some way, that his knowledge of the world is insufficient, which means that both men must rigidly guard their honor to protect their outward show of strength. Pullo and Octavian are aware of their personal weaknesses, but they are certain enough of themselves that they do not feel they have to control everything around them. When Maecenas tells Octavian someone is dishonoring him because the gold has been lost in episode 20, Octavian is unconcerned: "Someone somewhere is always dishonoring me." Petty dishonor is not reason enough to allow personal feelings to disrupt one's principles or larger concerns.

FRIENDSHIP AND COMPROMISE

The relationship between Pullo and Octavian, like the men themselves, survives through all the disasters and conflicts of the civil wars in Rome because each understands both the limits and advantages of their friendship. Their friendship is real, but it is circumscribed by their class status and social power. Octavian and Pullo share ten scenes over the ten episodes of Season Two, with half in the last episode, leading to the climax. These scenes are both a narrative device and a thematic device that create continuity in the second season of *Rome*. Thematically, the friendship between Pullo and Octavian shows the need for cooperation between classes to move past civil conflict and to establish peace in Rome. But the peace, like the relationship, is always tenuous, resting as it does on a basic inequality.

The first meeting between Octavian and Pullo takes place in the first episode (episode 13, "Passover"), after Caesar's funeral. The young Octavian and his teacher Pullo sit in the same courtyard where Pullo had trained Octavian in the first season, evoking their earlier relationship. Pullo has been a father figure to Octavian because he taught him to fight and took him to his first brothel. As the two now discuss the death of Caesar, Octavian confesses he revealed Niobe's secret to his sister, which is how the conspirators lured Vorenus away from protecting Caesar. Though Octavian is hesitant to admit his mistake, he asks Pullo for his forgiveness. "Of course," says Pullo, "You can't expect a young lad like yourself to be ... to be ...

It's done." Pullo is obviously disappointed. Octavian admits he is ashamed but asks Pullo not to tell anyone "because it will not look good with the people." Already Octavian knows where the support for his leadership will come from. He needs to convince Pullo, too, of his qualifications. When Octavian tells Pullo he is now Caesar's heir, Pullo offers to help avenge Caesar's murder. Thus Octavian maintains his superiority at the same time that he admits weakness. Pullo pledges his loyalty while keeping his own evaluation of the situation to himself. This scene foreshadows the last several scenes where the two friends meet because Octavian will need Pullo's help again.

The second meeting between Pullo and Octavian takes place on the battlefield after Octavian has defeated Antony at Mutina (episode 16). The power balance between Octavian and Pullo has shifted because Octavian is an adult now. When Pullo hears Octavian is victorious, he says: "I knew you had it in you." Octavian asks Pullo what brings him there: now Pullo needs Octavian's help to find Vorenus and rescue his children, which Octavian gives quickly and willingly. Although Vorenus has sided with Antony, Octavian values Vorenus' loyalty to the larger concept of Rome. Still, the fact that Vorenus has sided with Antony, while Pullo remains neutral in this case, solidifies the pairings among the men. Octavian always trusts Pullo, and rightly so since Pullo is a loyal friend. Moreover, Octavian treats him like a friend, though the class and power divide is always starkly present.

The third meeting between Octavian and Pullo takes place in episode 17 ("Heroes of the Republic") in the house Octavian inherited from Caesar. Octavian is now one of the three main leaders of Rome, which indicates his further victory and rise in status. After a friendly exchange about their personal circumstances, the two discuss the problems in Rome. Pullo tells Octavian that Vorenus is still under oath to Antony but that his friend will do his best to maintain order in their district. Pullo and Octavian are in agreement about the necessity of keeping peace on the Aventine. In some ways they have now become colleagues with a mutual interest in seeing order established in Rome. As Pullo leaves, he gestures around him: "Well done, by the way – all this!" The lavishness of Octavian's spacious urban house is a reminder of their differences in wealth, power, and status, in spite of their friendship.

Years have passed and the situation has changed drastically when Pullo and Octavian meet for the fourth time in episode 20. The grain situation in Rome is dire; the old and sick are dying, and even all the dogs have been eaten. As the leader of the Aventine, Pullo decides to go to Octavian for help: "I'll see if His Honor has any ideas." This statement seems to indicate that the two have kept up some kind of relationship. Octavian says he wishes he could do something, but even "the state's granaries are sparse." Then Octavian asks Pullo: "Tell me what the people are saying. Who do they blame?" Pullo answers truthfully: "You. They say you are the man in charge." "Not Antony?" Octavian questions. Pullo acknowledges the rumors that Antony is holding back the grain; still the people love him more than Octavian. When Octavian asks whether Pullo thinks he is heartless, Pullo hesitates only briefly: "I'll not say that, but you've never been the affectionate type." Octavian thanks Pullo and assures him he will do something about the grain. Ironically, though Octavian is perceived as cold, still he cares very much about the welfare of the people of Rome. The relationship between Octavian and Pullo has shifted once more in this scene. Octavian's authority as the leader of Rome has risen higher. He is more than ever Pullo's superior as his political and military commander. Still, Pullo trusts him enough to tell Octavian the truth, and Octavian relies on that. He also trusts Pullo for his loyalty and basic goodness, while Pullo knows he can count on Octavian's sense of good leadership.

It is at Octavian's request that Pullo meets with him for the fifth time (episode 21). The meeting takes place in the Senate House, where Octavian has just convinced the senators that Antony is a traitor because of his relationship with Cleopatra. Octavian asks Pullo to accompany him to Egypt to bring down Antony. Pullo agrees only when Octavian reveals he will also need to kill Caesarion, who is Pullo's secret son. Octavian smiles: "It will be like old times – an adventure together." It is important to note that Octavian almost never smiles throughout the *Rome* series, but he almost always does when he sees Pullo. His affection is sincere, as is Pullo's for Octavian. But this scene marks another shift in their relationship. Pullo realizes he must be more cautious and guarded with Octavian, obviously because of his son's life, but also because Octavian cannot fully understand either the vulnerability or plight of the lower class. Though Octavian has relied on Pullo for information about those he rules, Pullo knows that Octavian can only view the plebs through a utilitarian lens.

The gulf between Pullo and Octavian is more evident in their next four scenes together in episode 22 ("De Patre Vostro"). The setting is Alexandria where Antony and Cleopatra have holed up in their palace after their defeat. In three of the scenes, Pullo is a shadow in the background, standing at attention as Octavian's personal guard in the commander's tent outside the city. At first Pullo is only recognizable because of his familiar large frame. When Octavian commands a messenger to tell Vorenus he can still be saved if he opens the way for them into the city, Pullo steps forward to speak without being given permission: "You can tell him that, but it won't do any good." Obviously Pullo does not fear speaking up. But he remains a shadow until after Cleopatra's suicide. Finally there is free exchange between Pullo and Octavian. They are alone now in Octavian's tent, except for a slave in the background. Octavian is very angry at being outmaneuvered by Cleopatra and Vorenus, who has escaped with Caesarion: "Even now I would forgive him, if you could talk to him." Pullo says he is up for the job, trying not to sound too eager. While the old connection seems to be revived here, the audience knows that Pullo has a secret motive.

The last meeting between Pullo and Octavian takes place in the second to last scene in the series (episode 22). Octavian has finally had his triumph; he is now the sole ruler of Rome. When Pullo comes to Octavian's home to report on his mission, he has free access and so comes upon Octavian alone in his large state room. Octavian smiles and rises, surprised to see his old companion. He draws near: "Pullo! I'm very glad to see you alive . . . Old friends are a rare commodity." They clasp hands. Octavian continues: "It has been a long road we have traveled together." Pullo sits down before Octavian does. He explains how he killed Caesarion and how Vorenus did not survive. Octavian believes him; Pullo has always been trustworthy, so he has no reason not to. But there is some awkwardness. The scene ends with Octavian paying Pullo his reward.

In many ways this last meeting between Octavian and Pullo is a reversal of their first meeting in episode 13. Octavian is now the father figure, for he is the Father of all of Rome. Pullo now has something to hide, but there is no way he can confess, as Octavian did previously. The two men may be "old friends," but they are friends from different worlds, with the power all on Octavian's side, or so it seems. Pullo's secret does have the potential to harm Octavian, showing the complexity of power relationships. But Pullo wishes neither Octavian nor Rome any harm. Though Pullo lies to Octavian, he does not do so to destroy Octavian or to have an advantage over him. Pullo lies for the survival of the only family he has left. Octavian will have no son to succeed him, but Pullo will, if his son can accept the reality of his situation, as Pullo will point out to the boy in the very last scene.

Caesarion thinks he is the son of Caesar, but he is really the son of Cleopatra and Pullo, at least in *Rome*'s version. He stands as a symbol of the merging of classes and the illusive nature of the class structure itself. Caesarion will only survive if he gives up his pretensions of power, class superiority, and the need for revenge. The lighthearted tone in the last scene suggests Pullo may be persuasive. If so, he will prove his lasting friendship to Octavian by eliminating the emperor's rival and putting an end to the revenge cycle that family and personal honor have demanded, at Rome's expense, throughout the series. There is hope that Octavian/Augustus may establish his *Pax Romana* at the end of the second season of *Rome*, though not exactly for the same reasons charted by historians. The "Tale of Two Romes" in the series shows the two traditional social classes of ancient Rome sharply split into rich and poor, privileged and underprivileged, noble and ordinary, rulers and ruled. But it also shows the ways in which such polarities are undermined by common human behaviors and personal connections that break down, if subtly, this deep divide.

NOTES

1 Alföldy (1985) offers a solid introduction to the ways class structures defined Roman society. Shelton (1998) uses class structures as an overarching framework for understanding all aspects of Roman everyday life in ancient Roman sources.

2 For the complexity of class structures, especially in relationship to gender, see Toscano (2008).

3 See Pomeroy in this volume for the treatment of crime in the second season of *Rome*.

4 Alföldy (1985: 44–51) notes that there were "social climbers" in all periods of Roman history and that wealth was always a way to raise one's status.

5 For the treatment of women in the second season of *Rome*, see chapters by Augoustakis, McCullough, and Day in this volume.

6 See Alföldy (1985: 94–115) for the traditional Roman divide between the "upper strata" and the "lower strata" in this period. Ando (2011: 60–1) argues that as Rome moved from Republic to Empire after the disruptive civil wars, leading thinkers did not see problems in terms of "broad-scale inequities in the distribution of wealth" but rather in the relationship between personal ambition and "public-mindedness."

7 For more on the relationship between Vorenus and Antony, see Toscano (2013).

5 *Earning Immortality: Cicero's Death Scene in* Rome

Eran Almagor

Rome's fictional depiction of Cicero's death (episode 18, "Philippi") was one of the most awaited scenes in the second season, yet one that variously surprised some viewers.[1] It was greatly anticipated, as the death of Marcus Tullius Cicero on December 7, 43 BC is one of the best-known pictures of the late Roman Republic, and one of the most detailed among such descriptions in antiquity, which did not lack its share of morbid portrayals.[2] It would be interesting to explore the modern adaptation against the facts we already know of Cicero's death. But what exactly do we know? Not much, it would seem. As succinctly put by Andrew Wright, the paradox is frustrating:[3]

> The route of Cicero's flight from Rome, the precise manner of his death, the identity of his killer(s), the reception accorded Cicero's head and hand(s) in Rome, as well as the numerous other details attested in the historical material must remain in doubt. We are faced with the ultimate irony: that despite having a range of source material on this event which is, relatively speaking, extremely wide, we know very little indeed about what actually happened.

Thus, from the outset, Cicero's death is obscured by clouds of fiction. Our tradition of the famous scene stems from several strands. One is historical, and found in the extant history books of Appian (*Civil War* 4.19–20), Cassius Dio (47.8.3–4, 11.1–2), Livy (*Summary* 120), Florus (2.16.5), the anecdotal collection of Valerius Maximus (1.4.6, 5.3.4), as well as in Plutarch's biographies of Cicero (47–9) and Antony (20).[4] The other tradition comes from the rhetorical schools, and is evidenced mainly in Seneca the Elder's *Suasoriae* (6–7) and *Controversiae* (7.2). The episode attracted orators in particular and was deemed a suitable topic for what were called declamations (*declamationes*), exercises used in rhetorical training. In the schools, they included *suasoriae* (fictitious historical speeches) or *controversiae* (fictitious legal orations). The first were related to the deliberative variant of persuasion in political cases, based on historical or legendary situations; the second dealt with the forensic variant of oratory, addressing legal questions.[5] In the case of Cicero, we have two *suasoriae*, in which he deliberates whether he should entreat Antony for his life, and whether he should burn his writings to save his life;[6] we also have one *controversia* which involves Popillius, Cicero's killer, and the question whether he was right to act as he did toward his former benefactor.

Thus, only one strand in the tradition of Cicero's death is committed to the relation of facts; the other comes from the field of invention, a presentation of deliberative and legal dilemmas, in which imagination and fiction are given a free rein. Presumably, the scene became popular because of the political and ideological overtones related to the episode, reflecting, respectively, a line of propaganda directed against Antony and a presentation of Cicero as a fallen martyr for the Republic.[7] Yet apart from these aspects it would seem that the scene had a special appeal in that it exemplified the clash of rhetorical art and harsh reality, with Cicero as the great exponent of eloquence of his age not defeated in a debate but brutally slain.[8] It displayed the favorite theme of contrast between words and deeds, seen in the two completely different figures involved – an armed soldier vs. a defenseless orator/politican, whose chief weapon is eloquence. As repeatedly embellished by rhetors, the scene was designed to echo the play of fact and fiction.

FACT AND FICTION IN *ROME*

This is where the scene of the series comes in. *Rome* is an allegory of the manner in which fiction flirts with history, and is eventually allowed to penetrate it, appropriate it, and preserve the memory of real events, but not as facts. The two parallel worlds of the lower, fictional story of common Roman soldiers and the higher, political, and factual history of the Roman civil wars interact from its very beginning, and indeed form the core of any attempt to interpret the series.[9] At the juncture between fact and fiction stand the two characters of Titus Pullo and Lucius Vorenus, both historical,[10] but made fictional. The two are *Rome*'s own "Rosencrantz and Guildenstern," in that they are two negligible figures culled from a classical work (Caesar's *Gallic War*) to assume leading roles of their own in another fictional creation. The appearances of Pullo and Vorenus throughout the series function as markers of the points where the infiltration of fiction into history takes place[11] – rescuing Octavian from the Gauls, preventing Antony from entering the Senate House and making an important veto on the eve of the civil war, saving the life of Pompey after Pharsalus, fighting against Ptolemy's army in Alexandria, participating in the battle of Actium (Pullo), or being with Antony and Cleopatra in their last moments and rescuing Caesarion from Alexandria (Vorenus). The two figures are portrayed as if they are the instruments of fate to advance historical progress in a certain direction,[12] or agents of politics and history.

Pullo in particular serves in this role, as Monica Cyrino describes him: "In more contemporary cinematic terms, he is like the character Forrest Gump in his role as an incidental agent of high politics and history."[13] Indeed, episode 2 is called "How Titus Pullo Brought Down the Republic." To be sure, this forceful incursion of fiction into history is allegorized by Pullo's literal impregnation of Cleopatra. The ensuing child, Caesarion, thought by all to be the son of the historical Caesar, is in reality the offspring of the fictional Pullo. The fact that Caesarion is kept alive at the end, contrary to real history and despite ostensible claims that he was murdered – and indeed, the very last words of the series which are to reveal the secret to him – all indicate the complete appropriation of history by this fictional narrative. The ending also wholly complicates the relation between factual truth and fictional lie, made to coexist with each other in the series' universe.[14]

It would not be surprising to find the same Pullo as the man entrusted to execute Cicero, in a death scene that ever since antiquity has been well entrenched within the gray area between fact and fiction. Since we know so little about what actually happened, it would not be right to call the scene transmitted by the series "ahistorical." If we mean to say that it does not follow the ancient sources, then this judgement is not altogether precise. It would seem that some effort has been made to model several of the modern scene's details upon items found in our texts. The particulars in our sources are contradictory, so choice elements are included in *Rome* among the many possible versions. The ancient rhetorical variety, as shown by Matthew Roller (1997), stems from the employment of certain oratorical devices, such as *color*, a technique that adds information, a framework, or an event to ascribe (or facilitate in attributing) intent to the party in question (either the defendant or the plaintiff), and thus enhances one line of argument.

For instance, one important detail is that Cicero's assassin was a soldier, in the service of Antony, though his exact military rank is not clear: a common soldier (Livy, Jerome, Cassiodorus), a military tribune (Plutarch), or a centurion (Appian). Wright proposes that the soldier assassin may have undergone a "promotion" for rhetorical effect, although he does not exclude the opposite possibility of demotion.[15] This is related to the question of his social status: in the declamations he lacks a cognomen. Valerius Maximus is the first to give his supposedly full name: Gaius Popillius Laenas, thus connecting him with the renowned aristocratic family of Popillii Laenates (which produced six consulares). Was Cicero's killer of noble descent or was he in fact a freedman (or of freedman origin) of the Popillii, who received a rhetorical social advancement after his horrid deed? Moreover, did the rhetorical embellishment groundlessly include the association of this murderer with one of the esteemed families in the first place?[16] Interestingly, the series might be seen here as *correcting* the false historical accounts. Rather than a centurion, Cicero's killer is presented yet again as a common soldier, and instead of being an aristocrat, he is of lower status. It is precisely in the fact that fiction can be and is used to correct history that the overall importance of *Rome* lies.[17]

Furthermore, the lost account of Bassus (Seneca, *Suasoriae* 6.18) had Cicero address his killer as *veterane* (veteran), and this is indeed reflected in Pullo's identification of himself: "Titus Pullo, sir. Late of the Thirteenth." The early tradition held that a conversation took place between Cicero and his assassin (Seneca, *Suasoriae* 6.20, *Controversiae* 7.2.14), in which the victim had a previous knowledge of his killer.[18] Note that in the series, Cicero has also already heard of Pullo.[19] Yet while in this early depiction Cicero is completely unaware of the purpose of the man he encounters, in the series he is conscious of his fate.[20] Some of the declamations and historical versions emphasize Cicero's brave stand in face of his killer. Livy has Cicero offering his neck; Bassus has him admonishing the soldier for his hesitation; Plutarch describes Cicero as looking steadfastly at his slayers. In opposition, Asinius Pollio gives a denigrating account of Cicero,[21] and Appian, while probably not following Pollio, still does not assign to Cicero such courageous behavior.[22] This variance is seen in Cicero's alleged cowardly flight, on whose details our sources are not wholly in agreement.[23]

The blend of brave resignation and cowardice appears in the *Rome* scene: on the one hand, Cicero is silently accepting his fate, on the other, he offers Pullo a bribe to dissuade him from his task. Pullo refuses, and claims he is bound to do so by Cicero's renown. This resort to necessity as governing the killer's act was a popular motif in the schools (Seneca, *Controversiae* 7.2.8–10, 14), where Popillius is compelled by the circumstances of the civil wars, or by Antony. In Plutarch's version, Cicero's servants rebuke themselves for not coming to their master's defense, and so decide to put him in his litter and carry him to the sea, which they achieve partly by entreaty and partly by force. In the series, Tiro (who is still portrayed as Cicero's slave) tries to offer armed resistance.[24] One particularly fascinating fictional invention in the ancient narrative is the sinister omen of ravens on Cicero's final day (Valerius Maximus, Plutarch, Appian). Surprisingly, this element is also carried into the series, where it is briefly portrayed, but is much denser; it is not viewed as a portending omen, but does seem to be employed to convey a transcendent layer of meaning. Through the use of the special medium of television, a different shot is used in the scene, done from Cicero's perspective, whereby we get a view of the sky and see a crow flying. This is done at the moment Cicero requests time to reflect and perhaps spells a bitter contemplation of divinity's abandonment, or else thoughts of life or immortality.

FATHERS, SONS, AND IMMORTALITY

One noteworthy addition of the schools was a fictive previous trial at which Cicero had helped Popillius to counter the charge of parricide for which he was arraigned. This entered historical accounts as well (Plutarch). The ironic result is that Popillius, acquitted of the charge of murdering his father, now kills his *patronus* and benefactor (a social "father"), thus incidentally proving the first charge true.[25] In the series, none of this occurs. Instead, we have a different sort of irony, perhaps even more subtle and sophisticated. Cicero tells Pullo that he will be famous because of this very act of killing:

> Cicero: I dare say your work today will earn you immortality.
> Pullo: How's that?
> Cicero: I will be in all the history books. My killer's name, no doubt, will live on also.
> Pullo: Oh, my name . . . Thought you meant me.

In other words, Cicero says he will grant fame to Pullo by the latter's deed, the killing of so prominent a person (Figure 6). By this favor, Cicero would become Pullo's benefactor (close to becoming his actual *patronus*), whom Pullo would then kill in an act of sheer ingratitude. By the very same act, therefore, Pullo both makes Cicero his benefactor and betrays him. Cicero's ironic relation to his assassin is thus made to work even better than in the classical sources, by positing one action instead of three (that is, an alleged parricide, a

Figure 6 Cicero (David Bamber) awaits his death at Pullo's hands in episode 18 ("Philippi") of *Rome* (2007). HBO BBC.

legal process in the past, and the murder of Cicero), while admittedly not resembling the binding legal connection that supposedly existed between Cicero and Popillius. The way the fictional series strains a particular act to have several meanings points at the manner in which fiction is understood to create its own reality. First, it entangles the name of Pullo with the killing of Cicero, as the fictional scene explicitly predicts. Second, in order to assign an added significance to the deed as the killing of a *patronus* who had helped the assassin, an act of assistance has to be postulated as real, or at least as having the same degree of reality as the murder – in the rhetorical declamations it was a previous trial which was to become real, here it is the killing of Cicero, which we *know* actually happened. The scene thus transposes the fictional elements to the historical occurrence and transforms it to become a new event. Our ancient sources' reworking of the killing scene as presumably done by a certain Popillius is not much different from what we get from the series. Needless to say, not only Popillius' trial but also his figure itself may be suspect.[26] Plutarch even has another individual altogether, Herennius the centurion (Plutarch, *Cicero* 48), as the killer. Why not our Pullo?

Perceiving Cicero as the would-be *patronus* of his would-be killer actually fits in well with a recurrent motif throughout the series, the significance of the father–son relationship. Pullo does not know his father, although Vorenus is older and is made to act in a fatherly fashion toward Pullo; he restrains and incarcerates him at the beginning, and on more than one occasion behaves like the responsible adult. There is an interesting comparison to be drawn between Pullo and Octavian, both orphaned at a young age,[27] and Pullo may even serve as a father figure to the future emperor.[28] Pullo's son from Eirene dies; the children of Vorenus are reported to be dead, and reappear again (anticipating the later fate of Caesarion, who will be presumed dead by all); the reconciliation of Vorenus' children with their father comes only in the last episode. The first season ends in the slaying of the Republic's father figure, Caesar (a point already alluded to in the ancient sources),[29] who was certainly a father figure to Pullo, and the second season ends with Pullo's disclosure to Caesarion of the identity of his real father.

The killing of Cicero, an elder statesman and another father figure in this respect (and ostensibly a *patronus*, etymologically a "father"), is therefore significant within the series. It is probably not accidental that the *nomen* of Cicero's killer in the ancient sources, Popillius, along with the *cognomen* Laenas attributed to him by some, is found among the assassins of Caesar.[30] Some connection between the two killings was thus felt among the ancients to persist, which the series spells out with an even clearer voice through the use of the father–son motif. Cicero was also honored as a *pater patriae*, "father of the country" (literally, "fatherland") at the end of his consulship, soon to be killed by one of its sons. Note that the series has Pullo being attracted suddenly to the fruits of Cicero's garden (more on this below). Before he plucks Cicero's life, he picks the peaches that Cicero had endeavored to grow. As a metaphor for offspring, the fruit taken by Pullo correspond to another produce he appropriates later on, Caesar's fruit, that is, his "son" Caesarion. Linked with the general import of the series, then, the father–son motif in the scene is a brilliant metapoetical allegory of the way fiction snatches history for its own uses. And if fictional history of the sort presented here is the progeny of real factual history, then the relation of the series to the history texts cannot be other than one resembling parricide and appropriation: it has to kill its progenitor in order to take over the events and give them a new significance.

Note that the lines quoted above from the dialogue have several other subtle ironic nuances. The first such insinuation is included in Cicero's promise of immortality. While it is ostensibly correct and reasonable that Cicero's murderer would gain fame in perpetuity, we know for a fact that Pullo's name is not immortalized as Cicero's killer outside of the series. He will be remembered as the fictional assassin, not the one appearing in the "history books" dealing with facts.[31] It is also ironic that the name of Pullo is indeed attested in the "history books," but in those dealing with Caesar, not Cicero.[32] Thus, the latter appears to be the victim of this irony of fate and of his own arrogance. Pullo is excited to hear he will gain immortality by an act of killing, but is then disheartened to learn that this eternity concerns his *name* and not himself. Pullo appears to perceive history and fame as virtual or unreal, without any relevance to his (fictional) life and being. This is a complete reversal of the manner in which we tend to think of the relation between facts and fiction, and here the visual medium of television is important in creating this illusion for the modern audience, exactly as the oral/aural medium of the rhetorical schools was in the time of the late Republic or early Empire. In both cases, it is accepted that fiction should correct history by the very fact of its being performed "here and now" rather than virtually written for immortality.

This playful reversal opens up new possibilities to explore. By ignoring Pullo, does history distort the real facts, and in so doing, does history become the fantasy world? Or does "fiction" invent its own facts, which should gain more prominence? This is linked to the relation of history or fiction to the possibility of changed personality traits. Cicero's arrogance is fully in character, as is corroborated by his own words and works. Yet he seems to be more courageous and reserved here than ever. Is Pullo's behavior in character as well? Over the series, we observe a change in him. From a violent man or a murderer, a breaker of bounds (for which he is incarcerated at the outset), a "drunken fool," as he is called by Vorenus, he becomes more restrained, more responsible (as Vorenus gradually becomes more unsound) and at the end he spares the life of Caesarion. Is this ostensible change factual, and reflected in fiction, or does fiction beautify historical reality and cover up problematic facts? Paradoxically, it would seem that Cicero and Pullo gain immortality by following fiction's own logic. Note that in the next scene, Pullo remarks to Vorenus: "He's not a bad fellow, that Cicero. Not stuck up, like you might think." The language is in the present tense, as if Cicero were still alive; but in a way he still is, within the fictional universe. Pullo's misunderstanding of Cicero's conceit is another tongue-in-cheek portrayal, which shows how fiction *mis*represents history. Or does it? What probably matters in terms of historical commemoration is the picture one gets from its last presentation, be it a fictional or factual depiction.

THE DEATH SCENE

In the ancient accounts, there is a discrepancy between the actual manner of the fatal blow and the way Cicero's body was mutilated. Livy, Bruttedius Niger, and Valerius Maximus have Cicero's head cut off immediately as he offers it; Plutarch distinguishes between the cutting of the throat and the severing of the head, and Appian has Popillius striking Cicero's head three times when sawing it off.[33] Some (Livy's *Summary*, Cremutius Cordus, Valerius Maximus, Plutarch's *Antony*, Appian, Cassius Dio) claim that Cicero's right hand was removed from the body and sent to Antony, to be placed on the rostra in the Forum, while others (Seneca's Livy, Bruttedius Niger, and Plutarch's *Cicero*) mention two hands. According to Cassius Dio, Antony's wife Fulvia inserted her hairpin through Cicero's tongue, and Appian has Antony placing Cicero's head on his dinner table.[34] Presumably, all these gory details were added in the rhetorical declamations. It seems that the severing of the head motif goes back to the depictions of the murder of Antony's grandfather in 87 BC,[35] or else serves as proof of the murder to Antony, as indeed is noted in one of the versions.[36]

The series presents a different picture, in that Cicero's head is not put on display, but this only highlights the fictionality of the ancient rhetorical tradition. Earlier in the episode Antony had given Pullo instructions to cut off Cicero's hands and nail them to the Senate door.[37] The murder itself is understated: Pullo gently drives his sword through Cicero's shoulder into his heart; and at first, the audience thinks the only thing that Pullo carries from Cicero's garden is a bag of peaches. Thus the contrast of this impression with the following scene in which Cicero's two hands are shown nailed to the Senate door succeeds in surprising the audience and stressing the horror of the act. Yet the final part of the death scene abounds in patent politeness and is infused with a sense of appropriate courtesy and respect.

> Pullo: Mind if I pick some peaches?
> Cicero: What? Oh, yes, take what you want.
> Pullo: Thank you . . . Nice present for the wife.
> Cicero: All right . . . Now.
> (Tiro cries)
> Cicero: Stop this at once! Resume your hideous wailing when I'm gone. Everything will be all right. You've been freed in my will. Take . . . take care of my people.
> Tiro: Yes, master.
> Cicero: Goodbye.
> Pullo: Easiest if you kneel.
> (to Tiro) You might not want to watch this.

In keeping with this impression of appropriateness, earlier on Pullo explains that he could not return without completing his mission: "Imagine the fuss . . . I get back and I haven't done my job." Also, Cicero chastises Tiro for his attempt to force Pullo's retreat with a drawn sword: "Really, old friend, if you could see how absurd you look, you would not protest." There is definitely an aura of decorum in the scene, of what might be or not be done in this situation, alluding perhaps to the propriety of accepting fate's decrees or one's role in the great unfolding of history, as Cicero's philosophical approach to his death might imply. Thus we have peaches on the one hand, and a lesson on the other. One is reminded of the dual aims of poetry in Horace's *The Art of Poetry* (333), that is, *delectare* and *prodesse* – to delight and to benefit, be useful.[38] In ancient Roman literary theory, fiction was related to entertainment and the act of *delectare*, while accounts conveying truth were connected with instruction and *prodesse*. Yet fiction was not only false but could also occupy a middle ground as *verisimile*, or apparently true. Thus a historical fiction series like *Rome* might be both instructional and delightful. The audience may enjoy it aesthetically, an outcome compatible with the enjoyment of the fruits of Cicero's orchard (the delight), and they may benefit from the scene's implied lessons on fate, history, or the relation between fact and fiction (the useful). Instead of tasteless gore – Cicero's head and arm publicly displayed – we get a taste of the significance fictional elaborations have for a modern audience, which is not far off from the ancient one. Seneca the Elder likened the inclusion of rhetorical declamations within historiographical discussions to the honeyed glass that eases the consumption of medicine (*Suasoriae* 16–17).[39] The metaphor indicating the taste of the modern viewer is similar: the viewer would prefer to see the addition of delectable fictional elements (such as peaches) to what is construed otherwise as factual in order to be able to gulp down the entire historical picture.[40]

The scene presents Cicero as having an almost mystic faith in the written record; he is certain that the letter he composes to Brutus will reach its destination, he believes in the ability of his posthumous will to change reality (for example, by freeing Tiro), and he is sure that "every history book" will include his name. The written word is presumably valued more than actual life and real actions because of its ostensible power to transcend the mundane and temporary: Cicero leaves written documents after his death (letter, will), and his name will be preserved on paper. But Cicero is wrong, as the tragicomic fate of his letter to Brutus makes clear. His messenger drops the letter, and Vorenus' little boy finds it and makes a hat out of it.[41] The written word is even more appreciated by Cicero than the spoken one, and contrary to what we might expect, given his famous wit and eloquence, Cicero is made to deliver no impressive last speech in the scene.[42] Matching Cicero's faith in the written word is Pullo's similar confidence in vision, or in its effect on the viewer. His advice to Tiro is not to watch his master's death. Yet this also shows the weakness of visual representations, parallel to the blemish of the written, since once the audience averts its eyes, the memory is lost. This dual failing corresponds to the flaws of the factual and the fictional. Facts surrender to fiction, as the latter transforms them or ignores them; the powerful metaphor here is an epistle of historical significance turning into a hat. Conversely, fictional representations surrender to facts, when they are easily discarded and degraded by the audience, who prefer history. Eventually, Tiro will write his account of the murder; others will too. But Pullo will be forgotten and never immortalized as Cicero's killer. The death scene of Cicero killed by Pullo, in more ways than one, is an occurrence where history and art meet, and are pulled in various directions, symbolizing the fusion and tension between fact and fiction.

NOTES

1 The second season was viewed by some critics as falling in quality and historical accuracy in comparison to the first: see Bianco (2007).

2 For the scene, see Homeyer (1977); Roller (1997); and Wright (2001). See also Petersson (1920: 679–82).

3 Wright (2001: 452).

4 See also Seneca the Younger (*On Tranquility* 1.6.1); Pseudo-Victor (*On Illustrious Romans* 81. 6); Jerome (*Chronicon* Helm, 158); Cassiodorus (*Chronicon* Mommsen, 626). See also Velleius Paterculus 2.66.3–5; Seneca, *Letter* 83.25; Eutropius 7.11; Orosius 6.18.11; Jerome, *Against Rufinus* 3.42; Augustine, *City of God* 3.30. The lost historical accounts are those of Tiro, Asinius Pollio, Livy, Aufidius Bassus, Cremutius Cordus, and Bruttedius Niger.

5 See Russell (1983); Fairweather (1984); and Kennedy (1994).

6 Quintilian 3.8.46.

7 Anti-Antony propaganda: Seneca, *Suasoriae* 6.14, 6.24. See Roller (1997: 117–18, 124); Wright (2001: 450).

8 Cicero as the *acme* of Roman eloquence and a martyr for the Republic: Roller (1997: 124 n.39). See Lacey (1978: 170).

9 See Tatum (2008); Cyrino (2008b: 6), who calls it "dramatic parallelism."

10 Attested by Caesar, *The Gallic War* 5.44, *The Civil War* 3.67; Cassius Dio, *Roman History* 41.40.

11 As Cyrino (2008b: 4) notes: "The characters of Titus Pullo and Lucius

Vorenus, the heart and soul of *Rome*'s narrative trajectory, are thus able to manifest both the realism of historical authenticity and the thrill of dramatic originality."

12 After they save Pompey's life, Caesar pardons them because of their luck; as he explains to Antony: "Those men have powerful gods on their side" (episode 7).

13 Cyrino (2008b: 5–6): "Like Forrest Gump, Pullo is either present at or the direct cause of several momentous occasions during this most bracing period of Roman history." See also Daugherty (2008: 141–2, 147–8, 151).

14 See Wiseman (1993).

15 Wright (2001: 446–7).

16 See Roller (1997: 126–7) on the futile attempts at prosopography.

17 Creator Bruno Heller states: "This series is much more about how the psychology of the characters affects history than simply following the history as we know it"; quoted in "Rome News," *HBO.com* (January 8, 2007).

18 See Moles (1988: 24, 200), who points at the resemblance of this fact to Demosthenes and his killer Archias (Plutarch, *Demosthenes* 29).

19 On Pullo's fame, the fame of a fictional character among historical figures, see Toscano (2008: 157).

20 Roller (1997: 121).

21 Seneca, *Suasoriae* 6.15–17, 24.

22 See Wright (2001: 440 and n.16); Gabba (1956: 222–9). On Dio's treatment, see Millar (1964: 47, 54–5).

23 Wright (2001: 447–8).

24 See McDermott (1972: 269) for the (unlikely) proposal that "[Tiro] . . . may have been with those slaves who, according to Livy and Appian, were ready to defend their master."

25 On the proposal that this is an invention of the schools, see Seneca, *Controversiae* 7.2.8; also Roller (1997: 125–7); Wright (2001: 437–8). See, however, Crawford (1984: 238–40), who postulates a lost *Pro Popillio Laenate*.

26 For Seneca's doubt about Popillius, see *Controversiae* 7.2.8. See also Gudeman (1902: 28); Wright (2001: 441–3).

27 Octavian's real father died when he was four years old: see Suetonius, *Divine Augustus* 3–4, 8; see also Cooke (2008: 79). On the consequences of the absence of a father figure for the construction of Octavian's character, see Boyd (2008: 92).

28 Yet Boyd (2008: 98 n.9) claims that "in *Rome*, Pullo's social inferiority to Octavian ensures that he cannot assume . . . the role of surrogate father."

29 The question is noted whether Brutus was the actual son of Caesar, who notoriously had an affair with his mother, Servilia Caepionis. Caesar in any case addressed him as son in his last words (*kai su teknon*?), quoted in Suetonius, *Divine Julius* 82.2.

30 Noted in passing by Roller (1997: 127), but this fact is significant if Cicero's killer was in fact unknown and the role was given to a Popillius, in an echo of the famous assassination of the previous year.

31 Pullo attained a life of his own in the world of fiction, outside of *Rome*. He is a minor character in the books of Colleen McCullough, *Caesar* (1997) in the *Masters of Rome* series, and he appears in the *Legion* tetralogy of the Videssos fictional universe in the novel series by Harry Turtledove (1987).

32 The manuscripts of Caesar's *Gallic War* have different forms of the name: Pulfio, Puleio, Pullio, Pulcio, or Pulcia.

33 See Wright (2001: 449–50).

34 Seneca, *Letter* 83.25; Plutarch, *Antony* 20 with Pelling (1988: 167–8).

35 On Mark Antony the grandfather, see Cicero, *On the Orator* 3.10: "It was then, too, that that illustrious head of Marcus Antonius, by whom the lives of so many citizens had been preserved, was fixed upon the very rostra on which he had so strenuously defended the republic when consul, and which he had adorned with imperial trophies when censor." See also Plutarch, *Life of Marius* 44.4. Cicero's end is not a case of an irony of fate, as Rawson (1975: 296) seems to insinuate, but probably a contrived attempt by rhetoricians to allude ironically to Cicero's description of Antony's grandfather.

36 Seneca, *Controversiae* 7.2.10, 14.

37 Antony had warned Cicero directly in the first season (episode 8, "Caesarion"): "If I ever again hear your name connected with murmurs of treachery, I will cut off these soft, pink hands and nail them to the Senate door."

38 See Brink (1971: 153).

39 See Roller (1997: 120).

40 Cyrino (2008b: 4) explains: "As 'ordinary' Romans, Pullo and Vorenus more easily invite the audience into the grand historical account that might otherwise have been difficult for some viewers to access." Observe the influence of *Rome*'s delectable imagery on Richard C. Titone's novel *Of Royal Blood* (Dog Ear Publishing, 2009), where the killer, called Pullar, picks up the peaches after he has killed Cicero (29–30).

41 This image reflects Plutarch's description of the message announcing Brutus' initial military success at Philippi that never reaches him (*Life of Brutus* 47.4–7), and the parallel scene of the messenger from Timocrates to Dionysius, who lost the wallet containing the letters (*Life of Dion* 27.6–9).

42 Again, the influence seems to be from Plutarch (contrary to Livy, for instance). See Homeyer (1977: 65–8, 85–7), who prefers this version as authentic.

6 *The Triumvirate of the Ring in* Rome

Barbara Weiden Boyd

INTRODUCTION: ENIGMA VARIATIONS

Suetonius reports (*Augustus* 50) that, early in his career, Octavian used an image of the sphinx to seal letters and other documents. In a discussion of engraved gems, the elder Pliny gives a fuller description of this seal (*Natural History* 37.10):[1]

> In the beginning, the Divine Augustus used a sphinx as his seal. He had found two of these among his mother's rings that were impossible to distinguish. During the civil wars, when he was away, his friends used one of them [i.e., the one he did not keep on his person] to seal letters and official documents which the circumstances of the time required to be rendered in his name; and there was a clever witticism among those receiving these documents to the effect that this sphinx brought riddles (*aenigmata*).

In a slightly different version of this anecdote, Cassius Dio emphasizes Octavian's agency: according to Dio, Octavian himself had a duplicate of his sphinx seal made for the use of Agrippa and Maecenas, so that they could reseal the letters he wrote to the Senate and others after reading and, when necessary, altering them (*Roman History* 51.3).

Taken together, the two anecdotes, brief though they are, nicely capture and characterize the studied invention of the Augustan mask, in all its impenetrability and ominous power, from the earliest days of the young heir's ascendancy. Pliny's allusion to the witticism regarding the sphinx's riddles relies on the anecdote's implicit reference to the Theban Sphinx, who killed the would-be solvers of her puzzle until trounced by Oedipus.[2] The replication of the image, whether fortuitously found by Octavian (Pliny) or consciously crafted by him (Dio), also invites interpretation: the literal duality of the sphinx simultaneously evokes a city's salvation by the dead king's son and hints at that city's experience of terror at the hands of the same son. Like Oedipus, Octavian will both save his city and allow terror to run rampant in it.

The creators of *Rome* use Octavian's early adoption of the sphinx as symbol and seal, much as, at least as our ancient sources suggest, Octavian did himself: to assert his authority, to signal his obscure isolation as a man fated to rule Rome, and to hint at the potential for malignancy behind his calmly enigmatic appearance. They also introduce the motif of the ring – with or without the engraving of a sphinx – to characterize the Romanness of those who wear it. This chapter suggests that three characters in particular, Octavian, Brutus, and Antony, constitute a "triumvirate of the ring" in a sequence of episodes that establishes important narrative connections between and among them. All three are depicted as possessing rings that have or take on symbolic importance in the sequence of events; only Octavian possesses the sphinx-ring, however, and the distinction ensures that only Octavian will prevail.[3]

OCTAVIAN'S SPHINX

The ancient evidence for Octavian's sphinx ring is suggestive but brief; both Suetonius and Dio are far more interested in the Augustus he would become than in Octavian's early self-fashioning as a worthy heir to Julius Caesar. As we have already seen with the creation from whole cloth of an identity for Octavian in the first season of *Rome*,[4] the absence of any detailed extant account of the youth's early years presented the series' screenwriters with both daunting challenges and rich opportunities for invention. The treatment of Octavian in the second season is accordingly confident and clever, as boy becomes man; indeed, the writers appear to have relished the opportunity to replace the adolescent Octavian (played throughout the first season and in the first two episodes of the second by Max Pirkis) with a mature young man (Simon Woods), the eighteen-year-old Octavian who assumes Caesar's name and power after the disclosure of the contents of the dictator's will.[5]

The "new" Octavian first appears in episode 16 ("Testudo et Lepus"), immediately after his army's defeat of Antony at Mutina. The moment chosen to introduce the new actor is telling: Octavian is reintroduced to the stage of Roman history no longer as a mama's boy or pleb's pupil, but as victor in the first of what would prove to be many conquests over a long career. Equally important is the first look we get at the new Octavian: we viewers share the perspective

Figure 7 Octavian (Simon Woods) wears the sphinx symbol on his cuirass in episode 16 ("Testudo et Lepus") of *Rome* (2007). HBO BBC.

of Titus Pullo, who has fallen to his knees to examine the corpse of a fallen soldier and, upon hearing his name, looks up into the hazy light. Out of this haze emerges a military standard topped by an eagle; and then, directly before and below the eagle, a young soldier wearing a helmet and cuirass comes into focus – as does the large depiction of a sphinx emblazoned on the cuirass (Figure 7). As Pullo struggles to focus in the bright light, the man looming above him recognizes him, greets him, and then identifies Pullo as an "old friend" to his attendants. Octavian's superior position is emphasized visually when one of his attendants stoops to serve as a stepstool for Octavian as he dismounts; the visual cue is then emphasized verbally when Octavian says, "They call me Caesar now."[6]

Several features of this scene bear further scrutiny. First of all, the relative postures of the two characters, one kneeling on the ground and the other looming above him, closely echo the postures of the same two characters when they first met in episode 1 ("The Stolen Eagle"). There, a cowering Octavian, whose kidnappers have just been defeated, identifies himself to his savior, the gruffly amicable Pullo; this initial encounter paves the way for their anomalous relationship throughout the first season. Now, the roles have been reversed, with a confident Octavian helping a fearful Pullo; the simultaneous repetition and reversal of a defining encounter both renews the friendship of the two and redefines it, establishing definitively the normative hierarchy that will prevail through the remainder of the second season.

A further echo of the earlier scene is the initial visual prominence of the eagle standard: the encounter of Octavian and Pullo in episode 1 was a result of the search by Pullo and Vorenus for Caesar's stolen eagle, and their successful recovery of the eagle was paralleled by their rescue of Octavian.[7] Now, the eagle standard is the first thing Pullo can discern, and seems almost to be perched atop Octavian's helmet; it thus neatly establishes the connection between Julius Caesar and his adopted son. Equally important, however, is the fact that the eagle recedes from view as the sphinx on Octavian's cuirass comes into focus: the symbol of Caesar's military power and authority has been definitively replaced by a new and more enigmatic symbol.

The image chosen by the creators of *Rome* to serve as a model for Octavian's sphinx is based on the reverse of a silver *cistophorus* (provincial coin) from Pergamum now in the numismatic collection of the British Museum.[8] This fine coin, with the head of Augustus (labeled IMP CAESAR) on the obverse, in fact postdates the battle of Mutina by more than a decade and a half; the name AVGVSTVS following the curve of the sphinx's wing is prominent on the reverse of the coin, and so offers a *terminus post quem* of 27 BC for its minting.[9] Aside from the absence of an accompanying inscription, the sphinx seen on Octavian's cuirass in episode 16 is a virtual replica of that on the Augustan provincial coin, and so is anachronistic from a historical perspective; its symbolic importance, however, is hammered home by the appearance in the same episode of other similarly prominent insignia, especially the head of Hercules seen on Antony's cuirass. Descent from Hercules was, according to Plutarch (*Life of Antony* 2.1–2), an important tradition of the Antonii; the visual association of Antony with Hercules in the early episodes of *Rome*'s second season emphasizes this tradition and, as discussed below, makes his eventual transformation all the more striking.

A second feature of the appearance of the sphinx in this episode connects it explicitly with the signet ring that Octavian used in his early career. Once Octavian and Pullo re-establish their connection, Pullo explains that he has come to find Vorenus and to deliver the news that the latter's children are in fact alive, though enslaved. Octavian offers Pullo a letter, marked with his personal seal, to use as a means to free the children; he thereby indicates that his name should be enough to guarantee the success of their mission. And indeed, when Vorenus and Pullo finally arrive at the slave camp, only the document from Octavian prevents them from being turned away. The camp's boss takes the letter proffered by Pullo and, after reading it, accedes, albeit reluctantly, to their request. Before doing so, however, he queries the strange image on the seal, wondering aloud if it depicts an otter; Pullo vehemently corrects him with the words: "It's a fucking sphinx! Mark of Caesar!" – and thus offers a biting and definitive interpretation of the image associating the sphinx with the ascendant son of Caesar. The meaning of the sphinx is difficult to interpret, and this difficulty itself is also a key to its power. Octavian shows himself from the outset of his career as *Divi filius* to be a lord of the ring – and not any ring, but one bearing the sign of the enigmatic sphinx, the malevolent potential of which is later signaled by its appearance on the cover of the *tabellae* which Octavian uses to record the names of the proscribed (episode 18, "Philippi").

THE RING OF BRUTUS

The establishment of Octavian's association with the sphinx-ring in episode 16 is soon thereafter complemented by Brutus' receipt of a family heirloom, a gold ring that his mother Servilia sends to him immediately before the battle of Philippi (episode 17, "Heroes of the Republic"). As Servilia's slave removes the ring from a box of treasured items, Servilia (in a voiceover reading aloud as she writes to Brutus) identifies the ring as that of Brutus' father, handed down from father to son over the centuries, and reminisces that Brutus' father used to say that the gold was from the crown of the last king. This memory associates the ring and its wearers with the first great Brutus, Lucius Iunius Brutus, a nephew, according to Livy (*History of Rome* 1.56) of the last king, Tarquinius Superbus, whose reign ended abruptly in 509 BC. In the dramatic episode with which Livy concludes the first book of his *History*, the tale of the rape of the noble and virtuous Lucretia by Sextus Tarquinius, one of the king's sons, and of her subsequent suicide, it is Brutus who takes up the bloody sword from Lucretia's body and declares his determination to drive out the king and bring an end altogether to kingship at Rome (1.59). His success associates him, and by extension every one of his male descendants, with the liberation of Rome from tyranny; and there is ample evidence that the Iunii Bruti of the first century BC knew and took advantage of the presumptive familial relationship to Rome's first great liberator.[10] The signet ring Servilia sends to Brutus is an explicit homage to this tradition, even as it evokes the inescapability of one's fate.

Brutus' receipt of the ring in his camp at Philippi is equally evocative (episode 18). Like his mother, he recalls the history of the ring and the link it suggests to his own father; Cassius, too, recognizes its symbolic importance, and assures Brutus that he is worthy to wear it: "It's a good fit." And Brutus does indeed wear it into battle: as he faces his own imminent death, he kisses the ring before going forward, as if to extract some strength from it or to assure it of his faithfulness to family tradition. Yet viewers are never given a clear image of the decoration on the ring – it remains always tantalizingly just out of view or just slightly blurry. Similarly, the insignia on Brutus' cuirass is never shown with great clarity or precision; rather, it remains always at an angle, and is never entirely clear to viewers, although in general terms it is clearly a portrait bust – perhaps a bust of the great ancestor Lucius Iunius Brutus, or a bust of *Libertas*. This blurring is curious, especially given the full-frontal treatment that the sphinx receives; yet it also invites a symbolic interpretation, as Brutus' attempt to liberate the Romans from a contemporary tyranny echoes that of his ancestor. Both attempts, we may infer, were successful, for a time: the first determined Rome's path for almost five centuries, while the second did so for only two years, but both promised an alternative to tyranny. Both accomplishments are soon to be virtually erased, however, from the historical record, with the defeat of Brutus and Cassius at Philippi and the definitive transformation of Rome from Republic to Empire under Augustus; the symbols of this resistance, as characterized by Brutus' link to his ancestor, have already begun to lose their potency as images in the course of the series and are thrown off – symbolically as well as literally – by Brutus himself as he walks, wearing no armor at all, to meet his death on the battlefield.[11]

The erasure of alternative possibilities to Octavian's eventual victory is reflected, too, in the manner of the disappearance of Brutus' ring upon his death. Once an external symbol of familial lineage pregnant with the promise of freedom, Brutus' ring disappears from the annals of history – as, indeed, do Cassius and Brutus themselves – at the close of episode 18. We see Octavian and Antony together, surveying the mass of dead bodies on the battlefield with a businesslike lack of emotion;[12] Octavian's greatest desire is to find Brutus' body so that its severed head can be returned to Rome. They never do find the body: but someone else does, a nameless scavenger searching the field for random treasure. Coming upon Brutus' body, he quickly notices the ring, whose value as the gold of a king or as a symbol of liberty has no sentimental meaning in the present situation. Instead, with a wild and toothless grin the scavenger quickly determines that the most efficient way to remove the ring is by mutilating Brutus' corpse; thereupon he does so, shearing off not only the ring but the finger that bore it.

This brutal finale bears no resemblance to historical accounts of the battle's aftermath. Plutarch reports that, upon acknowledging that his was a lost cause, Brutus committed suicide; the biographer goes on to note that Antony did indeed find the body, and after cremating it returned the ashes to Servilia – presumably in recognition of her loss as well as to offer her evidence of her son's death (*Life of Brutus* 52–3). The writers of *Rome*, taking advantage of the elasticity of our historical sources and of a lack of reliable evidence, offer an alternative version that heralds the loss of identity to be experienced by Rome itself as the Republic comes to an end. Brutus loses his ancestral talisman when Rome loses its ancestral past; a brave new world controlled by a sphinx looms.

ANTONY THE ROMAN

The association of Antony with Hercules is well documented in our literary sources, most prominently in Plutarch's *Life of Antony*.[13] Antony, Plutarch reports, claimed descent from Hercules through the latter's son Anton; this tradition parallels many others, including, for example, the claim by the *gens Iulia* to be descended from Aeneas through the latter's son Ascanius-Iulus, and the claim by the *gens Claudia* to be descended from Odysseus through Telegonus, the latter's son with Circe.[14] Abundant archaeological evidence as well as prominent literary testimony bears witness to the strong association in Roman tradition of Hercules with the city's origins;[15] Antony's ancestral connection therefore links him directly to a mythical hero whose importance for Rome equals that of a character like Aeneas. Plutarch also emphasizes another heroic association besides that between Antony and Hercules, that is, a likeness to Dionysus, most unforgettably drawn in the scene describing Antony's activities in Ephesus (*Life of Antony* 24) and paralleling Cleopatra's arrival at Tarsus in the guise of Aphrodite (*Life of Antony* 26). As in Plutarch, however, in the second season of *Rome* the symbolic transition from Heraclean to Dionysiac persona parallels Antony's physical transition from West to East, from Italy to Egypt. Let us turn first to the Herculean dimension of Antony as depicted in *Rome*; the Dionysiac will follow.

As noted earlier, the prominent sphinx on Octavian's cuirass is complemented by the appearance of the head of Hercules on Antony's cuirass in episode 16. Elsewhere in the first half of the second season of *Rome*, it is Antony's behavior rather than his use of insignia that establishes his Herculean nature. His attempt to take control of the situation immediately after Caesar's assassination and proposal of an amnesty for the assassins (episode 13, "Passover"); his violent physical attack on the young Octavian (episode 14, "Son of Hades"); the crude menace of his meeting with Cicero (episode 15, "These Being the Words of Marcus Tullius Cicero"); the *rapprochement* between Octavian and Antony, the latter clad in an animal skin (episode 16); his delight in the battlefield, evidenced in his words to Octavian as he leads the charge at Philippi: "Watch closely, boy: this is how history is made" (episode 18); and his voracious sexual appetite throughout the entire series – all contribute to his Herculean persona: larger than life, limitlessly indulgent in pleasure, both staunch friend and fearsome enemy, violent, courageous, rash, and passionate.[16] Against this background, the attempt at domestication embodied in Antony's arranged marriage to Octavia (episode 19, "Death Mask") is clearly doomed to failure. This marriage, enacted onscreen in solemn Roman ritual, is intended to solidify the new alliance between Octavian and Antony after their victory at Philippi; but a subtle visual cue hints that this alliance is as ephemeral as the marriage itself, and is indeed destined for failure. At the climax of the marriage ceremony, Octavian as *pontifex maximus* joins the hands of Octavia and Antony, putting his own hand over theirs as he does so; central to this visual gesture is the ring worn by Octavian. We never see the surface of the signet ring here, but can surmise that the enigmatic sphinx is at work.[17]

The Antony whom *Rome* presents in episode 21 ("Deus Impeditio Esuritori Nullus") is Herculean no longer; he is instead Dionysiac, but displaying only the most languid and enervated aspects of the Dionysiac persona. He wears Egyptian dress, not Roman, and his eyes are thickly laden with kohl. His demeanor is that of someone chronically drowsy from smoking opium, and his passivity allows Cleopatra to dominate him easily. Antony's loss of Roman identity is crystallized when Octavian, after learning the details of Antony's new will, rouses the Senate with news of Antony's Egyptianization: "Who would not weep when he hears that the great Mark Antony pays homage to foreign gods?" The foreign gods most easily suggested here are the Egyptian divinities Isis and her consort Osiris – gods already mentioned when Maecenas reads the will aloud to Octavian, noting that Antony identifies himself and Cleopatra with them. In the syncretism of Hellenistic religions, Osiris had come to be identified with Dionysus.[18] The constellation of ideas thus linked – association with the wild and exotic god Dionysus, identification with Egyptian gods and traditions, and the subordination of the consort Osiris to his nurturing savior Isis – is neatly captured in the shocking appearance of an "Egyptianized" Antony in episode 21, radically different as it is from the combination of intimidating *bonhomie* and energetic masculinity that the Herculean Antony embodied.

The final episode of the series (episode 22, "De Patre Vostro"), is devoted entirely to the battle of Actium and its aftermath, culminating in the deaths of Antony and Cleopatra, the triumph of Octavian, and the return of Vorenus and Pullo to Rome. Of the battle itself virtually nothing is shown; but the camera lingers on Antony's hand, hanging over the side of the ship as he lies there in defeat. Antony is once again clad in armor, and it is not Egyptian armor, but Roman; the ring he wears, and that we are invited to notice, is a part of that armor. Once back in the palace at Alexandria, Antony again appears in Egyptian dress, but only briefly; after learning of Cleopatra's (feigned) suicide, Antony decides to kill himself, and asks Vorenus for the use of his "good Roman sword." In the moments before using it, Antony confirms his reclamation of his Roman identity with his final words to Vorenus: "Tell the people I died well. I died Roman." Vorenus decides to translate these words into action by dressing the corpse of Antony in Roman armor once more; in addition to his cuirass, swordbelt, and the other usual accoutrements, Vorenus places not one but several rings on Antony's fingers, thus signaling again their Roman provenance and symbolism. The rings worn by Antony are external markers of his Romanness, and signify his resumption of a Herculean, or Roman, persona as he dies. Even Cleopatra confirms this suggestion when she comes to Antony's dead body after putting the asp to her breast: as her last act she clasps the ring-adorned hand of her Roman lover – only for Octavian, watching her death-throes, to pull their hands apart.

With this last view of Antony, *Rome* brings us full circle: our first view of the adult Octavian is symbolically "sealed" by the visual association with the sphinx he uses as his insignia on armor and ring; the end of Brutus, along with the end of the cause he represents, is "sealed" by the disappearance of the armor and ring that signify the beginning and end of the Roman republic; and the armor and rings that decorate Antony's corpse "seal" the end of the Republic once more, locating its final moments now not on the battlefield of Philippi but in the embrace of Cleopatra and of Egypt.

EPILOGUE

Let us return for a final time to Octavian's sphinx. As we saw at the opening of this essay, both Suetonius and Pliny note that Octavian's use of the sphinx seal was a feature of his early career; the most important word in this context, however, is "early," since Pliny concludes his description of the seal as follows (*Natural History* 37.10): "Later on, Augustus used an image of Alexander the Great as his seal, in order to avoid reproach for the sphinx." This move away from the sphinx as symbol is noted as well by Suetonius (*Augustus* 50), who comments in addition that Augustus eventually settled on a seal carved with his own likeness; in other words, he ultimately, and shrewdly, rejected images of both a mythological creature and the greatest of Greek conquerors, to make a Roman (the *first* Roman) his seal and symbol.[19]

In the aftermath of the deaths of Antony and Cleopatra, the writers of *Rome* draw our attention once more to the enigma of the sphinx, as well as to the eclipse of its power as an image (episode 22). Upon the death of Cleopatra, Vorenus realizes that Caesarion's life is in danger; he quickly leaves Alexandria, hoping to transport the boy to safety back in Rome. Pullo, sent by Octavian to find and kill the boy, is reunited with his old friend in the desert, where they plan their escape from Egypt. As they flee across the desert, they are stopped by a border patrol suspicious of their presence:

> Vorenus: Salve, captain.
> Captain: Romans, are you?
> Vorenus: Yeah.
> Captain: Don't see many citizens out here. What's your business?
> Pullo: Hunting sphinxes.
> Captain: No such thing as sphinxes.
> Pullo: Now you tell us.

This exchange marks both the end of a leitmotif and the beginning of an unwritten history. Pullo's reference to the sphinx as the basis for a witticism suggests an ancient ethnic joke of sorts, playing with the idea of the sphinx as a distinctively Egyptian pest; the captain's response suggests that the whole idea is remarkably silly, not even worthy of a laugh. The exchange deflates the enigmatic power of the sphinx; it is represented now as a mythical creature of no significance rather than as a real threat. Like Cleopatra herself, the sphinx is now an anachronism.

After a violent skirmish with the border guards, Vorenus, Pullo, and Caesarion ride off into an ahistorical future; but the writers of *Rome* have already offered a final, and playful, visual substitute for the Augustan sphinx that gestures to the very real changes to come. The scene in which Vorenus and Pullo set out in the morning with Caesarion opens with a broad shot, as the wagon crosses the screen from right to left; in the foreground on a raised embankment of sand crawls a scorpion, larger than life, gradually scurrying off to the right. Unnoticed and unexplained, it disappears: but it is real and alive, unlike the sphinx. The style of the frame successfully evokes the heat and inhospitable expanse of the desert, and emphasizes the smallness – both literal and historical – of the humans on the screen; but it also serves as a sign of what is to come. Suetonius tells us (*Augustus* 5) that Octavian was born on September 23, and so under the sign of Libra; and in the opening of his *Georgics*, Vergil makes a learned allusion to this date by associating it with the nearby constellation Scorpio. Vergil imagines the catasterism of Octavian, locating his future constellation in the position currently held by Libra (*Georgics* 1.32–5):[20]

> Or you might add yourself as a new constellation to the slow-moving months,
> where a space lies open between Erigone and the Claws
> pursuing her – hot Scorpio himself contracts his arms for you even now
> and has left you more than a fair part of the sky.

Vergil's reference to the "Claws" is a recherché allusion to Libra, identified repeatedly with Scorpio's claws by the third-century BC Hellenistic poet Aratus, whose *Phaenomena*, an astrological poem in dactylic hexameter, had a profound influence on the poets of Rome.[21] As the scorpion of *Rome*'s final episode first dominates the scene and then withdraws, we may well be reminded of the celestial Claws that Vergil's Scorpio prepares to contract to make room for the son of a god – and of the permanent transformation of history that will follow in the wake of the bygone sphinx.

NOTES

1 All translations of Pliny are my own from the Latin text of Eichholz (1962).

2 For ancient textual and visual sources for the story of the Theban Sphinx, see Gantz (1993: 23–4 and 494–8). The word *aenigma*, "riddle," is associated with the Theban Sphinx from at least the fifth century BC: Sophocles offers the canonical version of the association at *Oedipus Tyrannos* 391–4. A further allusion can also be teased out from Pliny's anecdote, not only granting Octavian the status of the mythical hero Oedipus, but recalling the Theban king's notorious incest with his mother. The suggestion of mother–son incest is not borne out in the ancient evidence for Octavian's relationship with Atia, but the boy's incestuous relationship with his sister as depicted in the first season of *Rome* (episode 9, "Utica") invites comparison; see Strong (2008).

3 The motif of a ring's ability to symbolize an individual's identity and power has a long history in folktales: the Magic Ring is type 560 in the catalogue of "Types of the Folk-Tale" compiled by Aarne-Thompson; see Thompson (1946: 70–9). A recent development of this motif is likely to have been familiar to the writers and producers of *Rome*: the cinematic adaptation of J. R. R. Tolkien's trilogy, *The Lord of the Rings*, a series of three hugely successful films (2001, 2002, 2003). In this narrative, a special ring gives its wearer great power but also carries the potential to do great harm; the phrase "fellowship of the ring" describes a group of companions who accompany the ring-bearer on a journey to destroy the ring. At least by implication, *Rome*'s "triumvirate of the ring" is a conceit that aptly characterizes the competitive power-struggle represented by the possession of rings.

4 Boyd (2008).

5 The adolescent Octavian appears in episodes 13 and 14, smoothing the transition to his more mature self in a number of ways. In episode 13 ("Passover"), after Caesar's will is read and his posthumous adoption of the boy is revealed, Octavian immediately begins to assert his new role, deciding to stay in Rome against the advice of Antony and reminding those around him that, aside from the property he has inherited, the name Julius Caesar is now his ("They cannot take the name"). In episode 14 ("Son of Hades"), the young Octavian continues to show his determination to step into Caesar's shoes by a generous distribution of funds to the citizenry; and he comments ominously to his sister Octavia, "Rome is in need of new leadership." Octavian's relative immaturity nonetheless prevents him from being able to stand up to an increasingly hostile and politically powerful Antony, and the youngster therefore decides to leave Rome and stay with his friend Agrippa in Campania. While this absence has no basis in the historical evidence, it provides the writers with a plausible reason for Octavian's absence from events unfolding in Rome throughout the next episode, and makes his reappearance in episode 16, now transformed into a mature young man, both believable and dramatically effective.

6 Compare also the display of authority here with that of Julius Caesar before his troops in episode 1.

7 See Boyd (2008: 95–6) for a fuller discussion of this episode.

8 The image is *BMC* Augustus 702 (*PCR* 344). The reverse, with sphinx, of this striking coin is one of three images included in the montage on the cover of Zanker (1988); a copy of the book may well have drawn the attention of *Rome*'s writers to the symbolic possibilities of the image. The abbreviation *PCR* is the standard acronym used by numismatists referring to Carson (1978). *BMC* is an abbreviation for *British Museum Catalogue of Roman Coins*, which makes the image available online: www.britishmuseum.org.

9 Octavian is agreed to have assumed the honorific Augustus at or shortly

after the meeting of the Senate during which he proclaimed the restoration of the Republic: see Lacey (1974).

10 See, for example, the *denarius* bearing on its obverse a bust of Brutus and on its reverse the cap of liberty between two daggers, *PCR* 274; and an *aureus* with a bust of Lucius Iunius Brutus, identified as PRIM COS, "first consul," on the obverse, and a bust of Marcus Iunius Brutus on the reverse, *PCR* 269.

11 This detail in the scene of Brutus' death has no basis in historical fact, but provides a visual parallel to the death of Caesar himself: just as the senators circled around Caesar with their knives, only gradually raining down their blows on him, so here the soldiers of Octavian and Antony surround Brutus, but make the first blow only after he provokes them.

12 Note, however, Antony's delight at "the smell of victory," an allusion to the famously chilling comment of Lt. Col. Kilgore (Robert Duvall) as he surveys a scene of carnage in Vietnam in Martin Scorsese's *Apocalypse Now* (1979): "I love the smell of napalm in the morning."

13 See Pelling (1988) on 4.2; in his Introduction (37–45), Pelling also notes the degree to which Shakespeare's *Antony and Cleopatra* develops the association with Hercules (as opposed to Dionysus) found in Plutarch. See also Appian, *Civil Wars* 3.16, 19; and Kleiner (2005: 180–1).

14 For the traditions surrounding Iulus, see Austin (1971) on *Aeneid* 1.267–8 and Ogilvie (1965) on Livy 1.3.2; for those surrounding Telegonus, see Gantz (1993: 710–12).

15 For the archaeological evidence, see Richardson (1992: 162–4) on the Forum Boarium and environs; among literary sources, Vergil's Hercules-and-Cacus narrative at *Aeneid* 8.184–305, offering an aetiological explanation for the ritual performed at the Ara Maxima, is of particular relevance in the Augustan context; Morgan (1998) offers a politically attentive interpretation of the episode.

16 For the classic treatment of Herculean extremes in myth, see Kirk (1974: 176–212).

17 Ironic acknowledgment of this inference comes in episode 21, when Atia and Octavia travel to Alexandria in an attempt to release Antony from Cleopatra's influence (and to bargain for a shipment of grain to Rome); as they sail back to Rome in defeat, Octavia removes the ring that identifies her as Antony's wife.

18 See Pelling (1988) on Plutarch, *Life of Antony* 24.4; on Isis and Osiris, see Witt (1971).

19 See also Dio Cassius, *Roman History* 51.3.6. But the image of the sphinx appears to have had lasting power: most notable are the twin sphinxes that decorate the shoulder-straps supporting his cuirass on the Prima Porta Augustus, the *terminus ante quem* for which is the return of the standards from Parthia in 20 BC: Zanker (1988: 188–92).

20 The translation of Vergil is my own from the Latin text of Mynors (1969).

21 See Aratus, *Phaenomena* 89, 437–8; Thomas (1988) on *Georgics* 1.32–5 offers details.

7 *Jews and Judaism in* Rome

Lisa Maurice

A subplot was introduced in the second season of *Rome*, involving Timon the Jew and his brother, Levi, who is freshly arrived from Jerusalem. This thread was intended to set up the situation for the anticipated fifth season, which was to deal with the rise of Messianism in Judea.[1] With the cancellation of seasons three through five, this subplot could not be developed further, but even as it stands the thread highlights some interesting points that reveal more about ideas and concerns about the role of Jews, Judaism, and Israel in the modern world than anything about ancient Rome.

TIMON THE JEW IN *ROME*, SEASON ONE

The figure of Timon first appears in *Rome* in the first season, where he is employed by Atia of the Julii as a hired thug and assassin. In this capacity, he provides a variety of services, ranging from protection to murder. He is also one of Atia's lovers, bargaining for sexual favors in return for providing the services she requires. In these early episodes the audience learn that he has a family,[2] but this family does not appear on screen, nor are we told any personal details about them or about Timon himself. He is described briefly once in episode 5 ("The Ram has Touched the Wall") as "Timon the Horse Jew," but it is still something of a surprise when in episode 9 ("Utica"), the following short dialogue occurs, while Timon is watching for Servilia.

> Friend: What's the hat for?
> Timon: Yom Kippur.
> Friend: Oh, is that today?
> Timon: You call yourself a Jew?
> Friend: What're you, my Rebbe now?

Suddenly there is a new dimension to Timon; although little indication of his ethnic identity has been given until now, it appears that he is a Jew. It is notable that this revelation occurs at the very moment that Timon first shows any discomfort with his lifestyle and job as Atia's henchman; as Servilia is dragged from her litter and attacked, Timon looks on with a troubled expression on his face, clearly uncomfortable with the proceedings. This discomfort is to be linked in the viewer's mind with the knowledge that he is a Jew, and perhaps with the fact that it is Yom Kippur, the holiest day of the Jewish calendar, whose nature is at sharp odds with the actions taking place before his eyes.

From this point onwards, his Jewishness is what defines Timon. The next time he is mentioned, in episode 11 ("The Spoils"), is when Octavian orders him to be fetched, referring to him as "Timon the Jew." Commissioned by Octavian to find a lawyer to represent Pullo, Timon is suddenly instantly recognizable by the locals in the Forum as a Jew. The first lawyer calls out as he approaches, "Moses? You need law?" – while another refuses the case, turning away with a dismissive, "On your way, Jew." So having spent the first two-thirds of the first season as a hired sword with almost no religious or racial distinction, it appears from episode 9 onwards that being a Jew is not only Timon's prime characteristic but also one that is obvious at first sight to everyone else he meets.

Physically Timon in the first season has little to mark him out as being a Jew. He is relatively short and has a beard,[3] both of which are often characteristics of Jewish men on screen, but in the earlier episodes there is no indication, physical or otherwise, of his racial origins. His occupation of hired thug/assassin is not one traditionally associated with celluloid Jews. Like other characters, he dresses in tunic and cloak, and he is bare headed until the mention of Yom Kippur in episode 9. The only real visible differences between Timon and the other characters in *Rome* are that he has facial hair and that he wears leggings under his tunic, both of which mark him out as different, but not necessarily Jewish.

Even after his Jewishness is revealed, there is nothing that portrays him as conventionally Jewish in his practices or behavior. The only custom he keeps is that of wearing a hat on Yom Kippur, hardly a universally accepted sign of Judaism. This is clearly a hat, not a skullcap and there are no other traditional distinguishing elements. There is no mention of him not eating pork, for example, or observing the Sabbath. Timon's Jewishness in this first season is a feature to be remarked upon, nothing more. It is only in the second season that this feature is developed sharply and becomes an independent subplot.

THE JEWISH SUBPLOT AND THE PORTRAYAL OF JEWS IN *ROME*, SEASON TWO

Timon appears in the first episode of the second season (episode 13, rather evocatively titled "Passover"), again wearing a hat, although given that it is the Ides of March this is clearly not because of Yom Kippur. He is as besotted with Atia as ever, concerned for her safety in the aftermath of Caesar's assassination and eager to be her protector, but to his chagrin, Mark Antony arrives, unharmed, and takes charge of the situation. Again Timon is marked out as a Jew by Antony, but the Jewish subplot is really introduced in episode 15 ("These Being the Words of Marcus Tullius Cicero"), with the arrival of Timon's older brother, Levi, from Judea. It transpires that Levi has fled Jerusalem as a result of his political involvements and rebellion against the local pro-Roman leaders. Under the influence of his brother, Timon – whom Levi calls by his birth name, Tevye – rediscovers Judaism and joins his brother in his revolutionary activities. Timon agrees to Levi's plan to assassinate Prince Herod of Judea but then has a change of heart on the day of the planned killing. The two brothers fight, which results in Timon accidentally stabbing his brother to death. Timon then leaves Rome for Judea with his family, who do not know of Levi's death, and he is not seen again in the series.

Whether on the big or small screen, there are several factors that recur if a character is to be instantly recognizable as a Jew. Beards are the most common mark of Jewishness.[4] This feature dates back at least to medieval times, when the mystery plays depicted Judas, based on New Testament references, with a red beard and hair. He was also given a large nose in these productions, another stereotype that has persisted in physical depictions. American vaudeville presented the stereotype of the bearded Jew in derby hat, complete with Yiddish accent and "grotesque gesticulation."[5] Side locks are also a common element, as well as a yarmulke or other head covering. The dark complexion of the Semite features prominently, in contrast to the fair-skinned western hero. Thus, as Halberstam comments: "If you are casting for a 'typical' looking Jew, you search for someone with curly hair, large nose, dark complexion and dark eyes."[6] A noticeably Yiddish sounding speech is often a prerequisite.[7]

Dress also has some typical elements. Hats or some other kind of head covering are essential. Jews in ancient times will typically be more covered up than the tunic-wearing Romans and pagans, donning desert-ready robes and garments that cover arms and legs, although more assimilated figures, or those who convert to Christianity, may dress atypically to mark them out as different.[8] White robes and shawls may be worn by those portrayed as pure or holy,[9] and prayer shawls (*tallitot*) are sported, usually in scenes of religious ceremony and in the synagogue. Women will similarly wear concealing robes, shawls, and particularly scarves or shawls over their heads.

Of the two actors playing the two main Jewish characters in *Rome*, one, Nigel Lindsay who plays Levi, is Jewish. The other, Lee Boardman, who plays Timon, is not. Whether either of these actors looks stereotypically Jewish is debatable; while Boardman is dark-complexioned and black-haired, Lindsay has lighter hair and coloring; interestingly, he wore a fairly light-brown wig for the part, rather than a more typically "Jewish" looking wig.[10] Both actors were contracted to grow beards for the roles, but the beards are short (especially Timon's), and neither has curly hair or side locks. Both men dress slightly differently from the pagan characters in the series, typically in full-sleeved, striped tunics that are longer than those worn by the Romans. Indeed, Timon's style of dress changes as he abandons Atia and turns toward his roots and religion, so that his clothing becomes more like his brother's and less like that of the other pagan characters in the series after this point. Timon's wife and children dress similarly, in long, often striped tunics of rough-looking material, and all of the Jewish characters wear dark and dull colors, in contrast to the vibrant shades of the others. Yesh, Timon's son, at all times wears a hat that looks very much like a skullcap. Deborah, Timon's wife, with her long brown dress, apron, and cap, has clothing more reminiscent of Golda in *Fiddler on the Roof* (1971) than the other females in *Rome*. All the Jewish females have their heads covered outside of the house, in contrast to the non-Jewish women whose hair is covered, if at all, with light, often brightly colored veils and scarves.

Other Jews in the series are portrayed in a similar way, with occasional nods toward more stereotypical depictions. The Jews in the synagogue wear long, dark robes and various forms of head coverings (hats, soft caps, turbans). They wear prayer shawls that are recognizable as *tallitot*, with black stripes on a white background, but they are rather more roughly woven than is usual on screen, in an effort to make them appear authentic. In one scene, both Levi and Timon are wearing phylacteries (*tefillin*), and have their *tallitot* over their heads. During the scene in which Levi and Timon oppose the elders of the synagogue in their support of Herod and the status quo, the synagogue leader has a long white beard, and is dressed in long white belted robes and shawl, with a turban on his head, strongly reminiscent of traditional depictions of the Jewish high priest.[11]

This figure also speaks in a heavy Yiddish-influenced accent, asking the assembled men rhetorically: "Would you have the Seleucids rule Judea? Or the Ptolemies? Ach, better one we know, one we can work with." Similarly, the other men in the synagogue, unlike most of the other characters in the series, have markedly foreign accents, although not all of them have Jewish accents. Indeed, Timon himself speaks in a different manner from his brother. In playing Levi, Nigel Lindsay was able to draw upon his own knowledge and experience to pronounce Hebrew and Jewish words correctly, and advised the other actors as to customs and pronunciation as well. Lee Boardman's Timon, on the other hand, speaks with a Mancunian accent (from the city of Manchester in northwest England) that has much less of the flavor of Jewish emphasis that Lindsay provides, an aural element that adds to his depiction as an assimilated Jew in Rome.

In addition to the clothing and physical appearance of the Jews in *Rome*, other elements contribute to the creation of a Jewish atmosphere in the series, and allow the audience to recognize scenes, settings, and issues as Jewish. The most obvious of these is the depiction of the synagogue. The synagogue in *Rome* is a place of prayer and meeting for the Jews. When Timon and Levi are seen praying there, both the prayer itself (the first paragraph of the Shema) and the manner of praying (individual as opposed to led by a minister or recited in unison) are instantly recognizable as Jewish. Inside the synagogue, an eternal light and ark for Torah scrolls can be seen, while the menorah, the seven-branched candlestick symbol, is depicted on the doors, in the iron window grates, and etched above the main entrance. Although it is likely that a synagogue in Rome of the first century BC would have been quite different from this depiction,[12] if indeed synagogues existed in Rome at all at this period,[13] all of these symbols are meant to indicate to the viewer the context and setting of the scene.

Jewish customs are also depicted outside of the synagogue, most notably in Timon's home. Timon's family have names that are noticeably Jewish; his wife is Deborah and his son, Yesh, presumably a shortened form of Yeshua, more commonly Hellenized as Jesus. Moreover, while the Greek name Timon was introduced unremarkably along with the character in the first season, now in the second season Levi calls his brother Tevye, the name of possibly the most famous big-screen Jew of all, the lead character in *Fiddler on the Roof*. The fact that this is a Yiddish name rather than a more authentic Hebrew version implies that the use of this name was far from a coincidence, and that it is intended to suggest an identification with Tevye the milkman. The indication in *Rome* is that "Tevye" assumed the more familiar name "Timon" as part of his intentional assimilation into the Greco-Roman environment of the city. As his "conversion" back to his Jewish roots takes place in the second season, he reverts to his birth name, but this is also a name that evokes the ultimate diaspora Jew, under attack by the world.

It is also notable that Timon's family are presented very clearly as a family unit, in particular sitting round the table eating together, underlying the fact that Judaism is a family-centered religion.[14] There is also a reference to Levi eating kosher food, while Timon comes home to find Levi with the children sitting beside him and on his lap as he teaches them to chant from the Torah with a distinctly traditional cantillation that would be familiar to modern viewers (Figure 8). The purpose of including these elements was surely not to argue that such components were part of the Judaism of the first century BC but to provide a feeling of identification and authentication for the audience, establishing these characters as Jewish.

Figure 8 Levi (Nigel Lindsay) teaches Timon's children Torah in episode 15 ("These Being the Words of Marcus Tullius Cicero") of *Rome* (2007). HBO BBC.

TIMON'S CONVERSION

The aim of all this scene setting is to provide the context for the subplot involving Timon and his conversion from amoral hired thug and killer to religious Jew and freedom fighter. While not developed in great depth, this conversion is intriguing. It perhaps reveals the subconscious and underlying attitudes of the makers of the program all the more for having been apparently thrown in as an added element of interest rather than as the main developed focus of the series. According to Boardman, the concept of Timon being Jewish was "incredibly important" to him as an actor, especially since "he (in my mind) was morally compromised from the beginning – the opening scene is of him having sex with Atia by way of payment." Boardman stressed that although the audience may not have been conscious of Timon's faith at the beginning, he himself was aware of it and it was vital to the characterization. It is clear that Boardman saw a link between being Jewish and behaving in a moral way, for his feeling that Timon's sexual encounters with Atia compromised his morality is intertwined with the fact that he was a Jew. He strongly felt that sex was a major motivating factor in Timon's behavior, especially his willingness to torture and murder for Atia, and he also felt that this was in conflict with his religion. That struggle between his religion-driven conscience and his lifestyle was developed much more strongly in the second season with the arrival of Levi, who provides that moral perspective engendered by his religious beliefs.

Before Levi's arrival, Timon has no scruples about using violence and even committing murder in order to carry out Atia's bidding. Although he begins to grow frustrated and humiliated by Atia's neglectful treatment of him, as she grants him an audience and then dismisses him unheard, this does not stop him torturing and even butchering a slave on her orders. It is clear that these actions leave him, unlike the witnesses Jocasta and Octavia, unmoved. On his return home, however, soaked in blood, Levi upbraids him:

> Levi: These treacheries you do for that Roman witch, does she pay you enough?
> Timon: I get what I need.
> Levi: She must lavish you with jewels and gold. What a rich man my brother is. Tell me, where do you hide such fantastic wealth?
> Timon: We both sell what we have to these people.
> Levi: All Rome's wealth is not enough to buy what Hashem has given me.
> Timon: Again with Hashem. Let Hashem make me a living. The money that witch pays me bought this fucking house, this fucking table, and that fucking dress my wife wears!

Levi: That makes you proud?
Timon: Proud as any free Roman.

Although the argument ends with Timon pulling a knife on his brother, it is soon apparent that Levi's words have made an impression, especially when Timon suddenly realizes that his young son, Yesh, is watching. Later in the same episode, Timon finally rebels against Atia, refusing to torture Servilia further. His words as he cuts her free echo Levi's earlier taunt: "I am not an animal! I am not a fucking animal!" His next appearance is the scene at the beginning of the next episode, where he is praying in the synagogue in *tallit* and *tefillin*. Timon has been converted back to Judaism, spurred on by Levi's attitude.

This conversion is as much political as it is religious, however, as the next scene to feature Timon (in episode 18, "Philippi") reflects. At the meeting in the synagogue, where the local Jews debate whether to support Herod, Levi interrupts forcefully: "How has it come to this? In this holy place you conspire in bribery so that idolaters can rule over your own people . . . This is our land. You are traitors to your own kind. May Hashem have mercy on all of you." Levi's cause is a religion-driven belief in Jewish independence, a conviction that Judea must be free, ruled by Jews, and that God supports him in this cause.

So indeed does Timon, and after the brawl which follows this exchange, it is he who declares his beliefs. When asked by one of his fellow brawlers what the point of the disturbance was, Timon declares: "Zion is the point, brother. We're redeeming the kingdom of Zion. Remember, friends! Remember who we are! We are the chosen people. Not slaves, not animals. The chosen people." For Timon, once again, the acceptance of Judaism is recognition that he is not an animal, that he is subservient to no one, and that he is one of the chosen people who are destined to fight for their freedom to rule their own homeland.

This is clear, too, in the decision to attempt to assassinate Herod. "He'll not stop until he's made our people slaves and idolaters. He should die. The bastard should die!" declares Levi, Timon's ironic response to which is couched in religious terms: "Well, it would be a *mitzvah*, no doubt." The audience also learn later that the two men have taken an oath on the Torah to kill Herod. Constantly, the link between their religious faith and their political beliefs is stressed. When Levi dies, therefore, at Timon's hand, as he tries to prevent his brother from carrying out the assassination, it is a form of martyrdom, as Levi dies for the cause in which he believes. Timon, meanwhile, having killed his own brother, whose dying words to him deny that fraternal relationship, is left to bear the burden both of guilt for that death and of the need to keep it secret. His manner of dealing with this is to leave Rome and return to Judea to continue his brother's work, fighting for Levi's cause. Thus the final glimpse we have of Timon is him pulling a cart piled with the family's possessions as they leave Rome for Jerusalem.

ZIONISM AND THE MIDDLE EAST CONFLICT

In the twenty-first century it is perhaps impossible to present a picture of Jews fighting for the independence of their homeland without being influenced by or making reference to the modern state of Israel and the Middle East conflict. This is only natural; no writer can divorce himself from the world in which he lives and in attempting to portray a different era, he will want to create connections with the modern world to which the audience can relate. This is certainly the case with the depiction of Levi and Timon, who are to be identified not only as freedom fighters, but also as Zionists, as is made explicit by Timon's declaration that they are redeeming the kingdom of Zion.

This is not the first production to make the identification between the Jews fighting Rome for political independence and the modern state of Israel; this is a direction taken by earlier epic sword and sandal movies. *Rome* is, however, markedly different in its portrayal from earlier epic movies. Nicholas Ray's *King of Kings* (1961), for example, reflects contemporary political and historical reality in the depiction of both Herod and Barabbas. The former is a true villain figure in this movie, claimed to be "an Arab of the Bedouin tribe," who is a savage oppressor of the Jews. Similarly, Herod Antipas, Herodias, and Salome are portrayed as "lurid, sadomasochistic" Arabs,[15] representing the contemporary view of the Arab threat to Israel.[16] Barabbas, on the other hand, is presented as a rebel leader, a messiah who presents the option of war as the solution to the Jews' woes, in contrast to Jesus whose message is one of peace. A cowboy figure, a traditional American man of action, he is a rare figure, the Jewish freedom fighter, rugged, athletic, and with an overwhelming commitment to the freedom of his people and homeland. This depiction of the brave Jew fighting for his country against oppression owes a great deal to the American view of the modern state of Israel in the 1950s and 60s.[17]

Similarly, the 1981 mini-series *Masada* emphasizes the brave, tough Jewish fighter, and identifies him with the modern Israeli fighter. This is reflected in the framing of the ancient plot with scenes from the modern state of Israel, in which modern Israeli soldiers are sworn in atop Masada. These scenes are accompanied by a voiceover that refers to Masada as "the inspirational heritage that has made the Israeli soldier of today the most daring and defiant defender of freedom in the world," and goes on to link the ancient Masada story plainly with the modern situation of the state of Israel. At a period when American Jewry consistently showed its support for the young state of Israel, especially after the six-day war in 1967, when Israel's popularity soared,[18] the commitment of Eleazar ben Ya'ir, the rebel leader at Masada, to that same ancient homeland of Israel identifies him with the modern state of Israel fighting against its Arab neighbors for survival.

While the twenty-first-century production continues the trend of identifying the ancient Jewish freedom fighter with the modern Zionist, the presentation is much more nuanced. Neither Timon nor Levi is an unequivocally "good" or "bad" character; and in place of the idealized valiant fighter, struggling against evil enemies for his deserved freedom, Levi is portrayed as a hothead and a religious zealot. He is an extremist who is prepared not only to murder, but also to die himself, in order to further his cause.

This cause involves murdering Herod, who, portrayed here as a Jew, is in fact far closer to the typical Jewish stereotype with his dark curly hair and deep-set eyes, beard, moustache, and prominent nose. He is also fabulously wealthy, and corrupt, openly using bribes to further his aspirations to power. Levi, therefore, in trying to overthrow the Herodian regime, is no longer a freedom fighter, struggling for freedom against an alien conqueror, but a religious extremist involved in an internecine struggle.

JEWISH ASSIMILATION VERSUS CULTURAL PLURALISM

The introduction of the religious Jew from Judea into the household creates tensions within this family. This is clear from the very first scene in which Levi appears, where he has not been offered supper because the family does not keep kosher. Timon's reaction is "Already we're not good enough, eh?" In later scenes, when Levi is teaching the children to read Hebrew, Timon is resentful and disapproving, defensive of his own irreligious way of life. His scorn is also in part due to the fact that Levi's religiosity is not something he has always maintained. Timon sneers to his wife: "Did he tell you of his righteous life back in Judea, eh? Did you tell her about that, brother? Thieving, gambling, chasing whores," facts not denied by Levi. Timon clearly resents his brother's newfound religiosity. Obviously this is prompted above all by his feelings of guilt about his lifestyle and his rejection of his heritage. As Boardman himself explains: "Levi's appearance pricks at Timon's conscience. He is so far removed from any childhood Jewish teachings and he hates himself for what he's become. Levi serves as a constant reminder of Timon's fall from grace."

This element should be understood within the context of twentieth-century diaspora Judaism, particularly in the United States, where many Jews who define themselves as "cultural" or "secular" Jews and practice Judaism as a religion only minimally react against the tide of Orthodoxy that has experienced a considerable revival in recent years.[19] The rejection of a secular way of life in these cases can create tension with family and friends who have not altered their lifestyle and feel rejected themselves.[20] Even in those families where the extremes are less polarized, there are usually a range of levels of identity and observance. Thus this depiction of Timon and Levi would ring very true for a modern audience.

Such questions of religious tension are also part of the wider issues of assimilation and identity in the modern Western world. Diaspora Jewry and in particular American Jewry have long struggled with the question of how far American Jews should assimilate and how far retain their cultural identity in a pluralistic society.[21] On the one hand, Timon, like many assimilated modern Jews, regards himself as a free Roman far more than a Jew; yet as Levi reminds him: "You breathe this fetid air of Rome, but you are not Roman. You walk her beshitted streets, you speak her mongrel language, but you're not Roman. You're a Jew. You may forget that, they never will." This difference leads to a sense of isolation within the host culture, an experience commonly felt by Jews. Thus, for example, the Jewish novelist Bernard Malamud remarked: "If you ever forget you're a Jew, a Gentile will remind you." Similarly the philosopher Isaiah Berlin commented: "In Israel I don't particularly feel a Jew, but in England I do."[22] Indeed Boardman himself felt something of this while filming, as he explains:

> I began to feel a sense of the Jews' separation in the Roman Empire and I can only imagine that feeling was present in many societies in which Jewish communities survived. Timon was treated with suspicion by other characters throughout the series and this led to an understanding of a feeling of isolation. This is partly due to his lifestyle choice . . . but also his . . . religion. Also, in Season Two HBO built a huge "Jewish Quarter" set for my character.

> My scenes were shot separately purely for logistical reasons and this compounded that feeling of "difference."

This feeling of being an outsider is of course compounded by anti-Semitism in the modern world, and *Rome* depicts this as part of the background to Timon's life in the ancient world as well. Not only is Timon marked out as Jew and therefore different by the non-Jews around him, but there are several references to Jews as money-loving and not contributing to the state. Mark Antony tells Timon (episode 13): "I expect no public service from a Jew"; while the slave he murders on Atia's orders in episode 16 ("Testudo et Lepus") says as he pleads for his life: "You're a Jew . . . I have money." While these comments perpetuate the stereotype of the Jew as money-grubbing, the motivation behind their inclusion in the series is not anti-Semitism, but rather to highlight Timon's own isolation in an alien world.

Such isolation has traditionally marked the diaspora Jew in particular. Indeed, the only Jews who do not feel this way are the Jews in their own homeland, and it is for this reason that Timon/Tevye's final scene in *Rome* shows him leaving the city to return to his true home, Jerusalem. Here he is seen dragging a cart piled high with the family's belongings, and accompanied by his family on foot, in a scene strongly reminiscent of that other famous diaspora Tevye, leaving Anatevka at the end of *Fiddler on the Roof*.

It is no coincidence that this thread in *Rome* echoes *Fiddler* so noticeably, for the theme of the two productions is very similar, namely how far can and should a Jew assimilate and how far should he preserve his culture and traditions in a non-Jewish world. As Raymond Knapp says of *Fiddler on the Roof*: "The political events that bring each act to a close – the pogrom-like 'demonstration' at the wedding of Tzeitel and Motel midway through, and the mass eviction of the Jewish population at the end – serve mainly as the backdrop to one of the central dramas endemic to race-based cultural conflicts: preservation vs. assimilation."[23] Strikingly, however, where *Fiddler on the Roof* presents Tevye and family leaving Anatevka for America, *Rome* shows the later Tevye and family returning in order to fight for their homeland in Judea. While this is of course partly a reflection of plot needs and historical reality, it also perhaps reflects contemporary perception of the modern state of Israel, not only as a haven for Jews but also as a place where religious zealots, freedom fighters, and terrorists flourish.

CONCLUSION

It is clear that the creators of *Rome* went to great lengths to create a picture of Judaism that the twenty-first-century audience would instantly recognize and to which it would easily relate. The two Jewish brothers are, however, a far cry from the standard stereotype of the Jew often seen on television and movie screens. There are no caricatures, no neurotic, narcissistic Jews, and no references, either visual or verbal, to the Holocaust. Timon and Levi themselves diverge widely from the usual physical depiction of Jews on screen; both characters are much more ambiguous in their portrayal, being neither outright heroes nor villains. Judaism itself is represented as a moral religion, and a force for ethical behavior, but it is also intertwined with zealotry and fundamentalism. More than anything, Timon is marked out as different and isolated because of his Jewish identity, and his personal struggle is to find a balance between his religion and the society around him. It is striking that, in a twenty-first-century global culture in which a melting pot perhaps now seems impossible, the solution to this problem that is presented in *Rome* is to withdraw from that society and turn to a form of nationalist fundamentalism, as symbolized by Timon's leaving Rome and returning to Judea to fight for his people and homeland.

NOTES

1 This was confirmed by Lee Boardman, the actor who played Timon, in email interviews conducted with him and with Nigel Lindsay, the actor who played Levi. All quotes from the actors in this chapter are from these email interviews. I am grateful to both for their generous help in this matter.

2 He threatens Atia (in episode 3, "An Owl in a Thornbush"): "My place is with my family. Say the word and I'll go to them!"

3 In the first episode of Season One, Atia makes reference to "short, goaty little men."

4 See Bial (2005: 18–19).

5 Erens (1984: 15).

6 Halberstam (1997: 78).

7 For an examination of a "Jewish accent," see Gold (1985: 280–98).

8 See Charlton Heston as Judah Ben-Hur in *Ben-Hur* (1959).

9 For example, the temple priests in *King of Kings* (1961).

10 These details were obtained from the email interviews conducted with Lee Boardman and Nigel Lindsay.

11 See, for example, James Tissot's painting *Annas & Caiaphas* (ca. 1886–94).

12 A great deal more iconography, for example, is notable in ancient synagogues, while the ark and eternal light only became standard at a later date. See Levine (2005: 198, 306–7).
13 Levine (2005: 274–6).
14 See Cohen (1972: 105); Jospe, Madsen, and Ward (2001: 141).
15 Humphries-Brooks (2006: 30).
16 Babington and Evans (1993: 131).
17 See Grace (2009: 76).
18 Grace (2009: 96–8).
19 See Heilman (1995: 62–8, 109–11), for a description of these two groupings of American Jews.
20 See, for example, Jaffe (2005); Baum (2010).
21 See Greene (2011: 1–13); Ritterband (1995).
22 Both quoted in Kofman (2007).
23 Knapp (2005: 219).

PART II

Sex and Status

8 *Revenge and Rivalry in* Rome

Stacie Raucci

INTRODUCTION: REEL REVENGE

"I will have my vengeance, in this life or the next." This line is perhaps one of the most memorable in the film *Gladiator* (2000), as it comes at a pivotal moment and focuses on the main character's principal motivation: revenge.[1] In this crucial scene, Maximus Decimus Meridius (Russell Crowe), by this point a celebrated gladiator, stands opposite the Emperor Commodus (Joaquin Phoenix) in the arena and removes his helmet to reveal his face, as music swells in the background. Commodus gasps at the shocking sight of him alive, and Maximus announces that he is "father to a murdered son, husband to a murdered wife" and he will have his revenge. While this line is now legendary among fans,[2] the general theme of vengeance has long been a mainstay of the sword and sandal genre, often providing the driving motivation for the male hero, as well as overall narrative stimulation.

Hence it is not surprising that revenge is also a major force in the action of the second season of *Rome*, picking up on and augmenting a minor theme from the first season. While the instances of revenge in the series are clearly inspired by antiquity,[3] the purpose of this chapter is not to trace their historical roots, but to consider them within a larger modern cultural and cinematic framework, in particular examining how the series has moved revenge out of the domain of men into that of women.

The involvement of women in intrigues is not a novel take on ancient Rome. One need only think about the scheming women of *I, Claudius* (1976), such as Livia (Siân Phillips) and Messalina (Sheila White), to see a pattern. But the sword and sandal genre typically has not depicted female revenge as the main focus of these schemes. Even in *I, Claudius*, women are more motivated by a quest for power than a desire for revenge. *Rome*, by contrast, clearly makes female revenge a major theme of its second season. The cover art for the DVD box of the second season sets up the theme of female revenge, even before the viewer watches an episode. On the cover there is a woman in profile view with long hair, wearing a flowing white dress and gripping a dagger at her side: the dagger faces outwards toward the viewer. Blood covers the ground near her feet, while blood drips from the "e" in the series title. This image seems to mirror the one from the DVD box of the first season in which a Roman soldier appears holding a similar dagger, showing a shift in the gender focus of the series from one season to the next.

But as this chapter will show, female revenge in the second season is of a peculiar kind: while *Rome*'s women engage in female-on-female rivalries, their behavior – in popular culture terms – belongs more to prime-time drama and reality television than the sword and sandal genre. As several critics have noticed, *Rome* "with its spitting catfights, is closer in spirit to *Dynasty*."[4] This chapter argues for a feminization of the *topos* of revenge in Season Two, based on current televisual and cinematic models.

MALE REVENGE

In order to understand how the women of *Rome* transgress the cinematic norms of revenge, one must first examine their male counterparts to see how revenge is distinctly gendered in the series. The dynamics of masculine revenge in *Rome* adhere strongly to the image of the Roman hero already established in the genre of sword and sandal films. Like the above-mentioned Maximus, the hero typically uses vengeance and violence as strategic tools to reclaim honor for wronged family members and/or to defend his country.[5] This type of male revenge has a triangular structure: someone has harmed someone else, who now seeks revenge in the name of a higher ideal, such as honor or justice. This higher ideal is the third element in the structure, and it transforms revenge from a pure confrontation of egos to a moral obligation. The use of vengeance in this manner offers narrative force and provides the audience with a clear protagonist whom they can support.

Long before Maximus avenged his family and restored the Roman Republic in *Gladiator*, Judah (Charlton Heston) in *Ben-Hur* (1959) swore vengeance for the horrible treatment of his mother and sister,[6] and the escaped gladiators in *Spartacus* (1960) desired revenge for their years as slaves.[7] Following both Maximus and *Rome* itself, the cable television network STARZ transformed the character of Spartacus from the traditional freedom fighter into a vengeance seeker in both *Spartacus: Blood and Sand* (2010, starring Andy Whitfield) and in the aptly titled *Spartacus: Vengeance* (2012, starring Liam McIntyre).[8] *Spartacus: Blood and Sand* even ends its season (episode 13, "Kill Them All") with a line focused on the honorable nature of Spartacus' revenge, as Spartacus kills the *lanista*, Batiatus (John Hannah), the owner of the gladiator school, for ordering the murder of his wife Sura (Erin Cummings): "I do this thing because it is just. Blood demands blood." These characters perform the masculine act expected of them as part of the genre: they kill to avenge their loved ones and fulfill their noble role as head of the family. Male revenge might have a cathartic function, but it is also the fulfillment of a duty.

Rome's men follow this pattern closely throughout the second season. In the first episode (episode 13, "Passover"), Lucius Vorenus starts on the path to avenge his family. He begins by finding Erastes Fulmen, the gang leader who took his children. Vorenus first kills Fulmen's gang members and by the time he reaches Fulmen himself, he is covered in blood and appears crazed. Despite his appearance, his words demonstrate a clear mind and show that he adheres to an unspoken code of the hero, with concern only for his family: "You have my children . . . Where are they? Where are my children?" Fulmen's reply suggests that he also functions within a culture of honor and revenge, but he stands on the immoral side of the exchange: "I took your children in payment for your many slights to me. I fucked them, then I killed them, and I threw them in the river." With these words, Fulmen has left Vorenus no other choice in the cycle of vengeance that must occur: the cycle will only be complete through the ultimate revenge: death. Vorenus takes this one step further by killing Fulmen in a particularly violent manner, decapitating him and then walking through the streets with the severed head in hand.

The public display of the severed head functions as a symbol of Vorenus' completion of his masculine duties, both internally to the bystanders in the episode and externally to the viewing audience. The camera focuses first on the blood-spattered face of Vorenus and then shifts to the head before panning out to the crowd gathered in the street staring at him. The head will continue to serve as a symbol for at least another episode. After the killing of Erastes Fulmen, Vorenus' revenge remains a point of discussion, since he retains the head in his house as a "memento."[9] In the next episode (episode 14, "Son of Hades"), Vorenus' friend Titus Pullo notes to Mark Antony that "it calms him to look at the thing [the head]," thereby confirming the status of the head as symbolic of his fulfillment of duty. Mark Antony, in an attempt to bring Vorenus out of his mourning state, throws the head out of the window of Vorenus' apartment, but the audience is given one last look at it as the scene ends with a close-up of the withered head with its mouth and one eye open, still staring at the viewer.

The final mention of male revenge (episode 22, "De Patre Vostro") marks the end of the series, firmly establishing revenge as the dominating theme of the season.[10] The closing shots show Titus Pullo and the boy Caesarion walking through the streets of Rome. Pullo has saved Caesarion from death at the hands of Octavian by means of a series of lies. Caesarion, now in the role of the adult male since both his mother Cleopatra and supposed father Julius Caesar are dead, turns to thoughts of revenge to guide the rest of his life, as he makes an oath: "Brother Osiris, let me live to spit in his [Octavian's] face and remind him of this day . . . It is my sacred duty. By my blood I will not rest until I have avenged my mother and redeemed my father's name." Caesarion's words describe revenge in an almost religious way, as well as something lodged deep within his very body and spirit. This boy, on the cusp of manhood, understands his role as the head of the family.

FEMALE REVENGE

Feminist film studies have examined female revenge onscreen as a sign of empowerment.[11] As Hilary Stringer sums it up, these women transform "from victim to vigilante."[12] Typical cinematic instances of revenge occur after the female character has been the victim of a serious crime, such as rape or the murder of a loved one, giving the character moral impetus for committing atypical, violent acts. *Rome*, however, does not follow this model of female revenge. Nor does it imprint the generic sword and sandal model of male revenge (such as the vengeance depicted in *Gladiator*) on to them. Instead, *Rome*'s second season focuses its female revenge on rivalries and issues of personal fulfillment.

Some critics have read *Rome*'s principal female characters as being masculinized. Tad Friend, for instance, notes that the second season's "brusquest and most soldierly characters" are the "highborn women."[13] Such a gender assignment would place them in line with the women of revenge films, that is, women who take power into their own hands, and who are sometimes said to act "just the way a man would."[14] Typically, the women of revenge films are physically active in their revenge, in the manner of men. For example, in *Kill Bill* (2003), The Bride (Uma Thurman) awakens from a coma and sets out alone to avenge her own attempted murder. She battles her way through numerous female assassins, overcoming seemingly impossible odds and being wounded many times. In *The Brave One* (2007), Jodie Foster's character Erica Bain retaliates against the killers of her fiancé, working outside the realm of the law.[15]

Rome could have applied this "male" type of revenge to its female characters, blurring in this way the distinction between male and female. In fact it does the opposite, and offers a depiction of women seeking revenge that rests on a stereotype of femininity. To begin with, instead of using physical violence, women have recourse to gossip and shaming. As Margaret Toscano argues concerning the narrative of the first season, Atia and Servilia use typical women's methods to harm each other, pointing in particular to the use of "gowns and gossip."[16] In addition, female revenge in *Rome* is not motivated by a higher purpose. It functions according to a simple dyadic structure (compared with the male triadic structure): two individuals and their feelings confront each other, without a higher purpose. Promotional posters for Season Two, with their focus on the faces of Atia and Servilia, present an outline of this dyadic structure. Servilia's tagline reads: "Revenge calms the pain of betrayal," while Atia's tagline reads: "Beauty veils the face of war." In another poster, this time for the release of the second season DVD, Atia and Servilia are pitted against each other as rivals: "The Venomous Backstabbing Mother vs. The Suicidal She-Devil. Hell Hath No Fury Like a Woman Scorned." Prior to the release of Season Two of the series, HBO–BBC explicitly set up a public rivalry between the two female characters by giving away t-shirts that said either Team Atia or Team Servilia. An ad director for HBO noted that this marketing strategy played into the cult of female celebrity cat-fighting that is present in the media, such as the constant tabloid speculation about the supposed rivalry between Angelina Jolie and Jennifer Aniston over Brad Pitt.[17]

Within the series, the cycle of female revenge begins in episode 5 ("The Ram has Touched the Wall") with Servilia writing curse tablets against both Atia and Julius Caesar. She discovers that Atia has commissioned men to paint sexual graffiti of her and Caesar on the walls of Rome. Caesar, as a result of this humiliating and politically dangerous graffiti, decides to end his affair with Servilia, thereby instigating her desire for revenge against Atia. Revenge on Atia will neither change her situation nor restore her name. It is merely due to personal anger that she writes the following curse:

> By the spirits of my ancestors, I curse Atia of the Julii. Let dogs rape her, let her children die, and her houses burn. Let her live a long life of bitter misery and shame. Gods of the inferno I offer to you her limbs, her head, her mouth, her breath, her speech, her heart, her liver, her stomach. Gods of the inferno, let me see her suffer deeply and I will rejoice and sacrifice to you.

Although in antiquity curses were made by both men and women, *Rome* limits them to women, making them part of the feminine domain.[18] Curses allow the female characters to take revenge without direct, physical intervention.[19] This sort of indirect activity is emphasized at the end of episode 12 ("Kalends of February") as Servilia reveals to Atia "what has happened" to Caesar as he is assassinated. She does not use physical violence against her rival, but instead uses verbal threats and taunts. Indeed, the series goes so far as to depict Caesar's assassination as driven by Servilia – who manipulates her weak son, Brutus – in her desire for revenge against her former lover.

Season Two reifies this rivalry further and raises the level of "indirect" violence. In episode 16 ("Testudo et Lepus"), Servilia attempts to have Atia poisoned and in return, Atia has Servilia kidnapped, raped, and beaten. In both instances, the woman does not take physical action, but instead has someone else perform the actions for her. Servilia has a slave, Duro, unsuccessfully slip poison into Atia's food, while Atia has Timon and his men grab Servilia at the temple of Isis. Although the women of *Rome* clearly suffer some of the same crimes as women in other films (such as rape, or beatings), these crimes are not necessarily the primary motivation of later revenge. Rather, women use these typical forms of violence against each other as weapons of their vengeance. Yet in their "indirect" violence, they do not become masculinized by the use of these male weapons, but feminize revenge itself.

The torture and subsequent revenge of Servilia is a curious twist on the typical rape-revenge films, and this twist highlights the nature of female rivalry. As in other films, the female body remains the site of violence and aggression, but in this case, another woman stands by as voyeur and overseer to the heinous crime. Before Servilia's torture begins, Atia asserts her position and circles her like an animal circling its prey. Servilia is tied and on her knees in a submissive position, while Atia holds the higher, dominating ground. Throughout the torment, Atia never touches Servilia directly, but rather orders others to harm her. Her only "action" is to yell: "Have you had enough? . . . [to Timon] Do something. Cut off her face." Servilia, although the victim in this scene, is not completely passive, since she continues to use her womanly words to hurt Atia: "You think it's me you degrade now, but it's not. It's you. As long as you live, you will feel degraded and defiled by this."

The subsequent revenge for the violent acts of episode 16 is contrary to the rape-revenge model of film and would only fit in with a feminine image of revenge. During the wedding of Jocasta, a friend of Octavia's, at the house of Atia (episode 19, "Death Mask"), Servilia can be heard outside chanting the same phrase repeatedly: "Atia of the Julii, I call for justice." Servilia calls Atia out in the most public way possible, drawing attention to the wrongs she has committed. In the world of rumor and gossip, a public shaming like this one would have great impact. Servilia waits outside for a long period of time, night and day, calling for Atia until her voice is hoarse and the crowd grows larger. She turns her body into a public spectacle, as she kneels on the ground and has her slave woman Eleni pour ashes over her head repeatedly. Once Atia appears outside, the camera emphasizes the female rivalry by panning back and forth between the faces of the two women (Figure 9). When it focuses on Servilia, with her hand raised toward Atia, finger pointed in an accusing manner, the viewer sees what Atia sees and participates in the scene.

Servilia's call for justice is not a reference to the higher ideals of fairness and duty, but an attempt to find satisfaction and relief in the ill fortune and ultimate demise of someone else. It is a call for *her* justice:

Figure 9 Octavia (Kerry Condon) and Atia (Polly Walker) observe Servilia's public call for justice in episode 19 ("Death Mask") of *Rome* (2007). HBO BBC.

> Gods below, I am Servilia of the most ancient and sacred Junii, of whose bones the seven hills of Rome are built. I summon you to listen. Curse this woman! Send her bitterness and despair for all her life. Let her taste nothing but ashes and iron. Gods of the Underworld, all that I have left I give to you in sacrifice, if you will make it so.

This new curse continues in a more dramatic fashion what Servilia had begun in the first season in written form on the curse tablet. She publicly establishes her status in Rome and uses it to gain power to curse Atia. After she completes the oral curse, she takes a dagger and stabs herself, dying in front of the crowd of gathered witnesses. Although she verbally directs violence upon others, physically the only person she harms is herself, using her very body to take revenge. Her act is a very feminine form of revenge, a perverted and elevated use of the female sacrificial body as weapon. When she stabs herself with the dagger, it replays for those gathered the violation that was done to her body by Atia's henchmen, but with this public spectacle, she controls the conversation by turning her body into a tool. In the DVD audio commentary, director John Maybury says that she "uses her death as the most powerful weapon she had at her disposal." The power of Servilia even in death is emphasized when Mark Antony states: "Now *that* is an exit!" Furthermore, the death of Servilia may be contrasted with the death of Antony (episode 22). He stabs himself in a similar fashion, but he does so in order to die honorably – with the desire to "die Roman" – rather than be captured by the forces of Octavian. His masculinity does not require a large audience to gather and he dies with only one witness, Vorenus.

The lack of actual physical action taken by the elite women against others makes the contrast with what these women say almost comical. While the audience never sees Atia hurt anyone physically, immediately after the death of Julius Caesar she asks Antony: "What did you do then? I would have ripped them to pieces with my bare hands" (episode 13). Yet the audience never sees her touch anyone. The only women who take physical action are those of the lower classes and this seems to be simply out of necessity. For instance, among the lower-class women, there is a similar "cat-fighting" between Eirene and Gaia over Pullo. Gaia, wanting Pullo for herself and angry with Eirene for earlier slights, poisons her tea with an abortifacient, which eventually kills Eirene and her baby.[20]

The series ends (episode 22) on multiple notes of revenge, retaining the gendered hierarchy of vengeance established in Season Two. One instance is in the final image of the imperial family. As the imperial women prepare to make their entrance to watch the triumph of

Octavian, Atia and Livia, Octavian's wife, exchange hostile remarks about who should take precedence, wife or mother. With barely controlled contempt, Atia states: "I won't let a vicious little trollop like you walk ahead of me. I go first . . . I know who you are. I can see you. You're swearing now that someday you will destroy me. Remember, far better women than you have sworn to do the same. Go and look for them now." These words are the last of the series spoken by a woman, giving them special emphasis and underscoring the theme of female vengeance. Directly following this scene, Atia watches the effigies of Antony and Cleopatra being paraded as "captives" in Octavian's triumph. The viewer, in light of her words about "better women," may associate the death of Cleopatra with Atia's earlier statement (episode 21, "Deus Impeditio Esuritori Nullus"), in which she tells Octavian to "crush Antony and his queen," as her revenge for Antony's refusal to meet with her at Cleopatra's palace in Alexandria.

ROME'S WOMEN AS (POST)FEMINISTS?

Rome depicts several of the principal men of *Rome* working together and having deep friendships, what popular culture might now call "bromance."[21] For example, a great deal of the narrative in both seasons is built around the deepening relationship of the soldiers Vorenus and Pullo, and the bond between the two men remains one of the most constant things in the series. No matter what temporary disputes they may have, they are always reunited and care for each other, often risking their own lives for each other.

The presence of such a strong male relationship makes the contentious female relationships all the more prominent. The women of *Rome* fight alone, without friends, and exist in individualistic realms. These are not the women of *Thelma and Louise* (1991) who have an everlasting bond and die together. These are not the women of *Sex and the City* (1998–2004) who support each other through all the crises of life. Having been removed both from the realm of sisterhood and from that of moral revenge, *Rome*'s women fit into postfeminist norms.

Postfeminism has proven difficult to define, yet it is a term widely used in media studies.[22] For many theorists, postfeminism is a move away from "victim feminism."[23] It can be read as a backlash against earlier waves of feminism, since instead of retreating from ideals of femininity, it shows an empowerment based on "increasing openness toward traditional notions of femininity and female roles."[24] Yvonne Tasker and Diane Negra note that the "girling of femininity more generally . . . is itself a characteristic of postfeminist representations."[25] This embrace of femininity has caused some concern. Theorist Angela McRobbie worries that "in a postfeminist context . . . women . . . return to old-fashioned school-girl styles of feminine bitchiness, rivalry, and bullying."[26] Patricia Mamie Peers, in her own feminist study of *Rome*, reads it as "pseudo-feminism" in which patriarchal ideals are co-opted and "feminist ideals are oppressed."[27] Even if these negative statements are valid, it is the kind of feminism to which an audience in 2007 was exposed.

Because of the existence of similar films and television shows involving rivalry and revenge targeted at different age groups, a significant number of female viewers of *Rome* could relate to its feminine feuds. The youngest viewers had the models of shows like *Gossip Girl* (2007–12) and films like *Jawbreaker* (1999) and *Mean Girls* (2004). The world of rivalry and revenge is even defined in *Mean Girls* by one of the main characters, Cady (Lindsay Lohan), as the life of "Girl World."[28] The cat-fighting of Servilia and Atia, after all, often dwells at an adolescent level, with their clear desire to be the "queen bee." Yet, again thanks to current popular culture, women of older age groups were also able to relate to the women of *Rome*. Not long before *Rome*'s second season aired, *The Real Housewives* (2006–present), a reality show about the lives and rivalries of upper-class women in various cities, began its run. Carina Chocano calls it a "televised postfeminist-feminine-status Olympics."[29] Another primetime show, *Desperate Housewives* (2004–12), was constantly plagued by reports of off-air rivalries among its female stars.

In remaking the paradigms of cinematic revenge, *Rome*'s women become a part of the latest cultural standards. Women do not need to rescue themselves from victimhood in order to take power. They do not need to act as others think they should. They do not need other men, nor do they need other women, to help them succeed. In the "Women of Rome" podcast, Bruno Heller, the series creator, describes Atia as an "anti-heroine, an arch-manipulator and schemer, stirrer of trouble." It is precisely the description of Atia as "anti-heroine" that makes her the ideal postfeminist figure. Thus the women of *Rome* use a stereotypical femininity to gain power; and in so doing, they speak to the audience.

NOTES

1 On this film, see in particular Winkler (2004); Cyrino (2005: 207–56); and Blanshard and Shahabudin (2011: 216–38).

2 For instance, in another HBO production *The Sopranos* (1999–2007), mobster Ralph Cifaretto (Joe Pantoliano) is obsessed with *Gladiator* and recites the lines (episode 32, "University").
3 In the DVD commentary to Season Two ("All Roads Lead to Rome"), historical consultant and co-producer Jonathan Stamp claims that the series bases its instances of revenge on ancient Roman concepts such as *fidem implorare* ("to seek aid"), *quiritare* ("to call for help"), and *vim vi repellere licet* ("it is permitted to drive back force with force").
4 Friend (2007). On *Rome*'s cat-fights, see also Schwarzbaum (2007) and Lowry (2007).
5 See Winkler (1985: 526–7) on the role of revenge as part of the quest in hero myths.
6 Cyrino (2005: 231) describes the use of violence in both *Gladiator* and *Ben-Hur* as a method to "validate an ideal of family and individual honor."
7 Note, however, that Spartacus (Kirk Douglas) chastises the other vengeful gladiators who want to see their former Roman captors fight in the arena as they did.
8 On the reception of Spartacus and his traditional image as freedom fighter, see Cyrino (2005: 100–2); Wyke (1997); and Winkler (2006).
9 "Memento" is the word used by Stamp (2007: 81) to describe Vorenus' relationship to Fulmen's severed head.
10 Another example of male revenge in the series occurs when the gang leader Memmio punishes Quintus Bubo with castration for defiling the nephew of one of his men.
11 Stringer (2011: 268–9).
12 Stringer (2011: 268, 280). Stringer does go beyond the traditional issue of empowerment and challenges the reading of the rape-revenge film as strictly feminist.
13 Friend (2007). See also Cyrino (2008c: 132) on Atia's "strong and almost masculine *virtus*."
14 Barnes (2011). See also Barnes (2010).
15 On female revenge films, see for instance Lehman (1993); Projansky (2001); and Stringer (2011).
16 Toscano (2008: 159–60). See also Augoustakis (2008: 126) on the transgression of traditional gender roles by the women in the first season.
17 Caluori (2007), who is an ad director with Deep Focus. See also Rodgers (2006).
18 Evidence for curse tablets shows that they were used to wish harm on rival factions in chariot racing and love rivals, among others. See Gager (1992).
19 Contrast how in the same episode (episode 5), Pullo and a young Octavian kill Evander in revenge for his affair with Niobe, Vorenus' wife.
20 Vorena, elder daughter of Vorenus, may seem to assume the typical

masculine path in trying to avenge the death of her mother by betraying her father's trust; yet she also takes action against him for banishing her into prostitution, a more typically female revenge motive.

21 This is in stark contrast, of course, with the historical political rivalries depicted in the series.

22 On the definition of postfeminism and its problems, see Genz and Brabon (2009: 1–50) and Fien (2009).

23 Genz and Brabon (2009: 71).

24 Press (1991: 4), as quoted in Lotz (2001: 112).

25 Tasker and Negra (2005: 109).

26 McRobbie (2008: 130).

27 Quotes from Peers (2009: 49 and iii).

28 In *Mean Girls*, Gretchen Weiners (Lacey Chabert) compares the teenage queen bee Regina George (Rachel McAdams) to Julius Caesar: "And when did it become okay for one person to be the boss of everybody, huh? Because that's not what Rome is about. We should totally just stab Caesar!"

29 Chocano (2011).

9 *Effigies of Atia and Servilia: Effacing the Female Body in* Rome

Antony Augoustakis

The first season of the highly acclaimed television series *Rome* unfurled the feud between Atia and Servilia by emphasizing the transformation of Servilia's body into the body politic.[1] *Rome*'s first season depicted Servilia, the former lover and then staunch enemy of Julius Caesar, pushing her son, Brutus, against the dictator, under the pretext of liberating the Republic and thus honoring his family tradition of tyrannicide, a tradition that goes back to his namesake ancestor in the sixth century BC. This chapter explores the role of female sexuality in the second season of *Rome* and demonstrates that Atia's and Servilia's bodies are shown to be used and abused, as the viewer witnesses the desexualization of these main female protagonists.

Undoubtedly, both women experience tremendous personal bereavement in Season Two that reflects on their loss of both political power and momentum: Servilia's son, Brutus, dies in battle, and she commits suicide asking for revenge in front of Atia's house, while Atia herself loses Antony forever to Cleopatra. The matriarch of the house of Octavian is now spurned by her former lover in Egypt and returns to Rome desolate, soon to experience her own son's triumph; this triumph, however, only emphasizes how Atia has ultimately been "defeated" by her own son, who will now officially be called Augustus. Servilia's death figuratively underscores and prefigures Atia's own "demise" as well, as the latter's power will be displaced from now on by the ambitions of an emerging young wife, Livia.

At the same time, this transformation of the two main female characters of the series into powerless "effigies" in Season Two highlights Octavian's control over the female body. The grown-up Octavian transforms the female body into a locus of political manipulation: when he addresses a group of women in episode 20 ("A Necessary Fiction"), Octavian is offering a history lesson on Rome's men and on old-fashioned Roman *mores*, traditionally upheld by the virtuous women of Rome's past.[2] Octavian thereby "fetishizes" the female body by turning it into a controllable medium, on to which the future of the Empire under the Principate will be mapped.[3] The control and manipulation of female sexuality by the *princeps* announces a new type of regime, a rather more conservative and phallocentric one, in which the Eastern otherness of Mark Antony and Cleopatra are no longer viable.

In an earlier study of the characters and narratives of Atia and Servilia in the first season of the show, I demonstrated that the two women "do not hesitate to use and abuse their 'traditional duties': while Atia exploits her charm and sexuality to seduce Antony in her desire to promote her family's interests, Servilia manipulates weaving by turning it into a trap to engulf Octavia, a ploy that eventually brings disorder to the house of the Julii."[4] Since that essay was completed before the launching of the second season of *Rome*, I hastened to conclude my previous exploration by saying that "there are no real winners or losers among the women characters: rather, it is the *res publica* itself that swiftly crumbles to pieces."[5] And although there is no doubt that we witness in Season Two this swift passing from the end of the Republic to the Empire as initiated and firmly founded by Octavian, I would like now to rephrase my former statement by emphasizing that the women, especially Servilia and Atia, are among the vanquished protagonists by the end of the second season of the show, together with the notoriously doomed lovers, Antony and Cleopatra.

SERVILIA'S HASTENED RESOLUTION

Episode 13 ("Passover") opens moments after Caesar's death: Servilia cannot hide her contentment as she declares her pride in her son's deed. "Our name is redeemed," she tells him. "The Republic is saved." As Brutus is shaking and washing his bloodied hands in a basin, Servilia proves to be an exemplary Roman mother: she holds him steady and insists: "We must be strong now. The Senate will look to us for leadership. The people will need a firm plan." Yet this scene sets the tone for Servilia's own downfall; Servilia becomes the victim of her own plotting, as cleansing can only come through death. This scene of Brutus' attempt at cleaning his guilty hands from the unlawful deed and Caesar's blood has a mirror scene in episode 15 ("These Being the Words of Marcus Tullius Cicero"), when far from Rome, a shaggy-haired Brutus rides his horse to a river, undresses, and, transformed, enters the water up to his waist. He lifts his hands to implore Janus, god of new beginnings, to bless his next step of action: in other words, Brutus, a tragic figure, begs to start his life anew. He submerges himself saying: "As the shore is scoured by the tide, let me be cleansed, as the seed becomes the flower, let me be born again." Brutus' second attempt at cleansing may be considered successful in that he becomes the symbol of the lost Republic by means of his death at Philippi, an atonement that could save the drowning state from what the anti-Caesarian forces deem as extinction.

When Servilia attempts to revitalize her plans to avenge the drowning Republic and salvage what is left (in episode 17, "Heroes of the Republic"), she repeats her crafty retelling of stories, just as she used weaving in the first season to lure Octavia: Servilia writes a letter to Brutus, in which she welcomes the news that her son might be returning soon. She encloses his father's ring, a ring that his father's father had once given him in turn.[6] Servilia notes that the father always used to say that the ring was made of gold from the crown of the last king. But she quickly adds: "Your father liked a good story. I don't know if it's true, but it is nice to think so. I hand it on to you with all love and respect." The ring serves as a token that will reappear at Philippi (episode 18), when a peasant does not hesitate to sever the dead Brutus' finger to get the precious ring. But here in her letter, Servilia acknowledges explicitly the fallacious nature of her own figments: she is good at fabricating stories, except that these stories are built upon a very unstable foundation, since we know that the identity of Brutus' own father – is it really Caesar? – was a matter of contention and speculation.

ATIA'S PYRRHIC VICTORY

When Atia hosts a party for the Egyptian delegation in episode 14 ("Son of Hades"), she offers Servilia terms of reconciliation, which on the surface are accepted by both women. The young Octavian prophetically acknowledges to his mother: "There is more at stake than your vengeance . . . The political situation is extremely delicate. Her death would throw the Republic into an uproar." The truce, however, is not as seamless as it seems on the surface: when Octavian acts of his own accord and plans to fulfill personally the terms of his adoptive father's, Julius Caesar's, monetary bequest to the people, an out-of-control Mark Antony enters the young man's room, accompanied by Atia. The violent argument quickly turns into a vicious fight, during which Atia sides with Antony; a resentful Octavian does not hesitate to curse his own mother. The alienation between mother and son seems permanent, and when, in episode 17, Octavian returns from Mutina, his sister Octavia tries to intervene between her mother and brother and make peace. But it is too late, as Octavian cannot forget that his own mother had once betrayed him by siding with her paramour, Antony: "You know what kind of mother she is! She put her lover to beating me! Her sweat was on him!" Octavian here reproaches Atia's intimacy with Antony, causing Octavia to chastise him for being too "pious," as she tries to justify Atia's behavior on the basis of her love for Antony.

The quarrel between Atia and her son brings to the fore a rift that is hard to remedy. Octavian has been undergoing both a psychological and physical change, from the boy that he was in the first season to the leader of his country now.[7] This transformation and growth become apparent when he demands that Atia speak in public with the utmost respect for him. Later in the same episode, Atia appears before Octavian at his headquarters, where she falls to her knees and asks for his forgiveness: "I have been wicked and cruel. Beat me! Kill me! I spit on that pig Antony for leading me astray. I have been a terrible mother." It is difficult to tell whether Octavian is moved: "I forgive you," he replies. But it is Atia who has to change, in order to conform to Octavian's new character; and her submission seems to reflect that of the women of Rome. Atia flaunts the newly bought rhetoric that Octavian sells when she rebukes Octavia, drunk and high on drugs, that while her brother is "selling piety and virtue to the plebs," she spends time in orgies together with her new friend, Jocasta, a tradesman's daughter.

The two women, Servilia and Atia, then, have lost their sons, both literally and metaphorically. Octavian is alienated from a mother who seems only interested in promoting Antony; his departure from the mother's nest signifies a complete transformation from boyhood to manhood, a return from a self-imposed exile and the emergence of his self as the future *princeps* of Rome. At the same time, Brutus seeks cleansing and salvation away from Rome, never to return home; his dive in the waters of the river absolves him of crime and sanctifies him as the hero of the dying Republic. But another parallelism takes place simultaneously, as the series *Rome* often parallels the lives of the elite with those of the lower classes: the "lost" and alienated sons, Octavian and Brutus, resemble the lost children of Vorenus, which forms another important thread in the show's second season. Although Vorenus as a father is reunited with his children, he remains alienated from them, as they no longer communicate at any level and there is a lack of love and trust between them.

ISIS, MOTHER OF ALL

As revealed in episode 15, Servilia plots to kill Atia by hiring the handsome slave boy, Duro, who manipulates his way into Atia's household. A crucial event in episode 16 ("Testudo et Lepus") sets in motion the events that lead to the climax of the feud between Servilia and Atia in the second season of *Rome*. Servilia's hired boy, Duro, fails to poison Atia in her own home, and is caught and tortured; the innocent victim of the effort was Atia's kitchen girl, Althea, who dies from the poisoned dinner as she sings the "Crown of Sappho." In response to this failed murder attempt, Atia's henchmen, led by Timon, go to kidnap Servilia. As they arrive at the temple of Isis and are about to arrest Servilia, the viewers are absorbed by the intensity of the ritual as Servilia kneels before a statue of Isis: the goddess holds a *sistrum*, while Servilia chants a prayer, with two priestesses standing nearby. Servilia wears a cloak with a mirror in the back, anticipating the events as they unfold in this scene: the audience can see what is going on in the background, unknown to Servilia herself, the events that will result in Servilia's kidnap and bodily punishment. At the same time, the mirror serves as a reminder for the viewers to look back to the first season, when Servilia was again vilified, tortured, and thrown out in the streets of Rome (episode 9, "Utica").

It is true that Servilia's attitude toward and treatment of Atia have always underscored her haughty character, as this character has developed over both seasons: Servilia has always been arrogant, with a strong sense of superiority over Atia. However, Servilia's Stoic *apatheia* – her lack of emotional or physical response – in the face of severe physical torture signifies the transformation of the role of the female body in the show's second season: the female body no longer represents the body politic and is no longer the carrier of change for the populace at large, but is rather transformed into the vile, cheap medium on to which violence and torture are unleashed. In the exchange between the two women, this transformation of the female body becomes clear: "A slow and painful death, that's what you promised me," Atia pointedly remarks. "That's what you deserve," Servilia answers, even as she clearly fears what is coming next. But Servilia goes on to taunt her: "I think that you're a sad, lonely little creature; I think at this moment you are more afraid than I am." Even though Atia professes to be very happy at that moment, Servilia retorts: "Then why do you keep talking? Kill me." Servilia views her corporeal torture as Atia's own degradation: "You think it's me you degrade now, but it's not. It's you . . . As long as you live, you will feel degraded and defiled by this." Timon and his henchmen torture Servilia with rape and beatings, while Atia watches impassively. Servilia still has enough force to spit in Atia's face, and even Timon's allegiance finally wavers: "I am not an animal!" he exclaims as he clutches Atia by the throat, and then leaves. Atia is defeated because she has reacted beyond the boundaries of what was required by the circumstance. Servilia may have been tortured, but Atia is the one who is exhausted by the long feud; and it is Servilia who will have the ultimate word.

MASKS OF DEATH

In episode 19 ("Death Mask"), outside the house of Atia, the sounds of Servilia's grieving and her austere voice interrupt the otherwise everyday activities. As director John Maybury remarks in the commentary to the episode, the nature of the scene in public is "ritualistic," as Servilia is really a "chthonic" character here; in her own commentary, actress Lindsay Duncan adds: "Servilia sends herself into the future."[8] As the slave woman Eleni sprinkles ashes over her head, Servilia's words have a resounding effect: "Atia of the Julii, I call for justice." Servilia invokes the ritual of *fidem implorare* ("to ask for restitution") in her squalid appearance; as co-producer and historical consultant Jonathan Stamp observes, Servilia's actions reflect the act of *summittere capillos* ("to let down one's hair") and *vestem sordidam habere* ("to wear dirty clothes").[9] Nothing could prove more embarrassing for Atia, when she gets a glimpse of Servilia through a window hatch: her enemy embodies utter humiliation, anger, and resentment; she prefigures death. Stamp describes the scene: "Paradoxically, it is not the mud-smeared, unkempt Servilia who is humiliated by her vigil, but the coiffed, ever-immaculate Atia. It is Atia's dignity that has been lost. And that's what ultimately brings her to the door . . . Atia wants to face down her accuser, while she still has some face to save."

After two days, Atia can stand it no longer: she rushes to the door to confront Servilia. Atia's own reputation is on the line; her house has become a locus of spectacle and ridicule as the crowd gathers to watch Servilia, once a noble woman, now on her knees, humiliated and in a filthy state (Figure 10). But Servilia's voice is still strong. As Stamp notes: "Servilia's curse *manu cornuta* is delivered directly, eyeball to eyeball. It is terrible, withering, comprehensive, and sealed with her own blood. It doesn't come worse than that, it shakes Atia to the core." Duncan adds that Servilia is "like someone who's hardly

Figure 10 Servilia (Lindsay Duncan) delivers her final curse in front of Atia's house in episode 19 ("Death Mask") of *Rome* (2007). HBO BBC.

there anymore; the greyness, the ghostliness ... she is occupying another world already." With her public suicide and bloody sacrifice of herself, Servilia casts a permanent curse on Atia. Nothing will be the same again, after Servilia makes a thunderous exit from her life and from the series. Her final words perfectly encapsulate and evoke her character in both seasons of *Rome*:

> Gods below, I am Servilia of the most ancient and sacred Junii, of whose bones the seven hills of Rome are built. I summon you to listen. Curse this woman! Send her bitterness and despair for all of her life. Let her taste nothing but ashes and iron. Gods of the Underworld, all that I have left I give to you in sacrifice, if you will make it so.

Servilia's suicide marks the approach of Atia's downfall. Atia's own demise has just begun: in this same episode, Octavian promotes a wedding-pact between himself and his fellow triumvir, Antony, with Octavia serving as the bride-pledge between the two prominent men. As the newlywed couple consummate their first night together, Atia stands outside staring at the spot on the street where Servilia died, remembering the awful curse pronounced by her enemy. Soon Atia will be vanquished again when she loses Antony utterly to the Egyptian queen.[10]

OCTAVIAN AND THE FEMALE BODY

This transformation of the two main female protagonists of the series into powerless effigies in the second season also highlights Octavian's control over the female body, as he turns it into a locus of political manipulation. When he addresses a group of women in episode 20, Octavian proposes a history lesson on Rome's men and on Roman traditional *mores*, by ancient custom upheld by the virtuous women of Rome's past. "In the dawn of Rome's history, we men of Rome were strong and fierce but uncouth and solitary creatures," Octavian the educator points out. Then, he says, the men of Rome went on to acquire wives, a point when "our rise to greatness truly began." Octavian praises "the steely virtues and chaste morals" of the women of Rome: "It is by their virtuous light that we men have trod the perilous paths of glory . . . It is the women of Rome who guarded hearth and home while we men burnt Carthage." In Octavian's speech, women are raised upon a pedestal for helping to build a nation of leaders and warriors. Hence Octavian promises that "when the time is right," he will ensure laws are enacted to reward fertility and sanctity in marriage, while severely punishing "adultery, promiscuity, and vice of all kinds." However, at the same time as Octavian is delivering his speech to the attentive Roman *matronae*, just a few villas away the camera reveals his mother having a vigorous sexual encounter with Mark Antony, and his sister enjoying intimate erotic moments with his general, Agrippa; then the camera turns to another female figure, Gaia, who leaves the shop of the poison-seller, intent on her malevolent plan to poison Eirene in order to make Pullo her own mate.

Thus the series reveals that the realities of everyday life for women in Rome seriously undercut the message about feminine propriety that Octavian strives to communicate. Moral reform is shown to be meaningless for the moment; Octavian surely has a program he would like to enforce, and this is just an early preview. While Octavian's female audience stands silent, one of his most intimate associates raises a subversive voice to comment on what Octavian has to offer: "Strong stuff . . . Very amusing . . . They bought it wholesale," Maecenas pronounces at the end of the gathering. A disturbed but composed Octavian insists that he meant every word he said.

By slowly emerging as the sole ruler in the state, with power over everyone around him, Octavian gradually proves to be a control-freak, the *princeps* who "fetishizes" the female body by turning it into a controllable medium on to which the future of the Empire under the Principate will be mapped. Yet Octavian's statements are undercut by the realities of his own family and of his associates, Maecenas and Agrippa, neither of whom necessarily subscribes to Octavian's new rules of morality.

It is not coincidental that after his speech to the women of Rome in episode 20, Octavian meets the young Livia, his future wife. Livia is fashioned as a submissive woman, who is shown as immediately accepting of her future husband's sadomasochistic tendencies and strange sexual tastes. At his villa, Octavian asks his new fiancée if her husband or her father ever beat her, warning that he will on occasion beat her "with a hand or a light whip," not because she may have caused him offense: it is only for his sexual pleasure. A submissive Livia responds with a simple "Yes, sir," and submits to her future husband's wishes without a blink. Series producer John Melfi explains in the episode commentary that these are the early moments of Livia before she becomes the monster we see in *I, Claudius* (1976).[11] According to director Carl Franklin: "She is a charming, innocent girl, a little too forthcoming." As both producer and director agree, Octavian at the same time is growing into his own ambition, hunger, and desire.

In the following episode, episode 21 ("Deus Impeditio Esuritori Nullus"), Octavian and Livia are shown engaged in vigorous intercourse: as they pause for a moment, Livia slaps Octavian across his face to increase his pleasure. Sex and politics intertwine, since after their lovemaking Livia asks Octavian why he would send his sister and mother to Egypt, knowing in advance they will be denied a meeting with Antony. Livia figures out the reason: it is clearly a trap. Octavian will subsequently be able to renounce any ties with Antony, after the insult suffered by his kinswomen. The two women return to Rome spurned but accompanied by Posca, who possesses the document containing Antony's secret will.

In the final episode of the season, episode 22 ("De Patre Vostro"), after defeating Antony and Cleopatra in Alexandria, Octavian returns to Rome and heads to Atia's villa to report to his mother and sister the news of Antony's suicide. One month later, on the day of celebration for Octavian's official return as first citizen, Atia is miserable; she does not even want to dress for the occasion. "I don't know what I shall do if you give up," Octavia affectionately pleads with her mother. "Today is your triumph as much as his . . . Mother to the first citizen." The women of Octavian's house – Atia, Octavia, and Livia – are about to come on to the platform and be seated next to the conqueror of Egypt in a place of honor. But before they emerge on to the dais, Atia is explicit to her new daughter-in-law: she has figured out Livia from the moment they first met. "You are swearing now that some day, some day you will destroy me . . . Remember: far better women than you have sworn to do the same. Go and look for them now." This is the first reference on the day of triumph to Servilia and her noble death. Clearly, in Atia's mind, Servilia holds a special place: she has been her arch-enemy, and yet she has been a worthy opponent.

As the triumphal parade passes by the emperor's platform, Atia exchanges looks with her powerful son, but a wave of past memories and regrets overtakes her. While this is the day of Octavian's triumph that will forever change history, it is also Atia's biggest moment, a time of realization of past mistakes and current realities. Atia's dark garment is juxtaposed to the brightly colored linen worn by the rest of the women on the platform, while her gaze is directed away from the effigies of Antony and Cleopatra as they pass by in a wagon of spoils, to Octavian, and then back again to the effigies as they are lost in the parade and the crowd. This is a stark reminder of what Atia has lost, a son as well as a worthy enemy, Servilia. Jonathan Stamp's commentary on this scene impeccably summarizes the essence of the changed presence of women in the final season of the show: "As the effigies of Antony and Cleopatra bobbed past Atia in the triumphal parade, the camera crept in on Polly Walker's face. It's a truly great close-up, so much being said with so little. Ineffable sadness. She's the one who, at her moment of achievement, is mourning what she's lost."[12]

As Octavian takes over as the sole ruler of a vast empire, the women of *Rome* have to change and become the controlled wives and respectable mothers that exemplify the best of Rome's glorious past and promising future. Worthy female opponents perish together with the Republic: those who will survive have to learn the new rules of the game, as they now become pawns on the new chessboard of Rome's powerful men.

NOTES

1 The centrality of the feud between Atia and Servilia in Season One has been discussed by Augoustakis (2008). On the role of women, gender, and sexuality in *Rome*, see Cyrino (2008c); Raucci (2008); Seo (2008); Strong (2008); and Toscano (2008).

2 Similar speeches made by Octavian/Augustus can be found throughout Cassius Dio's account of the life of the emperor; see especially *Roman*

History 56.1–10, where Octavian addresses the married men and bachelors of Rome, explaining by means of historical examples why he passed his legislation on marriage.

3 On the fetishization of sex as visual spectacle in the first season of the show, see Raucci (2008) and Strong (2008).

4 Augoustakis (2008: 126–7).

5 Augoustakis (2008: 127).

6 See Boyd in this volume.

7 On the young Octavian as portrayed in the first season, see Boyd (2008).

8 Quotes from Maybury and Duncan are from the audio commentaries for episode 19.

9 Quotes from Stamp are from the DVD feature for episode 19, "Inside the Episode."

10 On Antony's "otherness" and his performance of masculinity, see Kelly (2013; 2014); Toscano (2013).

11 Quotes from Melfi and Franklin are from the audio commentaries for episode 20.

12 Stamp's description of Atia's final close-up is from the DVD feature for episode 22, "Inside the Episode."

10 *Livia, Sadomasochism, and the Anti-Augustan Tradition in* Rome

Anna McCullough

In two of the more notorious scenes from the second season of *Rome*, Livia and Octavian are discussing and enjoying sadomasochistic sexual activities together, with Livia as the dominant and Octavian the submissive.[1] Octavian may have been guilty of a number of things in and out of the bedroom, but he is not described in the ancient sources as possessing this particular kink. This discrepancy raises a few questions. Why did the creators of the series choose this sexual behavior in their portrayal of Livia and Octavian? Was this choice in any way informed by the historical or cinematic tradition regarding the pair? And finally, what messages are aimed at the audience through the use of sadomasochism, and are those messages different from the ancient reception of Livia and Octavian? In answer, this choice of S&M does indeed reflect historical tradition, particularly the anti-Augustan one as presented by Tacitus, and was also chosen as the most effective and efficient way of communicating the alleged dominance of Livia over Octavian to a modern audience more generally accepting of gender equality in public life.

THE FIRST COUPLE AND THE HISTORICAL TRADITIONS

We will begin with a brief background on Livia and Octavian as a couple. Rather than the match being arranged seemingly on a whim for pure political expediency, as suggested in the series, ancient accounts speak instead to the passion that preceded the marriage. The two had apparently met while she was married to Tiberius Nero, and she was pregnant with her second child, Drusus, when she went to Octavian. There were rumors that the two were involved in some way prior to her divorce from Nero, or that at the very least Octavian was smitten with her (Suetonius, *Augustus* 69.1; Tacitus, *Annales* 5.1).[2] The haste with which he courted and married her was considered unseemly in some circles,[3] and the two seemed to be aware of this, as they consulted the state priests to determine if the marriage would be legal and pleasing to the gods (Tacitus, *Annales* 1.10). Suetonius uses the verb "carried off" or "seduced" (*Augustus* 62.2) to describe the marriage, echoing Tacitus' own description of "the abducted wife of Nero" (*Annales* 1.10), a word choice meant to hint at the moral scandal involved with the affair and his having all but kidnapped her from her (rightful?) husband; but this haste is justified to some degree by the statement immediately following: "and he steadfastly loved and esteemed [her] alone" (*Augustus* 62.2). The "abduction," in other words, was mere proof of his love and dedication. Such devotion is also evident in his death scene; he advises Livia to "live mindful of our marriage" (Suetonius, *Augustus* 99.1), perhaps an admonishment to her not to remarry, and he passes away in the very act of kissing her. Lastly, Livia is named as a chief heir (along with her son Tiberius) in the terms of his will (Suetonius, *Augustus* 101.2). These anecdotes collectively point to the passion and deep emotional bonds that attended their marriage from its beginning, a conjugal love that spoke well of both their characters and the harmony of the imperial household.

However, Livia did not figure in the public imagination only as the woman at Augustus' side. Her image and prestige stemmed not just from this role as spouse, but also from her own status; she was extremely wealthy in her own right, a product of her prestigious natal family, her position as empress, and its attendant facilitation of forming networks of influence and investment.[4] She possessed extensive landholdings in Judea, Italy, and Egypt, among other locales,[5] and as patroness sponsored a large number of individuals and communities.[6] Her name and image were used in AD 69 by those jockeying for the imperial office during the civil wars,[7] and "a Trajanic inscription from an unknown colony ... records that her birthday was still being observed [in the second century AD], with games and gladiatorial shows and a public banquet ... [and] Livia's name was used in the marriage oath for more than a century after her death."[8]

Despite this popularity and power, however, some elite Roman men such as the historian Tacitus retained reservations about her, given the paradox she represented regarding female gender roles and expectations. Though the empress and her relatives were still matrons in a *domus*, that "household" happened to be headed by the emperor and any children were thus potential heirs, making domestic acts political ones as well.[9] The resultant inclusion of women in public events and the proliferation of imperial women's images thereby created a problem first faced by Livia: how to reconcile her untraditional role as empress with public expectations of feminine behavior and the needs of the new Principate.

For the regime and its supporters, one solution was to acknowledge imperial women's potential for power, but to depict them as eschewing that power in choosing instead to limit themselves to traditional roles and interests.[10] Livia's official image thus combined both tradition and innovation, as exemplified in her public activities as a patroness. The Porticus Liviae, built on the site of a private luxury villa once owned by Vedius Pollio and near to a market (the Macellum Liviae) which she also sponsored, returned valuable land to public use, and included an interior garden and an art collection famed for its antiquities.[11] While her son Tiberius helped dedicate the new porticus in January of 7 BC, within it was a shrine to Concordia financed and dedicated by Livia alone on June 11 of the same year; this shrine not only symbolized the harmony of her marriage with Augustus, but also "her public identification, encouraged by Augustus, as the pre-eminent benefactor of family life, the first wife and mother in the state, and the exemplar of chaste and old-fashioned Roman womanhood."[12] She also sponsored restorations to temples or shrines of Bona Dea, Fortuna Muliebris, Pudicitia Patricia, and Pudicitia Plebeia, all goddesses associated with chastity, marriage, and fertility.[13] In these actions she was exercising very publicly her wealth and influence, but in such a way that they both supported Augustus' moral program of renewed, traditional family and marriage values, and represented herself as the first and most dedicated follower and proponent of the program. Livia thus used her nontraditional status to support traditional female virtues and roles:[14] to be the exception that proved the rule.

This solution was echoed by the unknown author of the *Consolatio Ad Liviam*, a roughly contemporary portrait of Livia as empress addressed to her upon the death of her son, Drusus, in 9 BC. While the author for the most part emphasizes Livia's strict adherence to traditional feminine ideals, he departs from her official image to acknowledge openly Livia's power and visibility. One striking example is when the author identifies her as a *princeps*: "You draw to you ears and eyes, we observe your acts, nor is the voice uttered by a *princeps*' mouth able to be hidden" (351–2).[15] This unusual application to Livia of what was normally the emperor's title does not automatically mean she was imbued with any similarly official powers: the word "could at this period still connote 'prominent person' without necessarily implying any constitutional status."[16] So, here it is superficially the author's private expression of esteem for Livia; but its inescapable political connotations also hint at his own interpretation of her true place and influence within the government.

This departure from tradition is temporized by the author's earlier praise of Livia's self-restraint: "To have neither harmed anyone, yet to have had the chance to harm, nor that anyone feared your strength? Nor that your power strayed to either the campus or the forum, and that you arranged your house within what is permitted?" (47–50). That is, although as a *princeps* she may have had power sufficient enough to ruin reputations and lives, and had the opportunity and perhaps also the cause to do so, she refrained. The author does not downplay this power with any disclaimer that her strength and influence were used at her husband's behest, or that her husband was their source; rather, her power and motives are her own, and she too does the work of a *princeps* (cf. 353–6). But this untraditionally public and expansive role is mitigated by the author's reminder that she deliberately limited her reach to her appropriate sphere of power as a woman, the home, and did not intrude on the male spheres of the campus and forum. For the author, then, Livia is living proof of the principle that it is acceptable for an empress to be powerful provided that her image projects traditional virtues, and that she refuses to use her political power for anything other than upholding those virtues.

This was not a permanent or universally accepted solution, however, and anxiety surrounding the role and influence of imperial women continued. An alternative, anti-Augustan tradition in ancient literature chose instead to emphasize the negative qualities of Livia as empress, as well as of her relationship with Augustus. Tacitus is the most notable and vocal critic of Livia, although fellow historians Suetonius and Cassius Dio also register complaints. After noting that "her chastity at home was in the ancient way," Tacitus labels her "a violent/unrestrained mother, an accommodating wife, and matching her husband in strategy and her son in pretence" (*Annales* 5.1). In other words, she rivals Augustus at political intrigue and Tiberius at political falseness, hinting at her intrusion into public affairs. Augustus is also characterized as too susceptible to her influence, deferring to her opinions and whims on various issues, even matters of state.[17] Elsewhere Tacitus is even more condemnatory: Livia is "a burden to the Republic as mother, a burden to the house of the Caesars as stepmother" (*Annales* 1.10). That is, not only did she bear Tiberius, who would be a scourge to Rome as emperor, but she also harmed the imperial household by (allegedly) assassinating Lucius and Gaius Caesar and Agrippa Postumus, potential heirs and thus rivals to her own offspring. This intervention in the official state business of succession on behalf of her son, Tiberius, represented a significant overstepping of bounds, as well as a failure of her domestic role.

In focusing on Livia's influence over Augustus and her role in the succession, these complaints encapsulate the main anxieties regarding Livia and Augustus: her proximity to power, the degree to which Augustus allowed her to use that power independently, and the degree to which she was able to manipulate Augustus himself. Tacitus and his contemporaries thus see Livia differently than the author of the *Consolatio*: she may have been a chaste empress, but she was still too influential and visible. For these anti-Augustan authors, this development reflects as negatively on Augustus as on Livia, and through the implication that he allows his wife to rule him and indulges her use of power, criticisms are thus made of Augustus, his moral character, and his masculinity.

SCREENING LIVIA

This portrait of a conniving, ruthless Livia was propagated most notably in the book (1934) and television miniseries (1976) *I, Claudius*. Robert Graves relied heavily upon Tacitus and Suetonius for his material,[18] and introduces Livia in the book as a "remarkable and . . . abominable woman" (4) who "was one of the worst of the Claudians" (15). In Graves' version, it was she who had always agitated privately for Rome's return to monarchy, and when her first husband refused to participate, it was Livia who sought out and seduced Augustus in the hopes he would fulfill her ambitions (16–17). From that point, "Augustus ruled the world, but Livia ruled Augustus" (19). Indeed, "for Graves, female power depends on male weakness."[19] Echoing the worst allegations about Livia's actions, Graves also holds Livia responsible for Agrippa Postumus' death, among others, and implies that Augustus himself suspected that she intended to poison him (168–72). Overall, Graves faithfully reproduces the anti-Augustan Livia with extra dramatic flair in *I, Claudius*; she is brutal, immoral, arrogant, ambitious, and overbearing.[20]

The television adaptation of *I, Claudius* by the BBC not only adheres to this print version of Livia, but goes even further to emphasize her malignant force; for example, where Graves' Livia only gives Julia an aphrodisiac, the BBC's Livia "devises a complex plot to promote Julia's adulteries and secure her exile."[21] Similarly, while Livia's involvement in numerous deaths is more implicit than explicit in the book, the screen Livia is actively depicted as murdering Augustus and his nephew Marcellus, among others.[22] More generally, the book also downplays sexual excess, and treats imperial women's sexual misbehaviors relatively briefly; in contrast, the BBC adaptation pays more attention to sex, forefronting Messalina's contest with a prostitute and Caligula's incest with Drusilla.[23] This strong emphasis of the BBC's *I, Claudius* on sex and female machinations is also displayed by the series *Rome*, even though it ends in 29 BC, before Livia's worst alleged offenses. Nevertheless, *Rome* provides a similarly negative treatment of Livia. Given these parallels and the fact that the popularity and quality of *I, Claudius* have ensured its influence on later portrayals of ancient Rome, Graves' work and its subsequent interpretation by the BBC seem to be the modern links between *Rome*'s Livia and Tacitus.

With these historical and historiographical contexts in mind, let us turn to the actual scenes from the *Rome* series. In episode 20 ("A Necessary Fiction"), Octavian is hunting for a wife, and decides on Livia as a suitable candidate. While discussing with Livia their upcoming marriage, Octavian informs her that he may on occasion beat her with his hands or a whip; but that she should not take this as any kind of rebuke or punishment, as he will do it for sexual pleasure, and not to discipline her for any wrongdoing (Figure 11). She acquiesces with a simple, "Yes, sir."

Figure 11 Livia (Alice Henley) and Octavian (Simon Woods) discuss the terms of their marriage in episode 20 ("A Necessary Fiction") of *Rome* (2007). HBO BBC.

The subsequent episode 21 ("Deus Impeditio Esuritori Nullus"), shows the marriage at work. After announcing his decision in a family meeting to send Atia and Octavia to Egypt to see Antony, Octavian and Livia are shown having vigorous sex in their bedroom. Octavian slows his thrusting, then stops, and he and Livia exchange a look. She then gives him two hard slaps to the face, after which he resumes intercourse; the scene then cuts to her choking him with forearm against his throat, pressing her weight down. She releases him, and it is implied that he reaches orgasm while struggling to regain his breath. While he recovers, Livia begins a monologue decreeing the kind of food to be served in the house (no eggs – eggs are "sordid"), and moves to unpicking the reasons for sending Atia and Octavia on this mission to Egypt. After carefully working out his strategy, she praises him for being a clever boy, and he rolls over to sleep with a curt, "Goodnight, my dear."

In the actual details, the historicity of this portrayal is certainly questionable; while nothing like S&M preferences are mentioned in the sources, Augustus was known for his sexual deviancy. He was not monogamous; Suetonius records that not even his friends denied his proclivity for adultery (*Augustus* 69). Mark Antony invokes the scandal of their courtship in accusing Octavian of all but stealing Livia (*Augustus* 69.1), later pointedly asking Augustus in a letter: "Do you then mount only [Livia] Drusilla?" (*Augustus* 69.2). Livia was apparently aware of Augustus' sexual tastes, which extended past mere adultery to a more specific fondness for deflowering virgins; Suetonius notes that she herself procured girls to satisfy this particular desire (*Augustus* 71.1; also Cassius Dio, *Roman History* 58.2). That Livia actively encouraged this aspect of his character, or at the least tolerated it, might equally be evidence of a loyal wife or evidence of ulterior motives. Cassius Dio reads her indulgence as a method of gaining leverage over Augustus, a kind of silent blackmail: she knows his more shameful secrets, allows him to gratify these passions without criticism, and does not interfere (58.2). This was perhaps meant to elicit from Augustus both respect for her restraint in not telling him what to do, and leeway to operate with her own degree of independence. But apart from this hint of manipulation, authors do not assign Livia an active role in Augustus' sexual deviancies; his vices in this regard are his alone.

Rome's depiction of Livia and Octavian's sex life is thus a significant departure from the ancient tradition. Why introduce this detail? Generally speaking, the series uses slapping as a signifier of control within social and familial hierarchies, and it is a particular characteristic of Octavian's complicated family unit. Atia slaps both her children in attempts to rebuke them for displeasing her: Octavia in episode 2 ("How Titus Pullo Brought Down the Republic"), after she pushes her mother in anger for sending away her lover, and Octavian in episode 14 ("Son of Hades"). After informing her and Antony of his large loan to fulfill the terms of Caesar's will, she slaps him, and he retaliates with a harder blow, at which point Antony attacks him. It is a symbolic (albeit partial) liberation from her attempts to dominate and manipulate Octavian, and foreshadows the future conflicts with Antony, whom Octavian is as yet unable to defy completely. Upon her son's return to Rome following victory over Antony in episode 17 ("Heroes of the Republic"), Atia begs his forgiveness for her actions in episode 14, kneeling before him and at one point pleading with him to beat her in return; she attempts to convince him that she has submitted to him and admitted her wrongs. However, after his acceptance and forgiveness, the camera provides a close-up of Atia's face, and reveals both the false nature of the tears, as well as a triumphant smile on her face – this is yet one more manipulation meant to reassert her emotional dominance of Octavian.

However, in episode 20, Octavian shows himself to be no longer beholden to either Atia or Antony, and the body is once again the battleground. He orders Atia to silence – a command she obeys – and physically restricts her to the house. After Antony is informed that he must relocate to the East, he puts his hands around Octavian's throat, but does not squeeze or strike him, despite Octavian's daring him to do so. However, despite having just broken free of those who had controlled him for so long, this is also the episode in which Octavian marries Livia; authority over him has been handed from mother to wife, in a perverse negative echo of the traditional Roman *manus* marriage, in which complete authority over the woman was transferred from father to husband. He has freed himself from one tyranny, only to enter another.

This gender reversal stands in contrast to the behavior of Octavian's Republican predecessors. In episode 5 ("The Ram Has Touched the Wall"), Servilia hits Julius Caesar when he informs her their relationship must end; he slaps her three times in response, sending her cowering across the room, in a strong message that he must be obeyed and cannot be deterred from his decision. And in episode 6 ("Egeria"), Atia slaps Antony after he rejects her proposal of marriage, and he returns the blow, leaving the house immediately thereafter. In both these scenes, blows are exchanged; the abuse is not one-sided, as it is between Livia and Octavian. Moreover, it is always the female figure who hits first, a challenge that neither Caesar nor Antony allows to stand unanswered. Their blows end the confrontations, and each man continues the actions from which their respective women had urged them to refrain: Caesar ending his affair with Servilia, and Antony joining Caesar in Greece against Pompey. Thus, Caesar and Antony clearly do not allow the women in their lives to dominate them; their lovers are secondary to greater political interests, and are not allowed to fully participate in political or personal decisions. This contrast between leaders' behavior in the Republic and Octavian's new Principate is hence a gendered one: in the Republic, men were men, but in the deviant Principate, women are allowed to dominate men, and play a larger part in politics.

Further analysis of the Livia–Octavian scenes in episodes 20 and 21 provides a few notable observations that enforce this impression of deviant dominance. The most obvious is the deliberate reversal of roles: the audience is led to believe at first that Octavian is the dominant, and Livia the willing submissive: "Yes, sir." That expectation is then graphically upended by depicting Livia as the domme and Octavian as the sub. Secondly, Livia is shown making decisions about domestic arrangements, all but dictating them to Octavian, and then is shown quickly reasoning through a significant and complex political move by her husband. This micromanaging of the household to her liking and her quick mind, while Octavian is gasping and incapable of speech, give the strong impression that she is well on her way to possessing the upper hand in their relationship. Thirdly, there is no cuddling after sex is finished; no sentimental gestures or comments on the part of either; nor does either express a desire for such sentimentality. In combination with her solid grasp of political strategy, this underscores the similarity of their personalities and their equal cunning. Thus, these scenes demonstrate a rather Tacitean portrayal of Livia as a cold, calculating figure willing to exploit her role as wife and sexual partner of the emperor to exert influence in the household and beyond. In this respect, the subtext of the scenes is certainly in line with the anti-Augustan tradition discussed above.

NEW INTERPRETATIONS

Popular reactions to the scenes reflect and comment on these particular impressions, although the aforementioned contrast between Republic and Principate went unrecognized. A series of Google searches yielded a general pattern in audience response, as seen through online comments, blog posts, and episode reviews. In general, three major groups of responses emerged. First, the scenes were interpreted as a commentary upon Octavian's character; while some felt that it was only a confirmation of his coldness and lack of emotion, others saw it as a humanizing factor in displaying a vulnerable chink in his external armor. That Octavian could submit to physical abuse and derive pleasure from his submission is in strong contrast to his firmly alpha behavior in public and with other members of his family, an indication that he may be like other masochists in "striving for states of feeling which are normally abhorred."[24] In other words, Octavian may find the appeal of being submissive lies in getting to be what he is not allowed to be, or cannot be, in daily life.[25] This does point to an emotional side of the man that he does not otherwise reveal, and the hint of hidden desires and emotional vulnerabilities evokes greater sympathy in the audience.

Another interpretation focuses on Livia, and what the scenes reveal about a woman largely unknown to the audience, her character only just having been introduced to the series at the beginning of episode 20, the episode in which Octavian informs her that he may beat her. Audiences read the determination with which she carries out the physical abuse and her dispassionate monologue that follows as revealing of her personality as being equally as cold and unemotional as Octavian's. Or, for those viewers who consider S&M activity an indication of mental instability or perversion, the fact that they share this defect shows them as meant for one another. Either way, they are truly a match made in heaven. One may recall here Tacitus' comment that she is a match for her husband's cunning, and that their similar characters and mutual affection for one another produced the conjugal harmony described at the beginning of this chapter.

This new information regarding Livia's character generates in turn another interpretation of the scenes. She not only proves that she is Octavian's match, but in taking the domme role, she proves that she may even be his superior. After all, we are never shown the process by which she convinces him to be on the receiving end of S&M activity, which he previously stated he enjoyed as the dominant. How did this conversion come about? The audience is left to assume that she maneuvered him into this role, and uses it as leverage. A few viewers assumed that he did not abandon the dom role completely, but rather that they switched roles as it suited them; but this is never shown or implied, and at the point when he could have taken the dom role and slapped her – that is, when the two are gazing at each during the pause in the action – he chooses not to take that initiative, and instead Livia slaps him. Her actions as a domme thus signaled to a majority of viewers that Livia is in charge of their relationship, that she now increasingly possesses the upper hand over Octavian – and who could accomplish that, if not another person like himself?

Or, in the eyes of some viewers, another person like his mother, Atia, the primary source of female manipulation and political infighting in the series. This interpretation sees Livia as the new Atia, running Octavian's life and scheming just as his mother did. A piece of fanfiction inspired by these scenes takes this association to its natural conclusion. The very short story is set after the end of the series and immediately after the death of Atia. It begins with Livia finding Octavian mourning in their bedroom:

> She is used to the terrifying blankness there, but not to what she sees cracking through beneath it . . . She takes a deep breath. "Turn around, Gaius." The switch is in its box by the side of their bed. "Take your tunic off. And I think it would be best, during this, if you called me mother."[26]

This short piece neatly points to the dysfunction in Octavian's relationship with his mother: how her questionable morals, sexual excesses, and attempts to use him for her own political ends have served to undermine, but not entirely destroy, their emotional bond as mother and son. It also illustrates how that dysfunction continues to color Octavian's relationships with other women, and perhaps why he gets along so well with Livia: he has been searching for another Atia after throwing off her influence, and has found one in Livia, but one with better morals and goals consonant with his own. Truly, a woman he can respect and to whom he can submit without shame.

The modern reactions discussed thus far all show similarities to the ancient reception of the couple: Livia and Octavian as a true match, reflective of each other's virtues and encouraging of each other's vices. But where ancient sources could merely cite political prominence, or a claim to political power, and be understood as condemning Livia for her presumption and Augustus for his permissiveness in allowing her to be so influential, such claims work less well in modern society. Women's public visibility is commonplace and it is not considered aberrant for a woman to become involved in politics. Similarly, the expectations of men to be sensitive, well-groomed, and involved at home have blunted the edges of masculine ideals, so that it is acceptable and even encouraged for men to care about what their wives say and to encourage them in pursuits outside the home. While there is still more progress to be made, more equal roles in the home and in public are now the norm.

However, total male submissiveness is still not acceptable, particularly in matters of sex: and a domme–male sub relationship most clearly illustrates to modern audiences the control a woman has over a man. In fact, the figure of the dominatrix has crossed over into mainstream popular culture, judging from the numerous appearances of such characters on television shows such as Fox's *House* (2004–12) and CBS's *CSI* (2000–), and common references to it in the fashion and advertising industries; to an extent, this has also normalized the dominatrix.[27] Nevertheless, it continues to retain its subversive character, as the dominatrix provides an exaggerated form of femininity,[28] and male submissives are thus still clearly bowing to female authority in an area where expectations of male aggression remain. So, the writers are sending the same message as was communicated by the ancient anti-Augustan tradition – that Livia is in charge, and that this is a bad thing – but that message is couched in terms of modern vice as opposed to ancient: female public visibility has been replaced by female sexual domination as a sign of male submission. That the series goes out of its way to reverse so explicitly the expectations set up in episode 20 to show Livia as Octavian's domme is the clearest, most efficient way to emphasize to a modern audience how thoroughly and how quickly Livia is establishing and exerting influence over her husband.

NOTES

1 This chapter developed from a paper presented at the Southwest Texas Popular Culture/ American Culture conference in New Mexico (February 2013) and the conference "Beauty, Bravery, Blood and Glory: Ancient Virtues and Vices in Modern Popular Culture" (June 2013). I would like to thank the participants of these conferences for their extremely helpful comments and feedback, especially Kirsten Day, Geoff Bakewell, and Monica Cyrino.
2 All translations of Latin are mine from the Latin text of Tacitus in Fisher (1922) and of Suetonius in Rolfe (1914).
3 Flory (1988: 343–59); Barrett (2002: 22–4).
4 Barrett (2002: 175).
5 Barrett (2002: 181–4).
6 Barrett (2002: 188–9, 197–9).
7 The Emperor Galba "issued several series of coins honouring her," and according to records of the Arval priesthood, sacrifices were performed in her honor by Galba, Otho, and perhaps Vitellius; see Barrett (2002: 223).
8 Barrett (2002: 223).
9 Severy (2003: 239).
10 Barrett (2002: 121–6).

11 Flory (1984: 326–7). See also Kleiner (1996: 32).
12 Flory (1984: 317).
13 Kleiner (1996: 33); Flory (1984: 317–18).
14 One may be reminded here of the behavior of First Ladies in the United States: historically, they have been limited (or limited themselves) to traditional roles of hostess, mother, or supportive wife, and have not often publicly weighed in on policy issues. When Hillary Clinton was tapped to do so officially by President Clinton on behalf of his efforts at healthcare reform in 1993–94, there was a broad backlash, and she subsequently retreated to focus on the less polarizing issues of children's health and development. More recently, Michelle Obama has chosen uncontroversial topics centered on children and the home, for example her Let's Move! campaign against child obesity and her support of military families.
15 Translations of the *Consolatio* are mine from the edition of Mozley and Goold (1979 [1929]).
16 Barrett (2002: 133–5); see also Schoonhoven (1992: 151 v. 261, 172 v. 352).
17 Tacitus, *Annales* 1.3; Cassius Dio, *Roman History* 58.2; Laurence (1997: 134–5); Purcell (1985: 94–5).
18 Woodworth (1935: 367). Two examples among many will suffice. In Graves' version of Augustus' death (1934: 172), Livia conceals his passing for at least a day, issuing regular updates on his condition to the public as if he were alive, all in order to ensure Tiberius' succession; this corresponds to Tacitus' version at *Annales* 1.5. Graves also includes correspondence between Livia and Augustus from Suetonius' biography of Claudius (*Claudius* 1.4.6), translating nearly directly in some places, for example, regarding Claudius' ability to declaim: Graves (1934: 120).
19 Joshel (2001: 123).
20 This venomous portrait was potentially inspired by Graves' own lover, Laura Riding; see Helmling (1992: lxxxi).
21 Joshel (2001: 145).
22 See Joshel (2001: 145–50).
23 Joshel (2001: 142).
24 Kolnai (2005: 198).
25 Lindemann (2012: 20).
26 Vaznetti (2007).
27 Lindemann (2012: 8).
28 Lindemann (2012: 153–73).

11 *Windows and Mirrors: Illuminating the Invisible Women of* Rome

Kirsten Day

When they were concerned with women at all, Roman historians focused almost exclusively on imperial women or other elites, so that those outside the highest levels of the aristocracy remain virtually invisible to history. Cinematic depictions of the Roman world, in contrast, *have* shown an interest in the lower classes, both men and women, but they typically adhere to the common stereotype of a virtuous and industrious lower class set against a corrupt, vice-ridden elite. The *Rome* series largely avoids these pitfalls[1] by not only acknowledging the diverse roles of non-elite women in antiquity, but also providing these female characters with individuality and complexity. Admittedly, the portrayal of women like Eirene, Gaia, and Vorena in *Rome*'s second season does replicate some ancient prejudices about the female nature that have become familiar components of modern depictions: women are scheming, duplicitous, and dangerous, both sexually and otherwise. The men of *Rome*, in addition, seem to impose on these women the familiar "goddess/whore" dichotomy prevalent in ancient literary accounts of their upper-class sisters. But while the series repeats some of these biases, it also takes pains to trouble them, revealing such binary divisions to be a function of individual male subjectivity and exposing the "Catch-22" nature of the dilemma whereby women who would exert agency were limited to channels that required them to enact the very traits used to justify controls on their behavior. The series thus demonstrates that in a world where they are largely disenfranchised, women must draw on the tools at their disposal – such as their sexuality and reproductive functions – to negotiate power and position. The non-elite women of *Rome* in Season Two thus provide an instructive complement to the historically attested elite female characters, offering both a window into the lives of women in ancient Rome and a mirror in which we might catch reflections of ancient biases about the nature of women lingering in contemporary narratives.

THE WOMEN OF *ROME*

Through its lower-class female characters, *Rome*'s second season suggests to its viewers many important social realities for women, such as their association with domestic duties and nurturing roles. In this series, lower-class women cook, clean, and care for the sick, and thus they hint at the ancient association of women with "inside" and men with "outside." These female characters are also, as in antiquity, deeply connected to rites for the deceased: they attend the dead through prayer, through preparation of the body for cremation or burial, and through formal mourning rituals, so that the series also implies a connection between women and death, which like childbirth, was seen as a dangerous transition between worlds, association with either of which was seen as "polluting."

Rome also calls attention to the more formal roles women inhabited. The institution of slavery and the disenfranchised, subservient position it entailed are illustrated through Eirene, who exhibits a deferential attitude toward Pullo, persistently calling him "master" for some time even after she has been freed. Gaia, on the other hand, who in episode 14 ("Son of Hades") takes over the slave role that Eirene has vacated, is anything but meek and servile, but despite her spunk, her example reminds us that Roman slaves were completely at the mercy of their masters, who could use them at their whim for sexual purposes or even kill them – as Pullo does in the end with impunity. Eirene and Gaia thus demonstrate some of the realities of slaves' lives in antiquity, while also reminding us that they were distinct individuals – a fact that in the upper-class storyline, where slaves largely appear as undifferentiated bystanders, can easily be lost. Eirene's move from slave to wife, furthermore, alerts the viewer that in the Roman world, upward mobility was possible, while the enslavement of Lyde and Vorenus' daughters and the forced prostitution this entails for Vorena the Elder demonstrate that fortunes in antiquity were precarious and social mobility worked in both directions.

Despite her death at the end of the first season, Niobe still looms large in the role of non-elite wife through Vorenus' memory. His grief reminds us of the tender, loving feelings that often developed between married couples in antiquity, even if love was not the usual motivation for marriage, as Niobe herself made clear in episode 12

("Kalends of February"): "Strange marriage it would be if you loved him from the start." At the same time, Vorenus' relentless, unresolved rage at his wife's adultery suggests the extreme importance attached to women's fidelity in a world where identity and status were so intimately tied to paternity. Niobe's daughter, the elder Vorena, demonstrates further the limitations surrounding women's sexuality: a conversation between Vorenus and Lyde in episode 18 ("Philippi") informs us that, having been prostituted, the role of respectable wife is now closed to his formerly middle-class daughter. For women, sexual contact outside of marriage, even when forced, was a cause of shame and devaluation.

With Niobe's death and her own manumission and marriage, Eirene emerges as the main example of a lower-class wife in Season Two. Her pregnancy and Pullo's delight over the prospect of having a (legitimate) child suggest the important role of women as child-bearers, while Pullo's clear preference for a boy signals to the audience the ancient bias toward sons. And although Eirene's fatal miscarriage is triggered by poison, this event, which echoes the death of Julius Caesar's daughter in childbirth in the opening scenes of the series, reminds us of a common danger for women before the advent of modern medicine; indeed, the ease with which Gaia gets away with murder here emphasizes the unexceptional nature of mortality in pregnancy and childbirth. This development, however, leaves *Rome* without a non-elite example of another important role for women of all classes: that of mother. This omission seems puzzling, but signals a key social difference when viewed in light of the prominence of aristocratic models of maternity like Atia and Servilia, who are deeply concerned with their sons and their political careers: though children, particularly sons, may have been valued in the lower classes, for the elite, dynastic considerations greatly intensified the importance of male offspring.

Finally, Lyde's entry into and Vorena the Elder's later participation in the cult of Orbona in Season Two provide an example of the sole conspicuous public role for women – priestesses in female-oriented cults[2] – while also working well thematically: as patron goddess of orphans and of parents who have lost their children and want to be parents again, Orbona is a deity appropriate to a family in which parents are estranged from their children through death and disownment. The series also signals the dangers that offering women a public role of this sort entail: when Vorena wants to sneak out to meet her lover in episode 19 ("Death Mask"), she uses a visit to "Lyde's temple" as a pretext.

KALON KAKON

As Vorena's deceptive use of an accepted role for women suggests, in depicting their lives, *Rome* replicates ancient notions about the scheming, sexually voracious nature of women and the danger they posed to men as a result. In Season Two, Vorena maintains the veneer of a dutiful, respectful daughter, but this front masks resentment and malevolent intentions toward her father, as she blames him for her mother's death. Her "feminine weakness," moreover, allows the henchman of her father's enemy Memmio to exploit her sexually and manipulate her into using her domestic duties as a cover for eavesdropping and gathering information to wield against Vorenus' interests. In that her beautiful, virtuous exterior masks a "bitch nature" and lack of sexual self-control, from the perspective of the *paterfamilias* she exemplifies the *kalon kakon* ("beautiful bad thing") that dates back to Hesiod's first woman.[3]

The elder Vorena also provides an example of how "women's concerns" were imbued in antiquity with deeper meanings relating to chastity and virtue. In the Roman world, beauty was a feminine ideal, but the use of cosmetics to achieve it was not only regarded as deceptive, but also "expressly associated with aberrant sexual behaviour," and thus with the rejection of traditional female roles such as wife and mother.[4] Because of these threatening associations, Vorenus is upset when he finds Gaia giving his daughter a makeover in episode 18; the audience knows, however, though her father does not, that Vorena is already enacting these negative qualities, pretending love and respect for her father to disguise her hatred and willingness to betray him to further her own goals. Thus Vorenus' anger at seeing his daughter "painted" suggests his own unspoken fears while demonstrating for the audience the symbolic meaning of women's adornment.

Spinning and weaving is another area of feminine activity rife with symbolic meaning: as these activities suggest industry and domesticity, they were associated with women's virtue generally and recalled the chaste Penelope of Homer's *Odyssey* in particular. Significantly, when Vorenus discovers his eldest daughter's treachery, he bursts in on her as she is spinning. In light of her sexual betrayal, this image initially seems incongruous.[5] But Penelope was also a weaver of wiles, and *Rome* seems to be signaling here the two-fold nature of this activity: like Penelope with her shroud-trick, Vorena has used womanly industry and verbal deceit as a means of manipulating men. In the context of this series, then, spinning and weaving seem to signify not just conventional female roles and virtues, but also women's potential to betray, particularly sexually, their male protectors.[6] Because her sexual betrayal has deadly consequences for hosts of men, moreover, Vorena also recalls the quintessential dangerous female, Helen, whose infidelity prompted the Trojan War. And like Helen, who despite her *femme fatale* reputation was in some sense a blameless pawn of the gods (or pretense for a male-centered conflict), so too is Vorena tragically used by Memmio and his man to further their own masculine agenda.

GODDESS/WHORE

Through her associations with both Penelope and Helen, Vorena the Elder also evokes the goddess/whore dichotomy, whereby men in classical antiquity tended either to idealize women or position them as morally corrupt, duplicitous, and sexually dangerous. In *Rome*, this view is most clearly presented from the perspective of the focal non-elite characters, Pullo and Vorenus. Pullo venerates Eirene, consistently treating her with a gentle tenderness emphasized by its contrast with his generally gruff, often violent persona. At the outing where he proposes to her in episode 13 ("Passover"), Pullo fashions a laurel wreath for Eirene and places it on her head, visually symbolizing his idealization. This attitude is juxtaposed with the one he exhibits toward Gaia, whom he mistakenly takes for a "whore" on their first meeting in episode 14. Even in the throes of their later affair, Pullo characterizes her as a "cold-hearted bitch" (episode 21, "Deus Impeditio Esuritori Nullus"), and in his final judgment deems her worthy of execution, public humiliation, and bodily desecration.

Even more illustrative are the two scenes of Vorenus' sexual encounters, which draw particular attention to themselves because of his stoic attitude and insistent restraint from extra-marital sexual activity in Season One. Having been propositioned, Vorenus takes Gaia to bed in episode 17 ("Heroes of the Republic"), but afterwards angrily insists on paying her despite her indignant protests that she's "not a whore." The principled Vorenus is positioned here as uncomfortable with "betraying" his deceased wife, signifying her idealization in his mind: whereas paying for sex is not a betrayal, having intercourse with a woman out of any sort of mutual affection would be. Thus, in order to maintain Niobe's status as "goddess," he literally makes Gaia into a whore. Then in episode 21, in Alexandria, Vorenus dreams of lying in bed with a gorgeous, radiant Niobe, who clearly returns his adoration; but this fantasy is rudely interrupted when he awakens to the reality of a shaven-headed Egyptian whore who, with

Figure 12 Gaia (Zuleikha Robinson) clashes with Eirene (Chiara Mastalli) in episode 19 ("Death Mask") of *Rome* (2007). HBO BBC.

a grating voice in a foreign tongue, calls him a "hairy bastard" as she complains that he took the sheet again. By presenting this goddess/whore dichotomy from the perspective of the two "everyman" characters with whom the audience is expected to identify most closely, the series neatly suggests the Roman view of women as appropriate to one category or the other.

This dichotomy is complicated, however, by clear indications that none of the focal female characters fits unambiguously into either category.[7] Although Vorenus romanticizes the deceased Niobe, he is tormented throughout Season Two by the stinging memory of her infidelity and its repercussions for him and his children. Eirene for her part, despite the pedestal on which Pullo places her, is a full participant in the rivalry with Gaia, calling her "bitch, pig, whore," threatening her with physical violence, and asking Pullo to beat her regularly to promote good behavior (Figure 12). Gaia, on the other hand, despite reluctantly taking post-coital payment at Vorenus' angry insistence, repeatedly asserts even from her first appearance that she is "no whore." And despite Pullo's merciless final judgment, in her last scenes Gaia not only risks her own life to save Pullo's, she also expresses real love for him, along with a belated regret of sorts for her crime. In addition, her deathbed self-recrimination – she berates herself as a "she-wolf" in contrast to her assessment of Eirene as a "good woman" – prompts the audience's sympathy, but also has deeper implications. During their first sexual encounter, Gaia had characterized Pullo as a "lion" and scorned Eirene as a "mouse." Now, by providing at last an answer to Pullo's query – "What sort of animal does that make you?" – Gaia reminds us that she is indeed a better match for the likeable Pullo than was Eirene. Her final scenes thus complicate Gaia's character while making her a complement to the very man who would negatively categorize her. In this way, *Rome* clearly troubles goddess/whore divisions by presenting them as a function of the individual male perspective and by deliberately creating sympathy for and lending humanity to a woman who initially seems "wicked," while drawing attention to serious faults in another primarily cast as "good."[8]

NEXUS OF RELATIONSHIPS

The Roman view of a goddess/whore dichotomy is not limited to the lower classes, as is demonstrated in episode 20 ("A Necessary Fiction"), when Octavian's ennobling speech to a group of elite women on the role they and their virtue have played in shaping the character and history of Rome – an allusion to Augustus' future laws on morality – is overlaid with images of his mother Atia being entered from behind by her now-son-in-law Mark Antony; of his newly married sister Octavia making adulterous love to Octavian's right-hand man Marcus Agrippa; and of Gaia exiting the apothecary's shop with poison intended for her mistress and rival Eirene. Afterwards, Octavian privately asserts that he meant every word, while his friend Maecenas offers the opposing view: "Myself," he says, "I suspect that the women of old Rome were a parcel of whores and termagants." *Rome* thereby clearly signals that the tendency in antiquity to idealize or vilify women crossed class boundaries.

Gaia's inclusion in this montage, moreover, is an interesting disruption of the high/low divide. A closer look reveals that the series in fact consciously undercuts the class divisions prevalent both in antiquity and in cinematic depictions of Rome by introducing a network of parallels between elite and non-elite women and between women and men as well. This nexus of relationships is initially signaled by the deaths of Niobe and Julius Caesar, which events serve as a bridge between the first and second seasons and are clearly meant to be read in conjunction with each other. In the final episode of Season One, Vorenus' discovery of his wife's infidelity enables Caesar's assassination by compromising his guard, but it also prompts Niobe's suicide as a response to Vorenus' murderous fury, so that the two deaths are intimately linked. The first episode of Season Two underscores this parallel by juxtaposing scenes of mourning for Caesar with those for Niobe. The effect of this is two-fold: it calls into question the notion of women as less important and reminds the viewer that while the great events of recorded history were taking place, ordinary people were living and dying at the same time. While these revelations may seem self-evident now, it was only in the fairly recent past that the scholarly subfield of women in antiquity was enabled by just such insights.

Another of these parallels becomes readily apparent as Season Two continues: the deadly rivalry that develops between Eirene and Gaia clearly echoes the one already established between Atia and Servilia in Season One. Just as Atia and Servilia are intended to reflect one another – both red-haired beauties are prominent Roman matrons profoundly interested in advancing their family positions – so too are Eirene and Gaia: they are both foreign-born slaves compelled to adopt Greek names; they are both first enslaved to and later sexually involved with Pullo; and they both die violent, bloody deaths as Pullo attends their deathbeds. In addition, Atia and Gaia are paralleled as strong, forthright temptresses who do not let scruples interfere with their goals, while their seemingly self-interested natures are contrasted with the softer dispositions of Servilia and Eirene. Although they too can be brutal, Servilia and Eirene are more clearly motivated by traditional "feminine" amatory concerns – Servilia by spite in response to Caesar's erotic rejection, which Atia had taken measures to ensure, and Eirene by jealousy over the clear sexual tension between Pullo and Gaia, which the latter takes few pains to conceal.

These somewhat neat pairings, however, are interestingly disturbed when the soft underbellies of both Atia and Gaia are revealed. Gaia, as noted above, expresses regret for her crimes and an earnest, even if misguided, love for Pullo on her deathbed; while some tragic humanity is lent to the otherwise strong, ruthless Atia[9] first when Maecenas wryly observes in episode 19 that Atia's distress at Antony's marriage to her daughter suggests that "the old girl's genuinely in love with him," and again later in episode 21 when she crumples in the streets of Alexandria after Antony's humiliating refusal to receive her. Further complicating these seemingly straightforward parallels are intentional cross-connections: despite the affinity between Atia and Gaia, Gaia is paralleled with Servilia when, in attempts to do away with their rivals, both use poison – a "weapon" associated with women in antiquity. Then, a verbal and emotional connection is established between Atia and Eirene: Eirene complains to Pullo in episode 17 that he loves Vorenus more than he loves her, and Atia echoes this complaint in episode 19 when she accuses Antony: "You love power more than you love me."

The series further disturbs simplistic categorizations, along with the high/low divide, in the pairings of slave women with their mistresses. Margaret Toscano has shown that Merula and Eleni serve as "psychological doubles" for Atia and Servilia, respectively, while Gregory Daugherty has positioned Cleopatra's personal slave Charmian as a "crucial foil" for the Egyptian queen.[10] Significantly, the class distinctions between the latter two are obscured in the series finale, when in response to Octavian's suggestion that she betray Antony by striking a deal with him, Cleopatra recoils from the prospect of sacrificing her honor to preserve her life. "Better than death," Charmian suggests, to which Cleopatra responds indignantly, "That is a *slave's* answer!" When Cleopatra subsequently accepts the deal, tricking Antony into suicide by faking her own death, she undercuts ancient notions about behavior-related class distinctions by enacting what she herself has characterized as the slave's response. In addition, because "mirrors are often symbols of female vanity and inferior identity in the Roman world,"[11] the distorted image of Cleopatra in the mirror as she contemplates her options in the former scene signals that it is not in fact honor, but rather vanity that motivates her, while simultaneously foreshadowing her upcoming self-abasement. This blurring of categories in the series finale acts as an interesting bookend to a similar strategy in the series premiere, where Atia, by having sex with the mercenary tradesman Timon in exchange for a coveted horse as a gift for her uncle Caesar, effectively makes herself into a prostitute, so that the series signals from the outset the intention to eschew hard lines and rigid categorizations.[12]

This complicated web of relationships has an additional important function in that it implicates in the larger fabric of history non-elite women along with lower-class men. Many have noted the "Forrest Gump" quality of Vorenus and Pullo, two obscure historical figures who here serve as "incidental agent[s] of high politics and history," as Monica Cyrino puts it, in order to "more easily invite the audience into the grand historical account that might otherwise have been difficult for some viewers to access."[13] This dynamic extends to the lower-class female characters as well: like the revelation of Niobe's adultery, which provided the distraction that enabled Caesar's assassination,[14] Eirene's death distracts her own husband from duty, which facilitates the theft of Herod's gold. For the male characters, such "Forrest Gump" moments revolve around activities like sex and military glory; yet for these women, they entail the sacrifice of their very lives. Nonetheless, the fact that this series binds the fate of these nameless women to larger political and historical events serves as a reminder that these forgotten women were important, and their actions perhaps as vital to the course of history as those of figures preserved in the written record.

SEX AS CAPITAL

The more complex view of women in antiquity that *Rome* provides with this nexus of connections is consonant with the work of scholars interested in feminist and gender theory, who have in recent decades familiarized the notion that in highly patriarchal societies like ancient Rome, women learned to manipulate their disempowered positions to achieve agency. The creators of *Rome* were certainly conscious of this dynamic, as the official series website explained that women like Atia built "networks and alliances" to promote their agendas, and in effect became the "shadow rulers" of Rome.[15] Despite the ancient view of women as categorically different from and indeed inferior to men, the fact that women like Atia and Servilia are clearly striving for goals similar to those of their male connections – political advancement for their families – suggests that they are not really so different from men after all: rather, due to their social constraints, they use different means to achieve the same ends, or as Toscano puts it: "Their weapons may be different, but the women's aim is equally sharp."[16] The *Rome* series is unusual in emphasizing that these sorts of strategies were not limited to elites, but that women of the lower classes likewise drew on whatever opportunities were available to them to exert power in their more limited realms.

Vorena the Elder again provides a useful example in a scene from episode 17 where she attempts to run away, taking her younger siblings with her. She is dissuaded by her aunt Lyde: "Where will you run that Vorenus will not find you?" Lyde then makes clear that assuming a false front is a necessary stratagem for operating within the constraints of her situation: "While you live under his roof, you may carry your hatred like a stone inside you, but you mustn't ever let him see it. Ever," she advises. "You must be an obedient daughter. Kneel to him. Tell him you love him." Vorena next tries to escape her father's authority, as noted above, by securing refuge with an alternate male patron, secretly taking up a sexual relationship with one of her father's enemies who offers false promises of an idyllic life together. *Rome* thus succeeds in hinting at a cruel irony governing women's lives in antiquity: by attempting to negotiate an acceptable existence for themselves through the limited means available within a system that disenfranchised them, women like Vorena played into stereotypes about the deceptive, sexually dangerous female nature that served to justify the patriarchal constraints that motivated these behaviors in the first place.

Gaia offers another striking example when she uses her sexuality and exploits her servile position to avoid a beating by seducing Pullo in episode 19. In this interchange, Gaia verbally signals her ability to control men sexually by asserting that her lover Mascius, although subordinate to Pullo, will nonetheless do "what *I* tell him." When she succeeds in shifting Pullo's intentions from beating her to having sex with her, her gleeful laughter suggests delight at the way she has manipulated him as well. Afterwards, when Pullo expresses his regret and insists it will never happen again, she makes the dynamic she just demonstrated explicit through her coy response: "But what if I misbehave again? You've got to keep me disciplined, haven't you?" and challenges him: "Where's it say a man can't have his slaves if he wants?" Yet despite her adroit handling of the situation, Pullo's reply that "I can kill them, too, if I want" grimly foreshadows her death, suggesting the dangers that pushing these strategies too far can entail.

Gaia's use of sex as capital recalls Atia's initial seduction of Timon to obtain the prized horse, and her later willingness to have sex with him again in episode 3 ("An Owl in a Thornbush") as payment for bolstering her guard. Gaia's manipulation of her slave status here also evokes a scene from episode 8 ("Caesarion") where Cleopatra employs a similar tactic: describing herself as Caesar's "slave," she shrewdly adopts a subjugated stance as a means of seducing him both to strengthen her position through an alliance and to secure dynastic succession through Caesar's implied paternity of her child.[17] As a slave who answers to a lower-class man, Gaia occupies the lowest, most disempowered position of any character in the series, while Cleopatra, as queen of Egypt, carries the highest rank possible for a woman in this world; yet these two are linked through their conscious manipulation of a servile stance to effect agency and bolster their positions. Gaia and Cleopatra are further connected through their use and abuse of women's reproductive functions: as noted above, Gaia makes use of Eirene's pregnancy as an opportunity to eliminate her as a rival by using poison to effect a fatal miscarriage, while Cleopatra exploits her own reproductive capacities to strengthen her political position and achieve her dynastic ambitions. Significantly, both women's strategies involve sexuality and duplicity, so that in capitalizing on the limited opportunities available to them in a male-ordered world, they, like Vorena, collaterally reinforce the ancient notion of women as tricky, sexually dangerous beings.

WINDOWS AND MIRRORS

Margaret Toscano has noted of the servants who inhabit the background of almost every scene focused on the elite characters in *Rome* that while they generally remain unnoticed, "most viewers were shocked by the watchful presence of slaves in the sex scenes, which shatters our modern notion of privacy and intimacy."[18] These characters thus provide a sort of window into the ancient world, highlighting difference by demonstrating that from the perspective of their aristocratic owners, these slaves were no more than furniture. Yet their presence in these scenes also acts as a mirror, reflecting our own position as voyeurs as we participate in the scopophilic process of filmmaking.[19] These scenes thus encourage the sort of self-scrutiny that leads to deeper insight into our own behaviors and ideologies.

This examination of the roles of the non-elite women of *Rome*'s second season and how they relate to their more famous historical counterparts reveals that this "windows and mirrors" dynamic is part of a larger pattern. Because our view of the somewhat notorious women of the aristocratic clans has been skewed considerably by the patriarchal agenda, *Rome*'s inclusion of significant storylines focused on lower-class women helps suggest important truths about the lives of women in antiquity. Certainly, *Rome*'s representation of these women's lives is not perfect: as Mira Seo has noted, the series minimizes both the physical and social separation of historical Rome, along with relaxing patriarchal hierarchies, since depicting these would "seem alienating and create significant narrative problems for the contemporary Western audience."[20] But with its deeper interest in non-elite women, *Rome* succeeds in at least hinting at the varied roles that everyday women played in antiquity along with the limitations on their actions and behavior.

At the same time, the series creators draw on some of the stereotypical ancient notions about women's nature: for instance, women who lie or use subterfuge are presented as duplicitous and machinating, but when men do the same, it is framed as necessary, even if brutal, political strategizing. In their reactions to erotic angst, women come across as jealous and catty, while the responses of men like Vorenus to erotic disaster are anchored to notions of honor. Indeed, our ready acceptance of and familiarity with such gendered characterizations demonstrates their persistence, reminding us that these prejudices are still very much in play in narratives produced today. *Rome* clearly does replicate some of these biases, but it also disrupts them by challenging the goddess/whore division into which women have often been placed. *Rome* shows how such binary divisions can be a function of individual male subjectivity, and uncovers the dilemma faced by women who wished to exert agency.

Moreover, unlike many cinematic depictions of antiquity, *Rome* avoids black-and-white categorizations of class-based moral character, instead drawing intentional parallels between elite and non-elite women that disrupt such oversimplified class divisions. By introducing a complex network of connections and resisting hard-and-fast categorizations, *Rome* encourages us to consider the complicated dynamics that underlie women's behavior rather than presenting them simplistically and unproblematically. The presentation of non-elite women in *Rome* thus provides a window, murky and distorted though the view might be, through which we might start to glimpse some of the truths about how women lived in ancient Rome, while also catching a revealing reflection of our own presumptions.

NOTES

1 Haynes (2008: 51), in contrast, argues that *Rome* adheres to the stereotype of a "debauched upper class who provide titillation and shock value, and a sympathetic, hard-working lower echelon who embody 'values' we recognize."

2 Seo (2008: 170–1).

3 Hesiod, *Theogony* 585.

4 Wyke (1994: 137).

5 The spinning wheel Vorena uses is anachronistic, since it was not invented until well into the second millennium AD. The distaff and spindle used in antiquity, however, would be unfamiliar to modern audiences. Also, like the loom used in weaving, the non-portable spinning wheel is a better signifier for women's fidelity than the distaff and spindle, which, though connected with women's industry, provided less assurance about their fidelity because of their moveable nature. Thus the spinning wheel, perhaps inadvertently, provides an interesting two-sided metaphor for Vorena's nature.

6 See Allen (2008: 186).

7 Reviewers disagree on the complexity of the characters in *Rome*: Stanley (2005) called the characters "one-dimensional," whereas Monfette and Vejvoda (2009) praise the "humanity" and complexity with which they are drawn: "Never do these characters seem like mere statues in togas, as Romans have so often been portrayed in Hollywood productions."

8 *Rome*'s intentional avoidance of black-and-white categorizations

is emphasized in the final episode of the series when Cleopatra asks Vorenus whether or not the man who fathered her eldest son – that is, Pullo – was a "good man": "Define good," Vorenus responds.

9 For more on Atia's "almost masculine *virtus*," see Cyrino (2008c: 132).

10 Toscano (2008: 159); Daugherty (2008: 149).

11 Toscano (2008: 155).

12 The series tends to show characters drawn in opposition to each other also exchanging roles. For instance, early in Season Two, Vorenus and Pullo reverse roles: maddened by guilt and grief for his wife's death, Vorenus turns into an "angry, bloodthirsty bully," while the formerly "good-natured but violent lout" Pullo takes on new roles of responsibility both as husband and as caretaker to his "unhinged friend" (Stanley 2007). Likewise, in the first episode of Season Two, Eirene agrees to marry Pullo, her former master who brutally killed her fiancé in a jealous rage; in episode 21, Pullo has taken up with Gaia, who killed his wife in order to be with him.

13 Cyrino (2008b: 4–6). See also Stevens (2005); Daugherty (2008: 142, 151).

14 Toscano (2008: 160) positions the slaves Merula and Eleni as more active agents in Caesar's assassination.

15 Augoustakis (2008: 117); Cyrino (2008c: 130).

16 Toscano (2008: 159).

17 See Daugherty (2008: 142).

18 Toscano (2008: 157); see also Raucci (2008: 209).

19 Mulvey (1975: 8–11).

20 Seo (2008: 176). Yet as Tatum (2008: 30) notes, the Romans' own methods for transmitting truths about the past were more akin to the "creative operations we associate with historical fiction or historical drama," so that *Rome* can be seen as operating in a kindred tradition.

12 *Antony and Atia: Tragic Romance in* Rome

Juliette Harrisson

When Mark Antony left his wife, Octavian's sister Octavia, for Cleopatra, he provided Octavian with a propaganda gold mine. Octavia was painted as the chaste, proper Roman matron, abandoned by her irresponsible and increasingly emasculated husband for an exotic foreign temptress. *Rome* tells a similar story, but substitutes Octavian's mother for his sister in terms of narrative drive. This chapter will explore how and why *Rome* adapts a narrative over two thousand years old and why the emphasis is shifted from Octavian's sister to his mother.

ROME'S AFFAIR: ATIA AND ANTONY

Rome established an ahistorical affair between Octavian's mother Atia and Antony as early as episode 2 ("How Titus Pullo Brought Down the Republic"). In the first season, this relationship was portrayed as largely motivated by political interest as well as a fairly casual affection on both sides. Atia shows a glimmer of vulnerability in episode 6 ("Egeria"), when she first brings up the subject of the two of them getting married. When Antony asks why, she first says because she loves him, which he assumes is a joke. She then outlines political reasons for them to get married, in a conversation that quickly turns into an argument. Polly Walker's performance as Atia, first quietly suggesting that she loves Antony, then shifting into a more confident tone as she comes up with a political plan so unexpected and cold-hearted that it leads Antony to call her a "wicked old harpy," implies that it was the first reason she gave – love – that was the truth, and her political machinations were a cover-up to protect her hurt feelings. But the relationship is balanced out, to a degree, in episode 11 ("The Spoils"), when Antony enlists Octavia to help reunite them as a couple, placing himself, as Monica Cyrino has pointed out, in the position of the elegiac lover desperately pursuing his elusive mistress.[1]

In Season Two, however, the dynamic in the relationship shifts. The unequal affection hinted at in episode 6 becomes increasingly prominent and it becomes clear that Atia is more in love with Antony than he is with her. This is depicted at first through subtle shifts in their sexual activity. Atia, while displaying no objection to Antony's having sex with slaves and prostitutes, chooses for herself to reject Timon in episode 15 ("These Being the Words of Marcus Tullius Cicero"), apparently for no other reason than a lack of desire to have sex with anyone other than Antony. Antony, on the other hand, shows in the displeasure on his face in episode 13 ("Passover") when Atia refuses to have sex with him before Caesar's funeral and sends him a slave from the kitchen instead, that he resents the fact that even she cannot keep up with his sex drive.

By episode 19 ("Death Mask"), the audience are encouraged to judge Antony for his continued sexual proclivities in a way they have not been before, as he winks suggestively at a slave girl while Atia tries to talk to him about the two of them getting married. Although Atia has insisted throughout that she is purely motivated by politics, telling Octavian "love affair be damned!" in episode 14 ("Son of Hades") and, indeed, choosing Octavian's interests over Antony's in episode 13, she shows her true feelings to her trusted slave, Merula, when she thinks she and Antony are finally to be married in episode 19, smiling, excited, and genuinely happy. During Antony and Octavia's wedding at the climax of the episode, Maecenas spells it out for the audience: "I always thought her attachment to Antony was purely practical, but I think the old girl's genuinely in love with him."

Although Antony does not love Atia as wholeheartedly or as exclusively as she loves him, he is portrayed as feeling genuine affection for her. He runs to her when escaping his would-be assassins in episode 13, proving Octavian wrong after the younger man insists that Antony is already long gone and does not care enough about Atia to come to her. Octavian calling his mother a "fucking whore" is the final straw that provokes Antony nearly to kill him in episode 14. When Atia arrives at Antony's northern camp to negotiate a truce in episode 17 ("Heroes of the Republic"), he appears genuinely pleased to see her – and rather implausibly does not even seem to realize that she has come to negotiate on Octavian's behalf. Antony and Atia's final scene together in the series, in episode 20 ("A Necessary Fiction"), emphasizes their mutual affection and portrays their forced parting as a tragic romantic scene, Antony shouting for Atia from the street and kissing her hand as the guards will not allow any closer contact, promising to send for her "on my soul."

ATIA AND ANTONY AND CLEOPATRA

In most portrayals of Mark Antony's story, any other romantic relationship in which he might be involved pales in comparison with his famous affair with Cleopatra. If any of his wives appear, he tends to have no special affection for them, and he is not usually shown with other lovers. Although his relationship with Atia had been a significant subplot in *Rome* since early in the first season, it may be that if *Rome* had continued for four seasons, as originally planned, it would have been his relationship with Cleopatra that made a bigger impression on the viewer.[2] Yet because of the abbreviated storytelling required to get from Philippi to Cleopatra's suicide in the final four episodes, Antony and Cleopatra simply do not share enough screen time in comparison with Antony and Atia for their relationship to have the same impact, and the primary tragic romantic relationship in the story becomes that of Antony and Atia. Their relationship is portrayed as long-term (Cicero even asks after Atia as if she were Antony's wife in episode 15), loving, and "real" – Octavia calls Atia Antony's "real wife" in episode 21 ("Deus Impeditio Esuritori Nullus"), and Octavian assures her that he means to send both of them to negotiate with Antony, both "reality and appearance."

Much of *Rome*'s depiction of the end of Antony and Atia's relationship, and the whole of his relationship with Cleopatra, was determined by the series' abrupt cancellation. In episode 20, for example, it was necessary to find a reason for Antony to leave and go to Alexandria quickly, since there was no time to go into his decade-long relationship with Cleopatra in detail, nor cover his campaign in Parthia. *Rome* achieves this by adopting the same attitude toward living outside the city of Rome as the BBC series *I, Claudius* (1976) had: the series inaccurately associates going away from the city with political friction and displeasure – just as Agrippa leaving for the East is interpreted in the first episode of *I, Claudius* as the result of a rift between him and Augustus. *Rome* depicts Antony's leaving as an exile of sorts, following *I, Claudius*' depiction of not only Agrippa's time in the East but Tiberius' historically self-imposed exile on Rhodes as well.

The reasons for Antony's departure are represented, following this approach, in the light of Octavian's later actions as emperor. At the beginning of episode 20, Octavian gives a speech about the anti-adultery laws he plans to enact in the future. When he finds out that despite Antony and Octavia's marriage the sexual relationships between Octavia and Agrippa and Antony and Atia are continuing as before, he is furious with all of them. He confines Atia and Octavia to the house and compels Antony to leave the city – forcing him into the arms of Cleopatra in Egypt (Agrippa is both sufficiently contrite and too necessary to send away). There is historical evidence that Octavian did complain to Antony about his adultery with Cleopatra, but only toward the end of their relationship, in gearing up for war. Suetonius records a letter sent from Antony to Octavian in which Antony demands to know why Octavian has started to complain: "What has changed in you? Is it because I sleep with the queen?" (Suetonius, *Augustus* 69). He points out that their affair has been going on for nine years and Octavian has never complained before. Historically, then, Octavian's complaints clearly relate to Antony's rejection of both his sister and their political alliance. *Rome*, however, moves Octavian's desire for moral reform up to the 30s BC and makes the reason he secludes his mother and sister and virtually exiles Antony his desire to have his own family set a good example of the sort of lifestyle he insists everyone should lead.

It is important to emphasize that, although Antony and Atia's relationship has more time to develop and hold the audience's attention, this does not mean that Antony and Cleopatra's relationship is unromantic or unimportant. In the two episodes in which they are together, they are represented as passionately in love with each other and their deaths are suitably tragic.[3] In addition to the actors' performances, Heller and the other writers and creators achieve this effect partly by using popular culture to fill in the gaps left by the abbreviated runtime. At the end of episode 20, Antony arrives in Alexandria, to be greeted by Cleopatra wearing a translucent dress with a split that goes up to her hip. The only dialogue is the two greeting each other by name – "Antony" . . . "Cleopatra." Those names, in that order, tell the audience all they need to know about what is going to happen, allowing the following episode to jump forward in time and show their relationship fully matured. In relying on popular perceptions of Antony and Cleopatra's relationship to tell their story, *Rome* evokes the best-known representations of them, particularly Shakespeare's play *Antony and Cleopatra* (ca. 1607) and the 1963 film *Cleopatra* (directed by Joseph L. Mankiewicz).[4] In both these versions of the story, Antony's rejection of Octavia is represented as a choice of heart over head, of succumbing to a passionate love affair and rejecting his political alliance.

In reality, Antony and Cleopatra's relationship was political as well as romantic. Having earlier struck coins depicting himself and Octavia as a couple to celebrate his renewed alliance with Octavian, Antony later struck coins depicting himself and Cleopatra, a political alliance with a client kingdom as well as a sexual relationship.[5] In the 1963 *Cleopatra*, however, although the political advantages of Antony and Cleopatra's alliance are addressed, it is implied that they could have achieved their political aims with (and indeed, because of) Antony's marriage to Octavian's sister. Octavia herself is represented as a dull, weak woman. She chooses to leave the men to talk politics even when Antony asks her to stay; she does whatever she can to please him but offers him no challenge; she dresses in white, symbolizing her purity but also the lack of passion in her or in their relationship. Cleopatra, on the other hand, offers passion and intellectual challenge as well as beauty – and rather more exotic costumes. Cleopatra herself reacts with anguish to the news of Antony and Octavia's marriage despite the obvious political benefits it offers, feeling it as a personal betrayal. Throughout the second half of the film, Antony's love for Cleopatra (and to a lesser extent hers for him) is depicted as a tragic flaw that ultimately dooms him politically and mortally. In Shakespeare's *Antony and Cleopatra*, the point is driven home in Antony's suicide scene, in which the man helping him to fall on his sword is called Eros (Love) and Antony says, "Eros, / Thy master dies thy scholar: to do thus / I learn'd of thee."[6]

ANTONY AS ROMAN HUSBAND/EGYPTIAN CONSORT

This is quite different from the story historically told by Octavian. Although he emphasized Antony's attachment to Cleopatra, romantic affection or rejection was not the focus. He emphasized in particular Antony's rejection of a Roman woman as partner. Antony's rejection of Octavia, as well as being a political termination of their alliance, was, according to Octavian's propaganda, a rejection of Rome. Marriage was a central aspect of Roman foundation mythology, from the rape of the Sabines to the rebellion against Tarquin sparked off by the rape of Lucretia; this aspect would once more be emphasized by Vergil in the *Aeneid*, in which Aeneas rejects the African queen Dido for Lavinia. Affection between husband and wife sometimes plays a part in these stories; however, the love of husband

and wife is less important than the institution of marriage itself, which was one of the foundations of family-centric Roman society. When Antony rejected a Roman marriage, he rejected the Roman way of life.[7]

Rome deliberately follows Octavian's propaganda closely in its portrayal of Antony after he arrives in Alexandria, interpreting almost everything Octavian said about Antony as true. Both portray Antony as ceasing to be Roman once he becomes Cleopatra's lover, a fate ironically foreshadowed in episode 14, when Cleopatra insists that she was as a wife to Caesar and Antony smiles in amusement: "It's an odd thought, a Roman consul with an Egyptian wife – wouldn't do, you know." By the time they are together in Alexandria, he appears to have changed his mind; although he still cares very much about what the Roman people think of him, and is determined to force Octavian to declare war rather than doing so himself, he has completely given himself over to Egyptian style as well as living with Cleopatra as his wife. The series even includes the will Octavian claimed Antony had made declaring Cleopatra his wife, asking to be buried in Alexandria, and leaving Rome and the West to Caesarion and the Eastern provinces to his children by Cleopatra: *Rome* shows the will being brought from Alexandria by Posca, former slave of Julius Caesar, and Octavian's reading of the document in the Senate represents an authentic historical moment.

The transformation in Antony as a result of his relationship with Cleopatra is signaled by the changes in both Vorenus and Posca in the opening scenes of episode 21 – Posca is wearing eyeliner and smoking hashish and even the staid Vorenus has taken to having a "monthly debauch" with a prostitute. When Vorenus asks where Antony is, Posca replies: "Where is he – a deep question. His mortal flesh is in the throne room." When we see Antony, Posca's meaning becomes clear. Antony is high, drunk, or both, wearing eyeliner, Egyptian robes, and a henna tattoo, playing at shooting a slave.

The depiction of Antony in these Egyptian scenes is influenced chiefly by Plutarch's *Life of Antony*. Octavian's depiction of Antony as having succumbed to his vices as well as abandoning the role of a Roman leader of men offered the perfect material for Plutarch, whose biographies are designed to educate readers in moral values. Most of the *Lives* provide good examples of great men, but *Antony* is one of a small group designed to depict the worst sort of vice, as an example of what to avoid.[8] Plutarch offers great detail on Antony's behavior in Egypt and his rejection of Octavia, painting Octavia as a model of Roman womanhood, "fair" and "magnificent," whose conduct was so noble and impressive that, without meaning to, she made Antony look worse for rejecting her (Plutarch, *Antony* 54). While *Rome* depicts neither Atia nor Octavia as especially morally upstanding, it does follow Plutarch in depicting Antony's rejection of Atia as a rejection of someone who loves and cares for him in favor of someone who indulges his worst habits and is, ultimately, bad for him.

Vorenus tells Antony that he has "a disease in [his] soul" and that he himself has the same sickness: this is a very Plutarchian suggestion, as the biographer described the sight of Cicero's head and hands nailed above the rostra as "an image of the soul of Antony" (Plutarch, *Cicero* 49). Vorenus' symptoms are to all appearances quite different from Antony's (he is the only Roman in Alexandria still wearing uniform and no eyeliner) but he too has lost his sense of self – perhaps he had already lost it when he asked Antony to take him to Alexandria in episode 20, despairing of his own life, which he had only begun to live again when Antony ordered him out of bed in episode 14. He continues to live out of loyalty to Antony and, more importantly, to Pullo and Caesarion.

The Egyptian eyeliner and elaborate clothing also emasculate Antony: his body, so often on display throughout the series, is now covered in painted designs (Figure 13). In fact, he is rarely completely naked in these last two episodes, wearing a pair of decorative leather arm braces and some form of clothing, usually a skirt, at all times, sometimes with a red cloak as a mockery of Roman uniform.

Figure 13 Antony (James Purefoy) assumes the role of Egyptian consort in episode 21 ("Deus Impeditio Esuritori Nullus") of *Rome* (2007). HBO BBC.

Contrast this with episode 4 ("Stealing from Saturn"), in which Antony is shown fully naked, discussing business with Vorenus while male slaves clean him. Unlike the many sex scenes in which Antony is nude, there are no women in this scene and his nudity in fact emphasizes Antony's absolute masculine authority, shown not just through the literal display of his assets but through his confidence and the way in which all other men must defer to him: Vorenus is obviously uncomfortable but powerless.[9] He is presented to the female gaze of the audience as worthy of their admiration, but not to any female gaze within the scene[10] – unlike the nude male slave in episode 6, who exists purely to satisfy the internal female gaze of powerful female characters.

Thus, while Antony's nudity in Season One and the early parts of Season Two emphasized his masculinity, his lack of total nudity in his scenes with Cleopatra highlights the loss of his own identity, subsumed into hers. Octavian's propaganda underscored the idea that Antony had been bewitched and enslaved by Cleopatra. In *Rome*, Antony is similarly depicted as subservient to Cleopatra, who also remains slightly more sober and alert than Antony at all times. In the first scene in which we see them together in episode 21, he sits entwined with Cleopatra, shooting at a slave dressed as a deer. As Cleopatra takes the bow from him to have her turn, she moves to sit on his knee, placing her higher than Antony, who is now literally underneath her. Later, Jocasta tells Atia and Octavia that "no one's allowed to speak with Antony without *she* says so." It is only at the moment of death, believing Cleopatra herself to be already dead, that Antony recovers himself; he asks Vorenus to tell "the people" that "I died well . . . I died Roman." Vorenus then wipes the eyeliner off his face, removes the wrist braces, and dresses him in his armor, making him look Roman again, that is, like himself again.

Although *Rome* enthusiastically tells Octavian's story about Antony being no longer Roman, it is his cold rejection of the woman who loves him that forms the heart of this part of the narrative. He loves Cleopatra, to be sure, but this is not the simple choice of heart over head that Shakespeare and the 1963 *Cleopatra* portrayed, as Antony and Cleopatra's love is depicted as deep but unhealthy. Ultimately, the series suggests that when Antony is in Rome with Atia (or even Octavia) he is himself: naked, confident, and secure. He loses himself when he gives in to Cleopatra, losing what semblance of sobriety he had and becoming Egyptian. According to modern Western values, which emphasize the importance of being independent and true to yourself, his rejection of Atia is a rejection of an approved way of life for an alternative in which Antony's identity is lost. And so both Octavian and *Rome* tell a story of a man who has turned his back on approved cultural values and given in to a decadent Orientalism.

Central to this notion is the scene in episode 21, in which Octavian sends Atia and Octavia to visit Antony and ask for reconciliation; this is perhaps based on a historical incident in which Octavia got as far as Athens before Antony told her to turn back. Audience sympathies lie entirely with Atia, and Antony's rejection of her in favor of Cleopatra is given little political meaning. Antony is drunk, drugged, and, just as contemporary propaganda insisted, entirely bewitched by Cleopatra. His political rejection of Octavian resonates less with the audience than his cruel personal rejection of Atia, who is left outside in the sweltering heat while he refuses to set eyes on her.

There is another significant aspect to Antony's rejection of Atia in favor of Cleopatra. One of the key themes of Season Two is the conflict between romantic love and the desire for power. Antony observes in episode 14 that Atia objects to Cleopatra because Cleopatra is younger and higher-ranking than Atia herself (as opposed to the many slaves Antony has sex with, who may be younger but rank lower). When Antony marries Octavia and tries to convince Atia that it means nothing to him, she complains: "You love power more than you love me." Antony protests that "they are two completely different things," but in his relationship with Cleopatra, both are combined.

Although Antony's choice between Cleopatra and Atia/Octavia is played in *Rome* as a choice between two different forms of love, the old paradigm from the 1963 *Cleopatra* and from Shakespeare – that of cold-hearted politics defeating passionate romance – still appears through several stories over the course of Season Two. Every character who gives in to romantic love ends the series alone and disappointed because the desire for power will always defeat it: Octavia is rejected by Agrippa because he loves the power Octavian gives him more than he loves her; Vorena the Elder is tricked into falling in love with a rival of her father's who wants information from her; Pullo loses Eirene to Gaia's romantic jealousy and resentment of Eirene's superior position.

THE NEW ATIA: LIVIA

The apparent exception to this pattern is Octavian and Livia. Octavian's single-minded pursuit of power has been successful, and although he is a cold, increasingly unfeeling character (with a "rotten soul," as Cleopatra puts it in episode 22, "De Patre Vostro"), his marriage to Livia is depicted as a loving one. He seems to choose her almost on a whim, having checked her suitability as a potential wife, but once married he appears to love her as much as he is capable of loving anyone, caressing her hand as he talks about how the soft voice of a loving wife may sway a man in episode 21.

But by opening himself up even slightly to loving another person, Octavian may have condemned himself. In episode 20, Octavian tells Livia that he will beat her because it gives him sexual pleasure, but when they are shown in bed together in the next episode, it is she who slaps and chokes him. As they lie back, Livia declares that they will no longer serve eggs as she does not like them. She throws out a token, "unless you object, of course," but at that moment, Octavian is physically unable to speak. Octavian is therefore emasculated and the power dynamic in their relationship shifts – Livia is literally on top. This is a deliberate reference to the character of Livia as depicted by Robert Graves in *I, Claudius* (1934) and in the BBC adaptation of the novel for television. On the DVD commentary on episode 20 of *Rome*, producer John Melfi refers to the introduction of Livia as "the pre-*I, Claudius* moment," and says: "We get to see the early stages of the monster that Livia becomes." Her sex scene with Octavian in episode 21 is the closest viewers of *Rome* come to seeing the dominant Livia who "ruled Augustus" in *I, Claudius*, but there is an expectation that some viewers will read the whole story of *I, Claudius* into these scenes and interpret them accordingly – as with Antony and Cleopatra, existing popular culture is used to fill in the gaps left by the accelerated narrative.

This interpretation of Livia makes Atia's final scenes in the series distinctly double-edged. Much of the action in Season One was driven by Atia and Servilia, who manipulate their men into pursuing actions according to their desires. In Atia's case, as Cyrino has pointed out, her chief motivation is the desire for power, while Servilia is driven by anger at her romantic rejection by Julius Caesar, which develops into an ongoing feud with Atia.[11] However, with the shift in Atia's motivation in Season Two, she seems to be moving into a position more similar to Servilia, especially after the latter's death in episode 19. When Atia tells Octavian to "crush Antony and his queen" (episode 21), she is coming dangerously close to Servilia's obsession with crushing the man who rejected her. Livia, meanwhile, has taken on the role of the woman motivated by the desire for power. She cheerfully and without a second thought divorces her husband for the powerful Octavian, undeterred by her new sister-in-law telling her "you're marrying a monster" (episode 20).

Atia's final dialogue in the series consists of her asserting her authority over Livia. This scene reads drastically differently depending whether the viewer, like Melfi, considers the action a prequel of sorts to *I, Claudius*, or whether they are familiar with *Rome* alone. Atia refers to Servilia when she tells Livia that "far better women" than her have tried to destroy Atia: "Go and look for them now." Octavia smiles in delight as Atia takes her place at the front of the platform to watch the triumphal procession. For viewers of *Rome*, Atia has reasserted her power and authority over this upstart; but for viewers of *I, Claudius*, Atia's victory is temporary. Livia will murder Octavia's son and Atia's great-grandsons for the sake of her own child and even, eventually, Octavian himself. The cold-hearted pursuit of power will destroy them all.

This point is driven home in Atia's and Octavia's final, silent scenes in *Rome* (episode 22). As Octavia and Agrippa glance uncomfortably at one another, Atia watches effigies of Antony and Cleopatra go past in Octavian's triumphal procession. Earlier in the episode, Octavia told her she should be happy as it is her triumph as much as Octavian's, and notes that she has watched Atia strive for this moment all her life, but it seems, ultimately, that the sacrifice has been too great. The power Atia was looking for is a poor consolation prize for the loss of the love she has pursued throughout the second season.

ATIA AS THE AUDIENCE

This last twist in Atia's character development is the culmination of another shift in her portrayal across Season Two – the move to position her as an audience surrogate. In the first season, Atia was one of the characters who embodied Roman difference. Her comfort with nudity in front of her children and sex in front of her slaves, her ability to discuss group suicide calmly and practically, her obsession with her son's manhood, and her cold manipulation of those around her all marked her out as distinctly Other,[12] in contrast to Octavia, with whom the audience are encouraged to identify and who tends to act according to more socially acceptable, if misguided, motives in popular terms – chiefly romantic love for her first husband, and later for Servilia.[13] In Season Two, however, Atia increasingly becomes a much more modern-feeling character and much less Othered; she is nude much less often, she starts to prefer a monogamous relationship, and although her relationship with her son falls apart, she repairs her relationship with her daughter. Her torture of a slave and of Servilia and her adding Jocasta's father to the triumvirs' list of proscriptions maintain her ruthless, Othered status in the early part of the season, but by the end of the second season she is almost entirely sympathetic, as the behavior of both Octavian and Antony toward her becomes increasingly extreme.

Thanks to this softening of Atia, her relationship with Antony and his rejection of her becomes a tragedy that provides emotional focus during the dash for the finale. Just as Octavian Othered Antony into the emasculated slave to an Egyptian woman, *Rome* Others him into a drug-addled man whose lust for power and sex together in the figure of Cleopatra has ironically stripped him of both. Cleopatra is presented in a way that evokes some audience sympathy, but she remains inevitably Othered as the outsider, the foreign queen who has transformed not only Antony but his entire retinue into people barely recognizable to Atia and Octavia when they arrive in Alexandria. Octavian, always a distant and mysterious character, is increasingly unreadable and his ruthless actions separate him more and more from the audience's worldview and empathy. The rather sweet romance of Agrippa and Octavia appears to reflect a more modern relationship until the moment he leaves her because her brother tells him to, and so in terms of the elite story, by the end of the series it is the scorned women Atia and Octavia who hold the audience's sympathy and provide a recognizable Self to sympathize with against their Othered male relatives. The main audience surrogates in *Rome* are, of course, Pullo and Vorenus, who combine difference with more sympathetic actions – Pullo in particular is softened in Season Two – but the audience need a way into the elite story as well, besides Pullo's and Vorenus' involvement, and it is Atia and Octavia who provide it.

CONCLUSION

Romans are famous in Western popular culture for their degeneracy and sexual deviance.[14] They even told these sorts of stories about themselves: Octavian and Plutarch related wild tales about other people in order to prove that they themselves were different. In popular culture the emphasis tends to shift to the sexy, degenerate characters, but as Stacie Raucci has observed, even in the most exotic scenes of sexual deviance, a more moral character will usually be included with whom the audience is encouraged to identify.[15] Based on the first season of *Rome*, Atia would hardly seem destined to fulfill the role Octavia did in Octavian's propaganda, as the moral, noble Roman woman abandoned for the degenerate, exotic Cleopatra.

However, as the narrative speed increases and the number of elite characters available to provide audience surrogates decreases, Atia is increasingly less Othered and instead used as an audience surrogate, motivated by recognizable emotions and compared favorably to her exoticized Egyptian rival. And so, *Rome* finds itself telling the same story about Antony that Octavian did, of a man who rejects his upstanding Roman partner to fall into an unhealthy and vice-ridden relationship with an inappropriate Other.

NOTES

1 Cyrino (2008c: 138–9).
2 Bruno Heller, the show's creator, has stated that Season Two was originally to end with the death of Brutus (eventually moved to episode 18). The third and fourth seasons would have been "set in Egypt," and ended with the deaths of Antony and Cleopatra. When Heller discovered, "halfway through writing the second season," that the series had been cancelled, he "telescoped the third and fourth seasons into the second one"; see Hibberd (2008).
3 Both actors play them as passionately in love. James Purefoy observes on the DVD commentary for episode 21 that he and Lyndsey Marshal considered Antony and Cleopatra to be "soulmates."
4 According to Purefoy on the DVD commentary for episode 21, drapes from the 1963 *Cleopatra* were used as dressing in some of *Rome*'s Egyptian sets as an homage to the earlier film.
5 See Zanker (1988: 61–2).
6 Shakespeare, *Antony and Cleopatra*, Act IV, Scene 13.
7 Portraying Antony as non-Roman was essential to gaining public support for the war, officially a war against Cleopatra, not Antony. Contemporary poets like Horace emphasize the scandal of a Roman making himself subservient to a foreign woman; see for example Horace, *Epode* 9.
8 On Plutarch's moralizing in his *Lives*, see Duff (1999: 13–51).
9 See further Raucci (2008: 209–11).
10 Kelly (2013: 208) offers a different reading of this scene, suggesting that Antony's masculinity is elided by his subjection to the female viewer's gaze. But the total absence of any women in the scene and the manner in which Antony orders Vorenus from this position of absolute control suggests that it is intended as a display of his masculine authority.
11 Cyrino (2008c: 132).
12 See further Cyrino (2008c).
13 Note, however, that Octavia's most extreme action, seducing Octavian in episode 9, is clearly marked out as inherently wrong by everyone concerned, including Octavian himself; see Strong (2008).

14 There is substantial scholarship on this subject; see for example Cyrino (2013a).
15 Raucci (2013: 145–53), although she observes that the audience also vicariously enjoy the decadent side of the orgy sequences.

13 *Problematic Masculinity: Antony and the Political Sphere in* Rome

Rachael Kelly

"Running this damn city isn't *nearly* as amusing as I thought it would be," complains Antony as he reclines in a candlelit bath with his patrician lover Atia in episode 14 of *Rome*. His petulance is due to the fact that he is under mounting pressure from commercial and political leaders to deal with the chaos on the Aventine, Cleopatra is not the sexual pushover he had envisaged, and Cicero is uncomfortably cognizant of his own power relative to Antony's. Having seized control of Rome in the aftermath of Caesar's death, Antony expected that the strong-arm tactics that had served him so well as the dictator's quasi-political muscle would continue to reap the kind of financial – and authoritative – rewards to which he has been accustomed as the right-hand man to a political *force majeur*. That *true* power, power in its own right, has proven capricious is revealing of Antony's gender position within the text. This chapter will argue that the relationship of *Rome*'s Mark Antony to the public sphere – how he uses it and performs within it – is key to situating him on a continuum of problematic masculine performance that has ghosted Antony's position in popular culture for as long as popular culture has revisited his mythology. I will also argue that his incarnation in *Rome* is unique in terms of the way it chooses to structure his relationship to the political, and attempt to place this in the context of a wider socio-cultural debate about masculinity.

ANTONY AND MASCULINITY

Rome's Antony is a strange beast, and he defies simplistic evaluation. On the one hand, he can be situated alongside his previous incarnations on screen – Henry Wilcoxson (1934), Raymond Burr (1953), Richard Burton (1963), and Billy Zane (1999) – in that he evidences an engagement with wider socio-cultural anxieties around masculinity and a hegemonic masculine ideal. On the other, he deviates significantly from his predecessors in a number of key areas that, while the overarching message remains the same, demand closer engagement with his means of performing sub-hegemonic masculinity.

Hegemony itself is capricious; gender hegemony particularly so. Its nature is to be invisible, coded into the structures of societal discourse in a manner that allows it to be reproduced as something "everyone knows." Mike Donaldson provides a useful definition:

> Heterosexuality and homophobia are the bedrock of hegemonic masculinity . . . A culturally idealized form, it is both a personal and a collective project . . . While centrally connected with the institutions of male dominance, not all men practice it, though most benefit from it. Although cross-class, it often excludes working class and black men. It is a lived experience and an economic and cultural force, and dependent on social arrangements. It is constructed through difficult negotiation over a lifetime.[1]

As I have argued elsewhere,[2] the cultural function of Mark Antony, of which Antony-on-screen is only the most recent manifestation, is to act as a site for the interrogation and negotiation of gender anxiety; this is precisely because, as a white, heterosexual, economically privileged male, he *could* embody the western Warrior Hero archetype[3] but does not, and, as such, is supremely well suited as an avatar of the consequences of failing to police the boundaries of hegemonic masculinity. His construction follows a series of gendered tropes that can be traced directly back to Roman political discourse and the forms of rhetorical attack common to the public sphere of late Republican Rome, which are designed to position his performance of masculinity below the paradigm. This is partially informed by a discourse of gender reversal, enacted upon him by the presence of the Powerful Woman (Cleopatra), whose unnatural appropriation of the (masculine) position of power renders Antony symbolically emasculated. His failure to resist the reversal imposed upon him reinforces his positioning as gender transgressor, which in turn reinforces and informs his construction as performer of sub-hegemonic masculinity. This semantic loop positions him as an avatar of a host of anxieties about masculine performance and the encroachment of female autonomy on to the sphere of male dominance, and allows the key events of his life to be understood in line with this reading of him as sub-hegemonic.

Thus Antony's political decision to align himself with Cleopatra's wealth and influence in the eastern Empire is transmuted into an overwhelming, emasculating love that makes him abandon Rome.

His suicide, the last honorable refuge of a Roman nobleman in defeat, becomes an act of tearful despair in the wake of the battle of Actium. His appetites are excessive: he is prone to drinking himself into a stupor – particularly during his famous meeting with Cleopatra at Tarsus, which allows her to orchestrate his seduction to both the material luxury of Egypt and the pleasures of her own body. He loves to distraction and some of the more daring texts even hint at a robust sex drive: *Serpent of the Nile* (1953), for example, in which Antony is introduced to the audience mid-passionate embrace with an unnamed woman, quickly discarded and never seen again; or 1999's *Cleopatra*, in which Antony decides, with very little provocation, that Cleopatra wants to sleep with him as soon as he arrives at Tarsus. Finally, to underline Antony's position as sub-hegemonic performer of flawed masculinity, every text embodies the paradigm in a player that represents the potential masculine ideal, denied center stage for various narrative reasons, but always directly or indirectly compared to Antony. Often, this function falls to Caesar himself, but Caesar, as Maria Wyke demonstrates,[4] is an unstable avatar of hegemonic masculinity, and there is always an alternative – drawn from the annals or invented specifically – to underscore the message: in *Cleopatra* (1934), it is Enobarbus; in *Serpent of the Nile* (1953), it is Lucilius; in *Cleopatra* (1963), it is Rufio; in *Cleopatra* (1999), it is Olympos.

Rome is more complex. For one thing, the paradigm is embodied in not one but *two* men, acting co-dependently: Vorenus and Pullo, who, separately, often fail to achieve the ideal, but together tend to recuperate each other's flaws. For another, Antony's adherence to the standard tropology is considerably more problematic.

His tendency toward excess remains conspicuous – if anything, it is *more* pronounced in *Rome*, and more explicitly used to position him as sub-paradigm: in episode 13 ("Passover"), he refuses to rise from his bed on the morning of Caesar's funeral "until I've fucked someone" (Figure 14); while in episode 19 ("Death Mask"), he arrives late to a conference with Octavian and Lepidus, hungover from Posca's wedding, and explaining: "I could not get out of bed, no matter how hard I tried. I have the most shocking headache. So you must both speak very quietly or I shall shatter into a thousand pieces." He propositions Cleopatra in the middle of negotiations for grain shipments in episode 14 ("Son of Hades"), and bludgeons a senator to death as he reads out a paraphrased version of Cicero's Second Philippic on the Senate floor in episode 15 ("These Being The Words of Marcus Tullius Cicero"). His behavior is id-driven, of

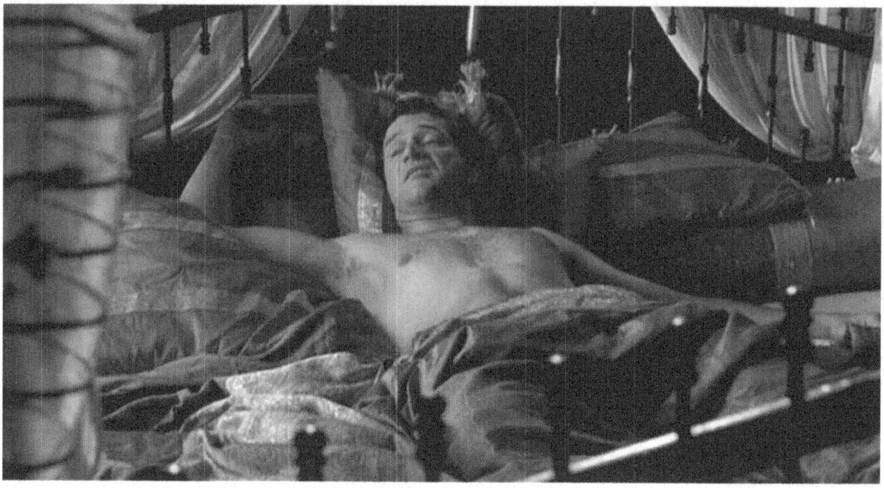

Figure 14 Antony (James Purefoy) indulges his excess on the morning of Caesar's funeral in episode 13 ("Passover") of *Rome* (2007). HBO BBC.

the moment, and uncontained – more so than ever before: Melanie McFarland's review of the series describes him as "an arrogant libertine who would willingly bugger the Senate with the same casual attitude as he does the help."[5] But the difference is that *Rome*'s Antony glories in his excess, where previous incarnations agonized over their inability to transcend their fatal flaws. Moreover, when he makes his final move East, it is not love that drives him, nor a sense that he cannot function efficiently in the masculine space of Rome. Rather, this Antony has to be forced to leave. This will prove to be revealing in terms of his positioning within the politicized world of the text.

THE POLITICAL SPHERE IN ROME, AND THE POLITICAL SPHERE IN *ROME*

Much of the structure that underpins Antony's screen construction can be traced to contemporaneous political maneuvering by his enemies. As Catherine Edwards argues in *The Politics of Immorality in Ancient Rome*,[6] gender discourse is key to establishing one's fitness (or otherwise) for political authority, and is the primary source of ammunition for political attacks. The public:male / private:female binary is enshrined in rhetoric: fitness-to-rule is inextricably linked to masculinity, since the public sphere is exclusively constructed as *male*, and therefore an attack on one's masculinity is equal to an attack on one's capacity for government. It is important, therefore, to understand the boundaries of masculinity within Roman convention. This is problematic, since the terms of reference are not strictly mappable on to modern gender discourse but, in general terms, Roman hegemonic masculine performance can be most usefully delineated with reference to two terms that describe its "other": *mollitia* ("softness" or effeminacy) and *incontinentia* (lack of self-governance). Both incorporate behaviors which are readily identifiable as items in Antony's standard tropology: *mollitia* does not directly translate, but may be read as a general charge of feminized behavior that, critically, can be mapped on to any subjugated population as a justification for dominance. Greece and the Hellenized world, being a particular locus of colonialist anxiety (as the source of what Edwards calls Rome's "cultural inferiority complex"),[7] is one such population. Consequently, "Egypt" is closely aligned, in Roman rhetoric, with "female," thereby allowing Antony's decision to ally himself with Cleopatra to be framed as the selection of female decadence over male order and propriety. Likewise, when Antony's pop-culture persona fails to curb his excessive appetites, when he allows himself to be incapacitated by love, when he fails to moderate his emotionality post-Actium, all of these are expressions of *incontinentia*, directly reproduced from Roman political propaganda where they are used to frame his masculinity as deficient. And, according to rhetoric, where his masculinity is deficient, he is discursively excluded from the political sphere.

This construct is visible throughout Antony's screen incarnations. In Cecil B. DeMille's *Cleopatra*, it is his manifest *incontinentia* that initially frames him as politically incompetent: during his first appearance on screen, fresh from a night of partying, the *mise-en-scene* signals his distance from the political elite by physically separating him from its representatives. Later, Cleopatra uses his bodily excess to lower his defenses: by plying him with alcohol and staging a dance spectacle featuring a multitude of beautiful women, she is able to seduce him and, thus bewitched, persuade him to join her in Alexandria, to Octavian's vitriolic chagrin. Likewise, Joseph L. Mankiewicz's *Cleopatra* contains the following exchange between Antony (Richard Burton) and Rufio (Martin Landau), performing the paradigm that Antony cannot achieve. Antony is startled to learn that Octavian has stripped Lepidus of command so early into the triumvirate, and laments his confusion:

> Antony: I wish I had not drunk so much today.
> Rufio: So do I.

> Antony: Do I trouble you, Rufio?
> Rufio: Yes you do.
> Antony: I'll wager you never found Caesar befuddled with wine. Nothing, no one ever befuddled Caesar.

With remarkable economy, the text has positioned Antony's political performance as inferior to both Caesar's and Rufio's, and offered his alcoholic excess as explanation for his failings.

Rome's Antony is different. In the examples above, Antony's behavior is used to position him outside of the masculine sphere through a direct projection of Roman gender norms. This is problematic in *Rome* for a number of reasons. For one thing, *Rome*'s Cleopatra is no longer the main focus of the narrative and is, in fact, reduced to a very minor role; by the time a discourse of emasculating love appears, it has only two episodes of the 22-episode narrative in which to play out. Related to this, and most importantly, *Rome* inhabits a much more overtly political space than any of the preceding texts, which tell, essentially, a love story set against an epic backdrop. Where the political intrudes in these earlier narratives, it is used mainly to contextualize the narrative and to afford it a level of historical verisimilitude. *Cleopatra* (1963) goes furthest in attempting to hang the plot upon the skeleton of the historical record, and the corpus as a whole pays lip-service to the political; but *Rome*, in taking as its core narrative the events of the end of the Republic, operates in a universe politicized to an extent not previously seen in Antony's screen mythology. This has the effect of re-focusing the thematic imperative and re-inscribing characters' motivation in such a way as to allow them to operate within the new narrative framework. When the central locus was Alexandria, to which Antony could absent himself for large portions of screen time on the pretext of overwhelming love, this effectively allowed the narrative to distance itself from any explicit interrogation of Antony's agency: the text, after all, was not interested in him except as his story intersected in a causative manner with Cleopatra's. It was enough, therefore, to allow that his feminized positioning equated to an inability to operate within the public sphere: the audience, after all, was given little opportunity to observe him in action, and his significant achievements – for example, his handling of the post-assassination crisis, or his power struggle with Octavian pre-Philippi – could be glossed over as tangential or inconsequential to the narrative. *Rome*, however, inverts the imperative: Antony's political career is subject to a lengthy, interrogative inspection across the 22-episode run; where previous screen texts have been free to ignore the question of how a man so manifestly out of his depth in the political arena might have gained and held a place in the team that ruled the known world, *Rome* is obliged not only to confront it head on, but also to offer some kind of convincing explanation.

This might have been framed as a demonstrable expression of political ability concomitant with Antony's position in the Roman world. That it is not, I would argue, demonstrates the gender anxiety that remains embodied in his pop-culture construction. However, the manner of his interaction with the business of leadership is fascinating: no longer explicitly feminized, Antony moves with a sense of entitlement within the political arena. Where Burton's Antony melancholically considered his inability to comprehend the niceties of political maneuvering, musing, "Make me to sit down, talk in whispers of this and that, with an emphasis here and a shrug there and I'm soon confounded and defeated," Purefoy stalks the Senate with a dangerous grin and an air of patrician confidence. Yet, as the opening quotation of this essay suggests, it would be wrong to mistake this for genuine political ability.

ANTONY IN THE POLITICAL SPHERE

Season One establishes the terms of Antony's inclusion in the public sphere. It is hinted in the first episode ("The Stolen Eagle"), where Brutus complains to Caesar, "I don't know how you tolerate that man," and Caesar sums up Antony's primary usefulness in four revealing words: "He likes to fight." However, it is in Antony's inauguration as tribune that his political participation begins to be quantified. Before Antony has left Gaul for Rome, at Caesar's instruction, to stand for office (episode 2, "How Titus Pullo Brought Down the Republic"), Posca – whose commentary on political matters frequently provides clarification and suggests a partisan position for the audience – expresses his objections in unambiguous terms: "I had understood the people's tribune to be a sacred office ... An office of great dignity and seriousness!" An amused Caesar concedes: "Perhaps you're right. We shall send Strabo along to make sure Antony behaves himself." Sanctity and dignity of office, however, hold little appeal for Antony: he rolls his eyes and sighs his way through his investiture, and complains loudly as it draws to a close, "About time! I need a drink." Later in the episode, during a senatorial vote on whether or not to declare Caesar an enemy of the state, Antony almost brings about civil war through his inaction. Seated apart from the senators, physically separated from them by the *mise-en-scene*, and semantically separated from them by his air of indifference, he is clearly bored by proceedings, and it takes the outbreak of chaos on the Senate floor, as Cicero and his supporters move to join the Pompeian faction, to rouse him from his lethargy. Cicero is unhappy about the gamble Pompey has chosen to take – Pompey's aim in proposing the motion is to show Caesar that he has no support in Rome, but he knows that the Senate cannot afford to provoke Caesar into war, and he is banking on Antony's tribunician veto to obviate catastrophe – but Antony, watching in panic as the congregation descends into anarchy, freezes at the critical moment, and it takes Cicero's yell of, "Antony! Veto the motion! Stand up! Veto the motion!" to rouse him into action. By the time he attempts to make his voice heard, however, the clamor is too great and he is ignored.

Judging by Antony's entry into the political arena, it is difficult to see why Caesar selected him. However, if we consider the scenes in which Antony's public sphere maneuvering is most effective, Caesar's motivation becomes clearer. On arrival in Rome, in the same episode, Antony attends a meeting of the *optimates*, where he offends Cato and Scipio by wearing his general's cloak within the city precincts. He removes it with an overly effusive gesture of contrition, but his dangerous demeanor during negotiations underlines his function: Antony is there to emphasize the physical risks inherent in crossing Caesar. Later, writing to his master, Strabo confirms his purpose in sending Antony to the city: "You will be pleased to hear that General Antony was as blithely arrogant and provocative as one could hope for," he says. Antony's political capabilities are moot: what Caesar requires of him, if anything, is the opposite – tactlessness and physical threat. Caesar is the political strategist: where Antony is successful, it is because Caesar has guided him.

This is clearest in Season Two, where Antony is lacking his *de facto* mentor and promptly either makes poor decisions, or is stopped from making poor decisions by other, more politically astute players (Posca, Octavian, Atia). It begins with the opening episode, where one of the historical Antony's greatest political achievements – maneuvering Caesar's assassins into a corner and turning the popular anti-Caesarian sentiment around – is essentially elided. According to historian John M. Carter:

> Antony's handling of this delicate situation compels admiration ... To the proposal advanced by the extremists, that Caesar's acts be annulled, Antony made a simple and effective counter. He pointed out that not merely had many important schemes been initiated by Caesar which it would be difficult or foolish to cancel, but that the vast majority of those assembled in the

Senate owed their past advancement, present status, and even future offices to Caesar's decision.[8]

Rome, however, depicts a panicking Antony determined to flee the city and raise an army for the express purpose of wreaking vengeance on Caesar's assassins. This is in keeping with previous texts, which have generally skipped directly from the Ides of March to the battle of Philippi, reconfigured as Antony's pursuit of justice for his murdered father figure. Alone among Antony's screen narratives, *Rome* chooses to display these negotiations, but, though Antony is once again required to lend his trademark brand of softly spoken menace to the proceedings, the strategy is not his. It is Octavian, still played at this point by a teenage Max Pirkis, who realizes that the conspirators have caught themselves in a legal loophole, and Atia, lured by the prospect of her son's potential wealth as Caesar's heir, who decides they will remain in the city. When Antony is sent to intimidate them into the pro-Caesarian way of thinking, he is repeating Octavian's words, at Atia's behest.

Indeed, Atia is often the political brains behind Antony's operations in the absence of Caesar and before his defection to Alexandria. In episode 15, it is she who determines that she would prefer not to uproot the family home to Macedonia, Antony's pro-consular province, at the end of his term as consul, and so reminds him: "Once you're gone from Italy, your enemies will no longer fear you . . . While you're swilling wine in Macedonia, do you think Brutus and Cassius will be idle?" Antony scoffs, "Those abject creatures?" to which Atia replies, "Abject only while you have power!" He immediately falls quiet and pensive, and it is clear that this has never previously occurred to him. Antony equates political authority with physical intimidation, not backstage maneuvering and, since Brutus and Cassius are currently physically intimidated, it has not crossed his mind to consider what will happen when they are out of his immediate reach.

Nor is this the only occasion on which Atia is obliged to do his thinking for him. She reads Cicero, for one, far better than does Antony: when it is necessary for Antony to intimidate Cicero into supporting his bid for a pro-consular province other than Macedonia (in episode 15), Atia is quietly unconvinced by Antony's blithe assurances that Cicero will toe the line because "I have my foot on his throat." Once again, Antony mistakes intimidation for authority, and it is, therefore, a shock to him when Cicero absents himself from Rome rather than be strong-armed into supporting his opponent. The scene in which Antony receives this news is particularly revealing of his political positioning: arriving late to the Senate with the same wanton disregard for custom that he displayed in episode 2 of the first season, Antony offers an apology for his tardiness that clearly indicates the relish with which he demonstrates his contempt for the proceedings. He is not the only patrician to subsume the good of the *res publica* to their own self-interest, of course, but the others – Pompey, Caesar, Octavian – are prepared to play the game. With their eye on the bigger picture, they use and abuse procedure in order to advance their own cause, but Antony holds the whole affair in contempt. He moves within the political sphere now, but he is no politician.

ANTONY, POLITICS, AND THE CHANGING GENDER PARADIGM

One way to consider this is to examine Antony's political performance against the series' treatment of politics as a whole, as it is clear that the narrative is as overtly concerned with issues of class, power structures, and corruption, as it is covertly concerned with issues of gender. Indeed, as briefly mentioned above, just as Pullo and Vorenus perform a dyadic ideal, Antony and Octavian perform a kind of inverse dyad, delineated along class lines. Pullo and Antony are id-driven and impulsive, Vorenus and Octavian are contained and authoritative, but the Antony/Octavian dyad is informed by a discourse of inner corruption that can be read as a commentary on the structure of the political elite. Moreover, there is a long history, in English-language filmmaking, of textual suspicion of the figure of the politician. While performance within the public sphere is unquestionably a key signifier of hegemonic masculinity within western socio-cultural discourse – Carroll calls it "one of the central arenas in which American masculinity has been experienced and enacted"[9] – politics-on-screen is an unstable quantity and can be used to evoke a wide range of responses in the audience. In their study of political messages in American cinema, Terry Christensen and Peter J. Haas discuss "the popular stereotype of the corrupt politician that would be reiterated throughout the history of American political film,"[10] and trace its lineage throughout cinematic history. Robert L. Hilliard expands upon the trope, interrogating a series of films that deal explicitly with politicians and political maneuvering and identifying not only the recurring theme of corruption at the heart of government, but also the concomitant archetype of the idealist whose scruples are eroded by the iniquity inherent in the legislative system.[11]

There are two candidates for this latter role: Brutus, who is manipulated into abandoning his principles by Servilia's bitterness and is required to undergo a figurative baptism in episode 15 before he can begin the process of recuperating his lost honor; and Vorenus, who is undefiled by the corruption of the upper classes until Servilia casually destroys his life to get to Caesar. Both are – almost uniquely – defined by their prioritization of the *res publica* over personal concerns, both are required to assimilate challenges to their own value systems by the demands of the public sphere, and both achieve the apex of their character arc when they give their lives for the greater good.

Again, the overtly politicized world of *Rome* allows for the performance of this kind of morality tale in a way that the earlier, de-politicized narratives did not. As such, with the public sphere – or at least, the key operators within the public sphere – rendered inherently corrupt, there is space for Antony's deficient masculinity within its de-idealized aegis. However, this is only part of the story. Corruption notwithstanding, these key players are at least able to *access* the political. Antony is not. For a fuller understanding of his position within the political space of *Rome*, we must look again to the way that the series constructs masculinity, and how this differs – substantially – from earlier constructions.

To claim that Antony's construction in *Rome* indicates a shift in the boundaries of hegemonic masculinity is unnecessarily polemical, and certainly beyond the scope of this chapter to prove. Evidence suggests, however, that the masculine paradigm itself has in fact been subject to a re-negotiation in recent decades,[12] perhaps in response to the feminist interrogation of gender roles in the latter half of the twentieth century. While the Warrior Hero archetype remains largely unchanged – according to Carroll, "strength, virility, control, power and dominance"[13] – the means by which the paradigm is embodied may be subject to a subtle re-negotiation in terms of the relative value afforded to each of its signifiers. Stephanie Shields, for example, explains how the use of "manly tears," if used with emotional control, may, in fact, be used as a marker of proper masculine performance.[14] This is important in terms of the manner in which *Rome* constructs paradigm masculinity. Antony's emotionality, in previous incarnations, is excessive and not subject to recuperation under Shields's paradigm, where tears are "not indiscriminate, nor are they profuse."[15] However, Shields' findings suggest that, to achieve the masculine ideal, a man must now perform appropriate emotionality.

This is part of a wider schema, collected under the "New Man" rhetoric, which also encompasses nurturant parenting and emotional availability – not *new* ideas, clearly, but not formerly applicable to the essentialized masculinity of the historical mythic space. Tim Edwards talks about the collapse of gender distinctions as a feature of this new paradigm,[16] and it is possible to see a blurring of the limits of feminized masculinity and idealized masculinity within this new structure. As such, a gender-reversed Antony, one whose *incontinentia* makes him susceptible to *mollitia* – and thereby effeminacy as a modern audience might understand it – is, potentially, no longer sufficient to perform the sub-hegemonic. Indeed, given Antony's previous tendency to exhibit characteristics consistent with Hare's seminal definition of psychopathy ("egocentricity, grandiosity, deceptiveness, shallow emotions with poor frustration tolerance, lack of empathy, guilt, or remorse, impulsivity, irresponsibility, and the ready violation of social and legal norms and expectations;"[17] it reads, in fact, like a character précis), his tearful despair in the final episode of the series, when he believes Cleopatra is dead, might actually evidence a degree of healthy psychosocial development.

As such, it is possible to see Purefoy's Antony in *Rome* coded as sub-hegemonic not through his failure to prevent the gender reversal enacted by the Powerful Woman or by his own characterological tendency toward feminizing behavior, but by a kind of hyper-masculinity, dangerously uncontainable, a pathologized version of the Warrior Hero, only exploded into hyperbolic excess. The mode of transgression is different: this sub-hegemonic behavior does not attract the same rhetoric of feminized shame, nor, consequently, the same reflexive self-loathing, and so Antony does not consider himself excluded from the masculine business of politics. But, though he does not realize it, his gender deficiency nevertheless continues to prevent him from participating in a structured, reasoned, and productive manner.

CONCLUSION

Rome remains one of the most fascinating examples of constructing Mark Antony on screen. There is much more that could be said about his political performance in this highly politicized narrative space: the mapping of the modern political arena on to the ancient world (indeed, one commenter at a conference suggested that Antony ought to be read as performing the present-day British Conservative peer); non-mainstream sexual practice among the political elite as a marker of gender deviancy; the Othering of Egypt and the positioning of Cleopatra in terms of reading Antony. Atia's attempts to influence the public sphere are intriguing inasmuch as they surreptitiously return to the patriarchal limits of female agency – private sphere intruding on public to the detriment of the *res publica* – even while ostensibly seeking to transcend them, and her affiliation with Antony, and her use of him in the pursuit of her own ends, is surely a rich source of information about his positioning within the narrative. Octavian's character arc is similarly instructive, particularly as it informs Antony's, and is certainly deserving of a more thorough investigation. The list is extensive, and this chapter is not intended to be an exhaustive investigation of Antony-as-politician. Rather, I want to situate his positioning in *Rome* as analogous to earlier incarnations, in keeping with his established tropology but singularly, significantly different in a manner that demands attention. *Rome*'s political bad-boy can be placed as the continuing avatar of hegemonic anxieties around the performance of masculinity, but his method of performing political masculinity also evidences a fascinating break with his previous, feminized persona. The rationale behind the shift, I suggest, is to be found in the tendency over recent decades to problematize the conventional model of hegemonic masculinity: but that's another argument for another day.

NOTES

1 Donaldson (1993: 646).
2 Kelly (2009).
3 Carroll (2003: 33) has a useful definition of this archetype.
4 Wyke (2007: 1).
5 McFarland (2007).
6 Edwards (1993).
7 Edwards (1993: 95).
8 Carter (1970: 17–18).
9 Carroll (2003: 362).
10 Christensen and Haas (2005: 64).
11 Hilliard (2009: 157–8).
12 See, for example, Clatterbaugh (1997); Connell (2005); Edwards (2006); MacInnes (1998); Whitehead and Barrett (2001).
13 Carroll (2003: 33).
14 Shields (2002: 125).
15 Shields (2002: 125).
16 Edwards (2006: 17).
17 Paraphrased in Hervé (2007: 50).

14 Rome, *Shakespeare, and the Dynamics of the Cleopatra Reception*

Gregory N. Daugherty

Almost at the end of Shakespeare's *Antony and Cleopatra* (ca. 1607), the tragic queen expresses her fears (5.2.214–21):

Saucy lictors
Will catch at us like strumpets, and scald rhymers
Ballad us out o' tune. The quick comedians
Extemporally will stage us, and present
Our Alexandrian revels; Antony
Shall be brought drunken forth, and I shall see
Some squeaking Cleopatra boy my greatness
I' the posture of a whore.

This metatheatrical prophecy is revisited in the second season of HBO–BBC's *Rome* as it begins and concludes with Antony's orgiastic excesses and a shrill Cleopatra's twin attempts to prostitute herself for survival. The Cleopatra scenes are indeed heavily indebted to Shakespeare's play but, as Jonathan Stamp and Bruno Heller note in the DVD commentary to the last episode, they do try to find "a new way into something familiar."[1] In doing so they have crafted a novel and modern reception of the Cleopatra story by invoking Shakespeare – and film – to underscore their departures, by emphasizing some frequently neglected parts of Plutarch, and most notably by attempting to tell the story of both Antony and Cleopatra while weaving their stories into the series' story arcs of Octavian and Pullo. The result is a creative and successful addition to the Cleopatra reception.

CLEOPATRA AND *ROME*

Cleopatra's appearance in episode 8 ("Caesarion") of *Rome*'s first season is discussed in depth by me elsewhere.[2] In this episode, the fictionalized core protagonists Pullo and Vorenus rescue the drug-addled princess from her brother's minions. On the way back to Alexandria, the slave Charmian detoxes Cleopatra and devises a plan to ensure her mistress' pregnancy by enlisting first Vorenus, who declines, and then a more willing Pullo. After emerging disheveled from a proper Plutarchan sack in a pose mirroring Claudette Colbert's in Cecil B. DeMille's *Cleopatra* (1934), she is able to seduce Caesar, secure her throne, and give birth to Caesarion, as Pullo cheers lustily for his progeny.[3] I have argued that this episode shows a keen awareness of Shakespeare, Plutarch, and several twentieth-century films. Her appearance, initial stupor, and serpent-like sensuality were quite a shock to many viewers. Cleopatra appears in the second season in episodes 14, 20, 21, and 22, which also bear witness to similar influences and offer their own novel depictions. Unlike many of her cinematic receptions, however, in *Rome* Cleopatra only appears in the context of her relations with Antony. Her own complex backstory and her monarchical competencies are largely ignored, but this is not her story: it is the story of Octavian's defeat of Antony.

There is considerable continuity between the two seasons of the series. Since Stephen Shill directed both episode 8 and episode 21 ("Deus Impeditio Esuritori Nullus"), there is close continuity in the Alexandrian sets, the unnerving costume and wig designs for the Ptolemaic court, and in the performances of Lyndsey Marshal, as Cleopatra, and Kathryn Hunter, as Charmian, who was an anachronism in the first season. And of course Pullo appears to rescue his (not as old as he should have been) son, Caesarion/"Aeneas." Cleopatra has not changed much. She still uses drugs, still wears daring outfits, and is quite comfortable with her sexuality, which she also still uses to her advantage. This dark, vicious, and vain Cleopatra is still a shock to many who are accustomed to the gentler, more romanticized versions of the 1920s Palmolive ads, Claudette Colbert in the 1934 *Cleopatra*, Elizabeth Taylor in the 1963 *Cleopatra*, and their numerous spin-offs.[4] But there has always been a dangerous side in the reception of the queen, for example in some Victorian novels,[5] in more recent comics,[6] and in films such as *Serpent of the Nile* (1953) with Rhonda Fleming or *Two Nights with Cleopatra* (1953) with Sophia Loren. This dark and dangerous Cleopatra belongs more to a nineteenth-century European reception than to a twentieth-century American version.[7]

It is not surprising that this largely British production would draw heavily from Shakespeare for much of what is familiar, but it is worth noting some themes which appear in more than one episode.

References to how "changeable" Antony is, Cleopatra's mercurial moods, and the imaginary theater the besotted pair substitute for reality owe much to the Elizabethan tragedy. As attested on the DVD commentary, the creators paid close attention to Plutarchan accounts of their personal excesses and deaths in Alexandria, while only alluding to the military losses in Parthia and Actium and to the political bombshells such as their marriage and the Donations of Alexandria. It is also quite evident that they were aware of aspects of previous filmed versions of the story.[8] The metal bra Cleopatra wears in the hunting scene in the palace is clearly a homage to the snake bra tradition begun by Theda Bara in *Cleopatra* (1917), continued in the Palmolive ads, and echoed numerous times in American popular culture.[9] From the Claudette Colbert 1934 film, we can see her smoldering sensuality, Antony's growing effeminacy, and the prominent thrones in the death scene. From the Elizabeth Taylor 1963 version, we have Antony's single combat challenge, the effect that Cleopatra's entrance has on the women of Rome, and even the re-use of curtains found at Cinecittá. And finally there is the impact that a series of stunning beauties in stunning costumes – Leonor Varela in *Cleopatra* (1999), Monica Bellucci in *Asterix et Obelix: Mission Cleopatre* (2002), Samuela Sardo in *Julius Caesar* (2002), Anne Valle in *Imperium: Augustus* (2003), and most recently Sofia Essaidi in a stage musical *Cleopatre: La Derniere Reine d'Egypte* (2008, DVD 2010) – have had on the sexualization of Cleopatra. The writers, producers, directors, consultants (especially Jonathan Stamp), and even the actors seem well informed about the historical queen as well as the ancient, Elizabethan, and contemporary receptions. As Marshal said in an interview about her youthful aspirations: "I would have been an archaeologist! I studied Classics at A level and then I applied to do Classics and French at university, but then I thought, 'No, I've got to try this out,' so I went to the Royal Welsh College."[10] In the DVD commentary, James Purefoy, who plays Mark Antony, notes the extent of his own reading and thought about playing his character.

Departures from the standard Anglo-American Cleopatra reception, then, are clearly not laughable blunders but thoughtful and innovative contributions to the tradition in service of a larger narrative vision. In a review of the relevant episodes, note the careful use of Plutarch as a major source for critical elements of the narrative. That narrative is designed to recount – through the linking devices of the fictionalized Pullo and Vorenus – the defeat of Antony, the victory of Octavian/Augustus, and the demise of the Roman Republic. This vast tale is held together and personalized by the linking and unlinking of numerous couples and pairs and their narrative arcs: for example, the relationships between Vorenus, Pullo, and Antony and their "families" and how they fracture in the beginning only to reconnect and reintegrate at the end. The parallelism between the themes of redemption, honor, and suicide in episodes 14 ("Son of Hades") and 22 ("De Patre Vostro") are very effectively highlighted.[11] Since relationships, especially dysfunctional ones, are a major motif of the series, it is not remarkable that Antony and Cleopatra are treated more as a couple than as individuals. Cleopatra will only appear when her story directly affects that of a principal Roman figure, whether he be Caesar, Antony, or Octavian. Even in effigy on a cart in Octavian's triumphal parade (episode 22), she is literally bound to Antony.

NEGOTIATION AND FORESHADOWING

Cleopatra's bond to Antony is precariously financial when they first meet in the second season. In episode 14, Cleopatra is in Rome, and their dialogue implies that she has just arrived. The precise chronology of her visit (or visits) to Rome are unclear, but since the setting is a little more than a month after the death of Caesar the historical scenario is possible.[12] This is drama, however, so her presence in this episode is essential to later plot developments and conflicts with Atia and Octavian in particular. Since her visit to Rome had not been included in Season One, the first mention of Cleopatra comes when Antony describes her to a suspicious Atia as "a dark skinny little thing who talks too much." This in itself is a clever allusion to Plutarch's assessment of her unremarkable looks (*Life of Antony* 27.3), although the author never claims that she was ugly. Cleopatra is confident, self-assured, and handsome, but hardly stunning. While this attribution has become quite frequent lately and has been taken too far by some fiction writers (notably Colleen McCullough), it is refreshing to see a Cleopatra played by an attractive, but not gorgeous actress.

When she meets with Antony, Cleopatra is not wearing the elaborate Ptolemaic clothing, headdress, or make-up from Alexandria, just a simple Greek-style dress and an ankh precariously balanced in an ample cleavage. He notes that she has changed: it is a nice touch for Antony to allude to their first meeting when he was with Gabinius in Egypt (Plutarch, *Life of Antony* 3) and for Cleopatra to fail to remember him. She says that the uniforms make all Romans look alike, yet he is in full armor when they meet again later in Alexandria in episode 20 ("A Necessary Fiction"). Her interview with Antony about grain pricing is terse but formal and conducted almost entirely by their alter ego servants, Charmian and Posca. It is an impersonal negotiation, although Antony is obviously intrigued by this powerful woman. He is put off by her mention of Caesar as her husband and remarks: "A Roman consul with an Egyptian wife. Wouldn't do, you know." This is a foreshadowing of his own PR problems for taking up with Cleopatra later on. When she brings up Caesarion, the tone sours even more, and the possibility that she might prostitute herself for what she wants is explored almost clinically. She refers to his "changeability" for the first time.[13] When she slaps him for touching her, Antony smiles: "Nice manners for a whore." She remains calm: "If I must prostitute myself for the good of my country and my family, I will," she fires back. "But the customer pays first, does he not?"

The Shakespearean themes have been established with this scene. Although it did not go well, she keeps her composure. As the camera follows her walking away from her meeting with Antony, looking like a conventionally Hellenistic woman, the shot gives a very clear impression of the impact she has had on the males of Rome: the togate elders step aside as she passes by. She flinches only when she sees the actual father of her child, Pullo, waiting to catch Antony (Figure 15). This sets the stage both for his reunion with his child and for the development of the relationship between Antony and

Figure 15 Cleopatra (Lyndsey Marshal) flinches as she sees Pullo, the "real" father of her child, in episode 14 ("Son of Hades") of *Rome* (2007). HBO BBC.

Vorenus, all motivated by a series of complaints about Antony's failure to deal with gang violence on the Aventine. At Pullo's urging, Antony rescues Vorenus from his grief and stupor and solves his own gang problem, setting up the mirror event for the final episode.

Continuing this framing device, Cleopatra goes to dinner at Atia's. Prior to this, Antony had given Atia an edited version of their encounter in which he played down the queen's appearance and demeanor. But this time she is dressed in the Alexandrian mode introduced in episode 8 of Season One. She makes a grand entrance to the dinner where she has the same powerful effect on the assembled men and women that Elizabeth Taylor's moving Sphinx had in the 1963 film. "Just as you described her," says Atia sarcastically: "Quite the little mouse." The montage of the dinner emphasizes Cleopatra's sensuality and attraction along with the growing interest and fascination of Antony. She immediately antagonizes Atia by implying that Antony had described her as "nice." To make matters even more tense, she introduces her son as the son of Caesar to the mother of Caesar's heir. In the course of the dinner, Atia shoots murderous looks, but not nearly as murderous as the ones Octavian has for a four-year-old Caesarion. This hatred rarely appears in the Cleopatra receptions, but is featured prominently here and in the film *The Son of Cleopatra* (1962), where Caesarion lives on to fight for his birthright under a new name. As Cleopatra proffers friendship, Atia whispers to her the prophetic line: "Die screaming you pig-spawn trollop." The Egyptian entourage, her revealing and exotic costumes, and especially her sensuous attention to food and drink foreshadow the "Inimitable Livers" of episode 21 (see below). What is more, this occurs in the context of a growing number of doomed couples coming together, such as Pullo and Gaia, Castor and Duro, and soon thereafter, Octavia and Agrippa. In this context it is clear that Antony and Cleopatra are to be another tragic couple.

ROMANTIC TRAGEDY

Cleopatra does not appear again until the end of episode 20 when Antony has finally gone to the East to take up his provinces and armies. He has married Octavia who is now completely involved in a relationship with Agrippa, which Octavian has used to blackmail Antony into going East and away from Atia. Vorenus, ashamed that he has failed Antony and almost strangled his own daughter, has chosen to go with him in a form of self-imposed exile. In an earlier scene, Pullo has beaten the rival gangs of the Aventine with the fearsome foreign witch Gaia at his side, having lost Eirene – the only source of peace in his life. This set-up provides the context for the sudden reappearance of Cleopatra. It is roughly 41 BC when Antony arrives at the court of Alexandria in full military kit, only to find the official throne room, later to be the place of his death, a child's playroom. To the side appears Cleopatra, backlit in a transparent gown of Coan silk.[14] Antony is sweating profusely from the Egyptian heat as his male gaze scans the essentially nude and coolheaded queen. The only dialogue they share are two words: "Antony!" . . . "Cleopatra!" In this brief but compelling exchange, another doomed couple is formed, with the whole barge scene from Tarsus condensed into two words, two gazes, two fates sealed (*Antony and Cleopatra* 2.2.204–6):

> With divers-colored fans, whose wind did seem
> To glow the delicate cheeks which they did cool
> And what they did undid.

In pronouncing the title of the tragedy, the Shakespearean section of the series begins in earnest. By the next episode (episode 21), as noted in the DVD commentary by Purefoy, they have cut out the courtship and they are shown in full debauch shortly before the "Donations of Alexandria."[15] The episode progresses to the revelation of Antony's will and the declaration of war against Cleopatra, or the rough dates of 35–31 BC. The campaigns in Parthia and Armenia are assumed but not mentioned, perhaps because they seemed to belong to a tale of Antony alone, not of the couple. Almost casually, but with the effect of emphasizing their partnership, *Rome* presents the fruits of their union, the twins Alexander Helios and Cleopatra Selene, although the youngest son, Ptolemy Philadelphus, is omitted: note that these progeny rarely appear in Cleopatra films. Moreover, the viewers are prepared for a changed Antony by seeing a literally haunted Vorenus (whose dead wife, Niobe, appears in his dreams) and a drug-addled Posca as shells of their former selves. Their declines contextualize the revels of Antony and Cleopatra as we see them at the height of Plutarch's "Inimitable Livers" phase (Plutarch, *Life of Antony* 28.2).

At the beginning of the episode, they are "hunting" a hapless slave dressed as a stag in front of a delegation of mortified Roman senators. According to the DVD commentaries, the actors Purefoy and Marshal had apparently discussed their roles at length, and had decided to play them as soulmates in a genuinely passionate but destructively abusive relationship. They felt that Antony and Cleopatra would have used any drug available, routinely abused alcohol, and continuously sought satisfaction for their appetites for sex, power, and food, especially foods that were, in Purefoy's words, "wet, moist, and sexy." Plutarch himself makes a connection between drugs and the relationship of Antony and Cleopatra (*Life of Antony* 37.4). The director Shill wanted the scenes to be packed with visual information about their excesses and their sadness, but also their profound attachment to one another (Plutarch, *Life of Antony* 53). In his visual appearance, Antony has become softer, effeminate in dress and make-up, and dissipated enough to shock the Roman emissary.[16] The snake tattoo on his chest foreshadows the end of their affair. The deer-hunting scene brings out the cruel and violent side of Cleopatra and the shocking effect of the scene gives credence to the Augustan propaganda summarized by the Newsreader at the end of the episode.

Cleopatra tries her best to egg Antony on to war. As she did in episode 14, she calls him "changeable." The only thing that forces his hand is the sudden appearance of Atia and Octavia, sent to procure more grain. Although this event is not attested in the historical sources, it is not entirely fictional either, being based on the actual grain shortage of 39 BC, on his wife's attempt in 35 BC to bring Antony supplies and troops, and on Cleopatra's subsequent jealous reaction and Octavia's useful public humiliation.[17] In a pivotal scene set in the now double throne room equipped with a giant bed/couch, the full range of Cleopatra's moods is on display: passionate lover, petulant wife, and arrogant autocrat are all artfully woven into one believable character. She even reveals the beginnings of doubt as to her choice of champions. In one drug-addled and remarkable exchange, Antony accuses Cleopatra of wanting "to play the queen" in front of Octavia. Enraged, she says: "I am the queen." This may reflect the fantasy theater that the Shakespearean protagonists construct for themselves. It builds as their dispute over how to handle the delegation goes from affection to passionate grappling to shouting and crashing pottery worthy of *Who's Afraid of Virginia Woolf?* (1966).

The true source of Cleopatra's anger is her realization that Antony is not willing to humiliate or kill his former lover, and she doubts both his love and his will to win. The embassy fails but mother and daughter secure even more when Antony shamefully sends them away, along with the desperate stowaway Posca carrying a copy of Antony's incriminating will. This plot point allows the series to make Atia and Octavia direct instruments of Antony and Cleopatra's downfall, as Antony deserts both his long-time lover (Atia) and his legal wife (Octavia). The episode underscores this theme as, back in

Rome, the symbiotic conjugal relationship of Octavian and Livia grows kinkier and the comparatively conventional coupling of Pullo and Gaia unravels in brutal violence. "Didn't end so well," as Pullo will answer Vorenus' inquiry in the next episode. The narrative of this episode offers a tragedy of doomed romantic relationships, emphasized by the unconventional success of the marriages of Posca and Jocasta and Octavian and Livia. What's love got to do with it?

CLOSING THE RING

Episode 22 ("De Patre Vostro") ties up the several storylines of the series, including the ones most relevant to this study: the ring begun earlier in episode 14 is now closed with the post-Actium redemption of Antony by Vorenus, the father and child reunions of both Vorenus with his children and Pullo with his son Caesarion/"Aeneas," and of course the union in death of Antony and Cleopatra, both perished on their thrones and as effigies on Octavian's triumphal cart. Antony returns from the naval defeat at Actium (31 BC) to a life of Alexandrian dissipation and an increasingly desperate and sober Cleopatra. The orgy scenes from the "Inimitable Diers" phase (Plutarch, *Life of Antony* 71.4–5) are certainly busy, staffed with Italian porn actors and volunteers from the crew: "whores, hermaphrodites, and lick spittle,"[18] as Antony describes them while debating flight or suicide with Cleopatra.

As noted at the outset of this chapter, the series creator Heller says on the DVD commentary to the final episode that he wanted to find a "new way into something familiar," and he succeeds in doing so by injecting some neglected items from Plutarch and the filmic tradition, by omitting one of the most familiar of all Shakespearean scenes, and by adding an episode from his own life. One of the neglected items from the tradition is Antony's challenge to single combat attested to in Plutarch (*Life of Antony* 75.1). While this appeared in the 1963 *Cleopatra*, here it is not invoked to redeem Antony's masculine bravery, but to show the depths of drunken effeminacy to which he has fallen, and to demonstrate to Cleopatra the desperate situation she is in, motivating her decision to yield to the invitation from Octavian that has been slipped to Charmian. She sees this meeting with Octavian after the death of Antony as the only way to save herself, her children, and her crown. The attempted seduction of Octavian – another relatively neglected episode and one not included in Plutarch – was quite popular in later Western painting and sculpture,[19] although it does not feature in Hollywood films. In *Rome* it helps to close the ring begun in episode 14 when Cleopatra, using some of the same lines, attempted and failed to seduce Antony during their negotiations. To meet with Octavian, she wears a diaphanous gown – as she did when she met Antony at the end of episode 20 – and oozes charm and promised cooperation. She fails to lure the soulless "monster" but at least manages to conceal her panic and her immediate resolve to follow Antony in death.

The item from Heller's own life comes in Cleopatra's last words, when she rises up and hisses to Octavian with her last breath: "You . . . have a rotten soul." Heller relates that this line was uttered to him one day in New York's Central Park by a random elderly woman, and here he redirects it toward Octavian.[20] In *Rome*, perhaps given the demands of the sudden shortening of the series, the story of Antony and Cleopatra is subordinate to the Augustan triumph and the death of the Republic. Finally, the narrative omission involves the character of Charmian who has two big scenes in Shakespeare: the fortune-teller and her answer to the Roman's query: "Was this well done of your lady?" Instead her role has been totally transformed into that of an intermediary, more like the Nurse in *Romeo and Juliet* (1597), when she appears to a hungover Antony with a bloodied dress and dagger. This must have been quite a change for Kathryn Hunter, an experienced Shakespearean actress, but it does set the scene for the rescue of Caesarion by Vorenus, after he has assisted Antony's final departure and has carefully outfitted his corpse as a real Roman.[21] This is the end of the notorious couple, but the episode and the series continue on to present the reintegration of three very odd families – Vorenus with his children; the elite Julii when Octavian gives his sister Octavia Antony's half-Egyptian children to raise; and Pullo with Caesarion/"Aeneas." The last words of the series are spoken by Pullo to his son: "About your father . . ."

The creators of *Rome* did find a new way into a familiar Shakespearean story, but they did it by re-reading and following Plutarch and emphasizing aspects of the existing reception that supported their themes. They did not shy away from invoking other films, especially those in which Cleopatra was played by Claudette Colbert and Elizabeth Taylor. The very beginning and the very end of the love affair between Antony and Cleopatra witnessed the highest level of creative fabrication, but the core of their depiction of the relationship was firmly based in Plutarch. Since Plutarch himself was but an early phase of the reception of Cleopatra, his account cannot be called factual – indeed, facts are hard to come by in the life of the queen – but it is at least not alarmingly anachronistic. The care with which that relationship was allowed to play out before the audience is what makes this one of the most exceptional and satisfying contributions to the Cleopatra reception. The series tells the story of the two of them as a flawed couple, against the backdrop of a world changing in ways they cannot understand or control.

NOTES

1 Quoted in the DVD commentary to episode 22, "De Patre Vostro."
2 Daugherty (2008).
3 See Plutarch, *Life of Caesar* 49.
4 For example, see Saylor (2005).
5 Such as H. Rider Haggard, *Cleopatra, Being an Account of Harmachis, The Royal Egyptian, As Set Forth by His Own Hand* (1889).
6 On Cleopatra in comics, see Daugherty (2009).
7 For a useful introduction to Cleopatra's reception, see Jones (2006).
8 For an exhaustive list of films, consult Wenzel (2005).
9 On the ubiquity of the snake bra in popular media, see Daugherty (2013).
10 Quoted in "20 Questions with Lyndsey Marshal" at *whatsonstage.com* (December 13, 2004).
11 See Toscano (2013: 134).
12 For a reasonable account and bibliography, see Roller (2010: 71–5).
13 Toscano (2013: 125).
14 See Lucan, *Pharsalia* 10.141; on Coan "silk," see Pliny, *Natural History* 6.20.
15 For the courtship, see Plutarch *Life of Antony* 25–7; for the "Donations of Alexandria," see *Life of Antony* 54.
16 On this aspect of the reception of Antony, see Kelly (2009: 9).
17 On the grain shortage, see Plutarch, *Life of Antony* 32; on Octavia's attempted interventions, see Plutarch, *Life of Antony* 53–4.
18 The line may be an allusion to Antony's famously coarse wit, what Plutarch calls *bomolochia* at *Life of Antony* 29.4.
19 An example of this scene in painting is *Cleopatra and Octavian* by Louis Gauffier (ca. 1787–88); in sculpture, see the William Wetmore Story neoclassical statue of *Cleopatra* (1858).
20 The New York story is noted in the synopsis for episode 22 in the trivia section on the HBO *Rome Wikia.com* site.
21 On this relationship, see Kelly (2010: 5).

15 *The Rattle of the Sistrum: "Othering" Cleopatra and Egypt in* Rome

John J. Johnston

This chapter focuses upon the representations of Cleopatra and the city and court of Alexandria in Season Two of the HBO–BBC series *Rome*. This exploration considers some of the significant production decisions, which appear to have been made in an effort to increase the sense of "otherness" in the depictions of the Alexandrian court, in both set and costume design as well as in casting and performance. My discussion highlights many of the actual two- and three-dimensional artefacts from which Carlo Serafin, the supervising art director, and April Ferry, the costume designer, along with their teams, evidently drew inspiration, while drawing certain parallels with the depictions of the Ptolemies and their city in earlier film, television, and stage productions.

EGYPT AS "OTHER"

From the outset, the producers of *Rome* were presented with something of a problem: their depiction of the city of Rome and its inhabitants was already a considerably grimier and more alien representation than the cinema-literate audience might expect from its more sanitized depictions in Hollywood epics such as Stanley Kubrick's *Spartacus* (1960) or, even more recently, Ridley Scott's *Gladiator* (2000). How, then, should the even more exotic and decadent city of Alexandria and its Egyptian queen be depicted?

First and most importantly, the designers took a clear tonal decision to represent the palace and its inhabitants as an almost entirely Egyptian society, eschewing the more obviously Hellenistic modes of dress, architecture, and internal décor which would have existed throughout the historical Alexandria of this period. No doubt this is a common problem for those attempting to visualize the Ptolemies and their world. Cleopatra VII Philopater, to give the queen her full name, was known as the first of her lineage to read and speak the Egyptian language, indicating that Greek was the more usual tongue and script used at the Alexandrian court. Sculptural representations show the ruling dynasty in both Egyptian and Hellenistic garb, depending upon the purpose for which the statuary was intended, although it is impossible to say which of the two modes may have been the more usual in daily life. It is normally suggested that Hellenistic dress would have been the general rule, while purely Egyptian dress was reserved for formal state occasions and more religious contexts. Certainly the Ptolemies are represented on their coinage in a fairly standard Hellenistic manner, while colossal statuary invariably depicts them as wholly Egyptian kings with similarly Egyptianized consorts.[1]

That the makers of *Rome* chose to take the purely Egyptian representational route is entirely understandable, however, in that it lends color and variety to the proceedings, while having a number of illustrious precedents in both film and television depictions of this historical period. Furthermore, such a standpoint decisively underlines the events in Alexandria as being both totally unfamiliar and apart from the events in Rome, whereas a more realistic portrayal may have resulted in a muddle of styles, causing confusion for a general audience. Consequently, as depicted in *Rome*, the Egyptians and their court are identifiably different from the Romans.

Before turning to Season Two, it may be instructive to begin by mentioning the introduction of the Ptolemaic court in the first season of *Rome*, wherein the designers make some interesting choices regarding the portrayal of the Alexandrian elite. The young Ptolemy XIII is a surly, obese child, seated upon a throne with a scalloped, feather-incised back, and his depiction is strongly reminiscent of two grotesque terracotta figurines from around 170–116 BC,[2] excavated in Memphis and now in the collection of the Petrie Museum of Egyptian Archaeology in London. These figures show "an obese man in a chariot . . . wearing a diaphanous garment that emphasizes his bloated form."[3] While the precise meaning of these figurines remains largely unknown – grotesque terracottas of varying types are a regular element of Ptolemaic art[4] – these particular figurines are often thought to be caricatures of Ptolemy VIII Euergetes, commonly referred to as *Physkon* or "Pot-belly." Euergetes' substantial bulk and arrogant exhibitionism in his meeting with the Roman envoy Scipio Aemelianus are charmingly described by Diodorus Siculus,[5] whose account of this awkward cultural interaction may well have provided a degree of inspiration to the producers of the Egyptian episode in the first season of *Rome*.

However, in their efforts to depict "otherness," the make-up and wig designers appear to have referenced a number of recent works of science fiction cinema in their presentation of Ptolemy, his advisors, and the other courtiers. Their faces are daubed with make-up in a manner unattested in ancient Egypt or the ancient Mediterranean, and the wig worn by David De Keyser's Theodotus, the tutor of Ptolemy XIII, has a rough woolen look, interspersed with stripes of red and green. It is an item of headgear the audience will later see adorning the pate of Caesarion's tutor and is evidently intend to denote pedagogical rank. But these are somewhat minor aberrations when compared to the wigs worn by Cleopatra first upon her arrival at court and later at the presentation of Caesarion to the troops. Neither wig type is attested from ancient sources. Conceivably, the former pale blue confection, which appears to be of corded rope tied high upon her head, is supposed to resemble the Egyptian *tjet* symbol, a common protective amulet usually fashioned from faience and referred to as the "knot of Isis." This may have been intended to reinforce Cleopatra's identification with that goddess. It was never, however, represented tonsorially. The latter, white-blonde wig has much in common with the somewhat festive wigs favored by Bella Darvi's Nefer in the epic film *The Egyptian* (1954) and is entirely ahistorical, but once again serves to reinforce Cleopatra's difference when standing next to Caesar: this depiction emphasizes the union of two identifiably distinct cultures.

Cleopatra as represented on stage and screen is traditionally attended by two female slaves, Charmian and Iras; however, in *Rome*'s retelling, only the former is represented, portrayed by the Greek-American stage actress, Kathryn Hunter.[6] Her casting is fascinating, for it seems that if Cleopatra is the personification of Egypt, Hunter's Charmian is the embodiment of Cleopatra's own Hellenistic and otherwise absent background. Charmian is the only character to share the queen's most intimate thoughts and moments. She is omnipresent and, although it is never stated, given their age difference it seems likely that she is here intended to have been Cleopatra's childhood nurse. At the same time, Hunter's performance as the fiercely loyal Charmian both contrasts with and thus calls attention to the alien qualities of the Egyptian court.

EGYPT IN *ROME*, SEASON TWO

When the series moves to Alexandria late in the second season,[7] Cleopatra has been reigning for some years and it is evident that more than the décor of the throne room has been reworked in the intervening period. There are a number of other, subtler changes in emphasis. The egregiously alien Egyptian design aspects of Season One have – like Cleopatra's own appearance – been supplanted by a rather more sensual and less ostentatious decadence. At the very end of episode 20 ("A Necessary Fiction"), Antony, at the head of his troops, manfully enters the throne room as he will shortly enter the queen herself, and Cleopatra's reintroduction here is both visually and narratively instructive. She is not enthroned as the Queen of Upper and Lower Egypt, and consequently both Antony's expectations and those of the audience are subverted by the first sight of her, standing to one side of the room, wearing a transparent shift dress, her left leg bared seductively as she smiles with her eyes only lightly outlined in kohl. The wig is present and is as un-Egyptian as those seen in the first season; however, it is considerably less flamboyant. Cleopatra's appearance contrasts with the more extravagant gaudiness of the preceding reign and signals that it is now she who rules rather than Ptolemy's advisors. As such, Cleopatra's softened appearance is reflected both in her throne room and its Alexandrian visitors.

It is worth considering the throne room at some length at this juncture, as the characters will spend considerable time there during the series' final two episodes and Antony's arrival has revealed it to the audience in some detail. The ornate door handles are enlarged replicas of the stunning inlaid gold uraeus of Sesostris II (ca. 1877–1870 BC), excavated by Flinders Petrie in 1920 and now resident in the Cairo Museum.[8] This rearing, fire-spitting cobra, the creature of the goddess Wadjet, is associated with the protection of the king and is ubiquitous on depictions of crowns and royal headdresses throughout Egyptian history. Its incorporation into the furniture of doors may be unattested but it is not inappropriate, given that the throne room is both the physical site and symbol of the monarch's authority.

The door surround, with its vignettes and hieroglyphic script that appears to have been cut from black granite or basalt, is recognizable from many of the architectural features excavated over the last twenty years by Jean-Yves Empereur and Franck Goddio in the harbor of Alexandria and surrounding submerged sites. In particular, the door design bears a marked resemblance to the working of the so-called

"Naos of the Decades,"[9] although on a monumental scale in keeping with the colossal royal statues evident in many scenes, which clearly find their basis in the statuary excavated by Goddio at Canopus.[10] These objects were, at the time of *Rome*'s production, receiving considerable attention from both the press and academic circles as they formed part of the major international touring exhibition, "Egypt's Sunken Treasures," and would have been an obvious and easy source of inspiration to the program's set designers.

The gilt and inlaid vignettes on the doors and the walls of the throne room owe much to the intricate and beautifully crafted royal jewelry of the XIIth Dynasty, excavated from the same site as the aforementioned uraeus of Sesostris II.[11] Although this material dates to some 1800 years before the Ptolemaic period, and thus nearly two thousand years before our Cleopatra, the Ptolemies were known to be keen to adorn their metropolis with monuments from earlier periods; so it is quite conceivable that their magpie collecting may have allowed them access to jewelry of the Middle Kingdom, if not the actual architectural objects themselves.

The image of the winged Isis dominating the back wall of the throne room in *Rome* reiterates Cleopatra's identification with this deity, and the fact that it supplants the more expected image of the god Horus reinforces Cleopatra's role as considerably more significant than as simply the maternal regent of Ptolemy XV Caesarion. The blue, inlaid face of the goddess is derived from the Middle Kingdom jewelry; however, the body and wings are substantially informed by the vulture collar found upon the mummy of Tutankhamun.[12]

The influence of Tutankhamun's funerary paraphernalia is clearly felt in the gilt and painted statues of the recumbent jackal deity, Anubis, flanking the throne dais. While elegantly rendered by *Rome*'s design team, such objects would have had no place in a throne room, given their mortuary significance; indeed, sphinxes would have provided a more expected and authentic royal architectural adornment in such a context. However, the jackal statues not only evoke the words of the Roman poet Propertius, whose derogatory description of the god is "yapping Anubis,"[13] but also serve to remind the audience of some of the fundamental religious differences between Rome and Egypt: Anubis, directly or otherwise, is mentioned several times in the dialogue of *Rome*, most notably by Titus Pullo in episode 21 ("Deus Impeditio Esuritori Nullus") and by Charmian in the final episode ("De Patre Vostro").

THE EGYPTIAN "LOOK"

The sense of unfamiliarity surrounding Cleopatra's palace is heightened by the inclusion of numerous "Nubian" guards who feature throughout the scenes set in Alexandria. While Ptolemaic troops would have been drawn from across the empire and from mercenaries beyond, the "Nubian" presence does seem a naive and somewhat simplistic attempt to signify "other" in visual terms through the use of racial stereotyping, which owes more to Nobel Johnson's baleful turn in *The Mummy* (1932) than to the racial politics of either the twenty-first-century television production or, indeed, Ptolemaic Egypt. The fact that the actors portraying Cleopatra's guard wear the so-called "side-lock of youth" as a means of further highlighting their alien nature is similarly problematic. This plaited lock of hair, worn on the side of an otherwise shaven head, was normally the province of boys (and sometimes girls) in Pharaonic society until puberty. The side-lock was never worn by grown adults, although there is a familiar cinematic precedent as both Charlton Heston and Yul Brynner, playing Egyptian princes, continue to wear theirs far beyond the normally allotted time in Cecil B. DeMille's *The Ten Commandments* (1956). In a conspicuous omission, the male children Caesarion and Helios, the characters most likely to wear the side-lock, instead have their hair combed forward in what is understood to be the standard style for Roman boys of patrician class. For the purposes of *Rome*, they lack the alien qualities displayed by their mother Cleopatra and are thereby presented as valid potential competition for Octavian.

Hair and its lack, to signify further the unfamiliar qualities of the Egyptians and their personal aesthetics, is rather shockingly utilized at the beginning of episode 21, when Lucius Vorenus wakes from a dream of his deceased wife, Niobe, and realizes the woman sharing his bed is an Egyptian prostitute – significantly her wrists and back are tattooed[14] – and the audience is intended to be taken aback by the woman's shaven head; her reference to Vorenus as a "hairy bastard" further reminds the viewers that total bodily depilation was a common practice for the ancient Egyptians. Her inclusion here is reminiscent of scenes from the BBC television serial *The Cleopatras* (1983), where the actress Amanda Boxer, whose head had been shaved for her role as Cleopatra Tryphaena, appeared without her wig in two brief but intentionally shocking scenes: as she initiates intimacy with her husband and at the time of her assassination. Publicity in British newspapers of the time surrounding the shaving of Boxer's head was designed to highlight, for modern viewers, the amusingly exotic elements of life in the Ptolemaic court, but also to emphasize the lengths that both producers and actors were prepared to go to in order to achieve authenticity. The appearance of the shaven-headed prostitute in the scene with Vorenus in *Rome* offers a similar shock, although with greater nonchalance, while the woman's inelegant donning of her wig, almost as if it is a winter hat, is clearly intended provide amusement for the audience while serving to depict the Egyptians as rather coarse and unsophisticated, even in the eyes of an ill-tempered boor like Vorenus.

It is worth noting that the producers of *Rome* expected no such tonsorial sacrifices from Lyndsey Marshal as Cleopatra. In spite of Cleopatra's range of remarkable and close-fitting wigs, her head remains unshaved; her natural hair is kept short, cut into a somewhat pixie-like style. Although her spikey cut has similarities with Helen Mirren's boyishly short, blonde hairstyle in the 1998 National Theatre production of Shakespeare's *Antony and Cleopatra*, it goes somewhat further than the mere practicality of Mirren's cut. Marshal's look, *sans* wig, is very much that of a sulky, spoiled teenage Goth, complete with kohl-rimmed eyes and gold ankh-shaped earrings, much beloved of this particular counter-culture but largely unattested in this form in ancient Egypt. The close-cropped Cleopatra is consequently "other," but nevertheless recognizable to the audience. While she may be unique in *Rome*, to a modern audience she represents an immediately recognizable type: her self-centered, shrill-voiced, somewhat neurotic behavior is rather less unique in the modern world. Thus, in place of the highly educated and adept politician, *Rome* delivers its audience the Cleopatra of myth and Roman dread. Marshal's portrayal of the queen as essentially a creature of instinct, embodying the twin attributes of *eros* and *thanatos* ("sex and death"), draws heavily upon the vampy, career-defining qualities of her early cinematic predecessor, Theda Bara in the 1917 *Cleopatra*, whose infamous metallic bra appears to be directly evoked in Marshal's costume during the "stag" hunt in the throne room.

In episode 21, Atia and Octavia are kept waiting in the brutal Alexandrian sun while Cleopatra and Antony fight and fornicate their way around the palace; as Atia's mounting frustration provides amusement for the audience, the scene also perfectly displays the differences between these two powerful women. For the elite Roman Atia, dignified display and adherence to etiquette are paramount; her power games are, perforce, reliant upon covert scheming and plotting, while maintaining the outward semblance of Roman matronliness. However, Cleopatra's substantially greater power and wealth mean that she has no such reliance upon deceitful behavior. Her power games are far more overt, intuitive, and largely unconsidered, allowing her to change tack with ease. Since the demise of her husband-brother, she is without peer in Alexandria and can give full rein to her considerable emotional excesses without ever losing face before her vassals. For all her power, however, Lyndsey Marshal's Cleopatra primarily responds to the actions of others. Opportunistically, she takes intuitive action and makes instinctive decisions, almost in the fashion of some feral beast, as the constant rethinking of her strategy – if it can be so described – ultimately culminates in her delivery to Antony of the line: "You'll be much happier when the war begins." Thus it seems as if she is convincing herself, finally, that she has made an appropriate choice given the options available.

The portrayal of Cleopatra as a creature of almost pure instinct is further developed during the final episode of the series, in the scene where she reads Octavian's letter at her dressing table. Perhaps a desk might have been more suitable, but again she is denied the intellectuality of such a setting and the emphasis is on her vanity. Her table is covered with toilet paraphernalia, including a wig on a stand, kohl pot, and a replica of the Hathor-headed mirror from the tomb of Sit-Hathor-Yunet.[15] More importantly, however, she is seen to be fondling a cat observably of the modern Abyssinian breed, one that closely resembles the *Felis chaus* or swamp cat, which would have been known in the Delta throughout the Pharaonic and Hellenistic periods.[16] The cat's involvement in this scene serves to identify Cleopatra with the goddess Bast, usually depicted in fully feline form, or in later periods as a woman with the head of a domestic cat, whose worship is first attested from stone vessels of the Second Dynasty (2890–2686 BC). Bast is a complex deity, appearing as both the nurturing mother, but with an alter ago: the terrifying and savage lion-headed Sekhmet who could represent the destructive power of the sun and the military power of the king. Marshal's Cleopatra perfectly embodies both of these, as Posca comments in episode 21: "When the Queen growls at me, I retreat." Moreover it is notable that the cat is foregrounded in the following episode at the point when Cleopatra most fully embodies both aspects of the deity – anxious mother and dangerously implacable foe. Cleopatra's feline nature is confirmed by Charmian's remark in episode 22: "Your Majesty has felt Anubis breathe on her before now." The implication of this remark is that Cleopatra has faced near-death situations in the past and survived; however, Anubis is properly the god of embalming and a pyschopomp; he does not represent death itself. As such, Charmian appears to be referencing his canine aspect, as the cat's natural enemy.

Marshal's performance further underlines the feline aspects of Cleopatra's nature. Vocally, she moves fluidly from low, purring murmurs to shrill howls of pique, while her large eyes coupled with her slight and sinuous frame reinforce her cat-like physicality. This is not an unusual representation of the character: the early scenes of Vivien Leigh as the young Cleopatra in Gabriel Pascal's *Caesar and Cleopatra* (1945) are replete with feline allusions, although Leigh, possibly the screen's most adept and fully rounded portrayal of the Ptolemaic queen, lacks Marshal's natural sensuality. Indeed, throughout the final two episodes of *Rome*, Marshal dominates many scenes with her wide, watchful eyes, most effectively during her meeting with Octavian, as she gauges his reactions and behavior while betraying nothing of herself – she is inscrutably feline.

FINAL IMAGES

During the last two episodes of *Rome*, the twin auras of sex and death appear to emanate from Cleopatra, infecting both Antony and those surrounding her. One compelling example is the "stag" hunt scene, mentioned above, which appears to draw its inspiration for casual cruelty from Alexandre Cabanel's 1887 painting, *Cleopatra Testing Poisons on Condemned Prisoners* (*Cléopâtre essayant des poisons sur des condamnés à mort*).[17] This image similarly portrays the queen erotically dressed upon an elegant divan, festooned with the skins of wild beasts, including that of a tiger. Notably, in episode 22 of *Rome*, it is Cleopatra who uses actual arrows to lethal effect, while Antony fires only sticks at their shared quarry. Thus the bloodlust and disregard for human life is revealed to be hers and not Antony's.

The final orgiastic gathering of the semi-naked members of the "Partners in Death Society," comprising what Antony bitterly calls "whores, hermaphrodites, and lick-spittle," is replete with both sex and death; Antony appears to have been corrupted by Cleopatra's bloodlust and callously murders one of the revelers before a company of scantily clad, blind (or at any event, blindfolded) female musicians, wearing full heavy wigs, which for the Egyptians would have been replete with sexual connotations.[18] Although the troupe contains no obvious harpists, there was an Egyptian tradition, attested in tomb scenes and papyri from the Middle Kingdom onwards, of blind harpists playing and singing *carpe diem* themed songs, the sentiments of

Figure 16 Charmian (Kathryn Hunter) looks on as a formally dressed Cleopatra (Lyndsey Marshal) greets Octavian in episode 22 ("De Patre Vostro") of *Rome* (2007). HBO BBC.

which seem singularly un-Egyptian but are entirely appropriate at this particular gathering:[19]

> "Make holiday,
> Do not weary of it!
> Lo, none is allowed to take his goods with him,
> Lo, none who departs comes back again!"

Later, following Antony's suicide, Cleopatra's meeting with Octavian presents the queen at perhaps her most formally regal. She is robed in a long white dress adorned with rosettes; the kohl around her eyes is more precise and she wears the wig, which we have already seen during the hunting scene. In its gravity-defying shape it appears to stand in place of the more usually employed White and Red Crowns of Upper and Lower Egypt, respectively, referenced on screen in the frequently used epithet, "Mistress of Sedge and Bee." It bears the feature of the apotropaic uraeus, and when wearing it Cleopatra is evidently formally garbed: note that the hunting scene, in which this wig earlier appeared, was simply a diversionary entertainment during the business of receiving a formal Roman delegation in respect of grain supplies. The scene where she agrees to meet with Octavian takes place atypically in the blinding Egyptian sunlight and serves to remind both the audience and Octavian that she *is* Egypt (Figure 16). Cleopatra is a ruler with a magnificently wealthy kingdom, and her decision to meet the enemy in the courtyard of her palace rather than within the throne room – quite apart from the fact that Antony's corpse remains there – is not only a deliberate flouting of conventional hospitality; it also connects powerfully with her affinity to Bast/Sekhmet through her deliberate exposure of Octavian to the pitiless heat of the sun, upon which most of the Roman characters have remarked at some point in their Alexandrian excursions.

In the final episodes of *Rome*, we witness a number of Roman characters "going native" after spending some time at Cleopatra's Alexandrian court. This appears to be more than mere expediency; all of the characters making the "conversion" have sufficient wealth to import Roman clothing and supplies, but appear instead to embrace their newly found lives. This is most evident, of course, with Antony, who now "blackens his eyes with soot like a prostitute," as Ian McNeice's Newsreader so decorously phrases it in episode 21; Antony has also taken to wearing a henna tattoo across his left pectoral, in imitation of Cleopatra's hennaed hands and wrists. Antony's "native" personal decoration is a symbol of his doomed love for Cleopatra. Posca, on the other hand, has taken to smoking opiates, wearing kohl on his eyes and dangling jewels from his ears, even though he distrusts and fears Cleopatra. Similarly, his wife Jocasta, in spite of her complaints about the heat and her boredom, now wears a heavy Egyptian-style wig and dress. This is clearly about more than simply fitting in: it is a direct representation of Octavian's propaganda about the emasculating and deleterious effects of both Cleopatra and Egypt upon the Roman mind. Of course, the design decisions made by the producers from the outset and discussed at the beginning of this chapter allow the audience to recognize this descent into Alexandrian decadence more discernibly than might otherwise have been the case: a more authentically Hellenistic representation of life within the Alexandrian court would have muddied the waters. It is a visual approach of which Octavian would almost certainly have approved.

In her last scenes with the cobra, Marshal wears copies of the gold rosette wig ornaments of the princess Senebtisi (ca. 1850–1775 BC)[20] upon a short black wig, as she reveals in her character's ultimate moments her continuing instinctive, somewhat bestial nature, emulating the cobra as she fondles it, extending her tongue to lick at the air. Gregory Daugherty has already commented upon her reptilian similarities during her initial appearance in the first season of *Rome* in episode 8 ("Caesarion").[21] If the cobra is the protector of the monarchs of Egypt, she makes one final connection with it in her attempt to prevent herself as monarch from becoming a spectacle for Rome's pleasure and to protect the life of her heir.

Before departing the Alexandria of *Rome*, there is one final element that is worthy of comment: the replica of the only known statue of Cleopatra VII, which appears in the background of a number of scenes set in the palace, most notably Caesarion's ball game with Vorenus. The original black basalt statue,[22] measuring only 104 centimeters, was for some time believed to represent Arsinoe II, wife of Ptolemy II Philadelphos, only being reattributed to Cleopatra – on the basis of the triple uraeus on the forehead and double cornucopia in the left arm – as recently as 2001, when it played a major role in the British Museum exhibition *Cleopatra of Egypt: From History to Myth*. Although the replica in *Rome* is more than life-sized and heavily gilded, it is a valuable visual reminder of the difficulties inherent in successfully pinpointing this apparently most accessible but, in truth, most elusive of Egypt's queens.

NOTES

1 Rausch (1998: 103–4).
2 Petrie Museum of Egyptian Archaeology, University College London, Accession numbers: UC4632/3.
3 Trope, Quirke, and Lacovara (2005: 38).
4 Torok (1995: 20).
5 Walker and Higgs (2001: 64–5).
6 Three years after completing her small but important role in *Rome*, Hunter portrayed Shakespeare's version of the Ptolemaic queen for the Royal Shakespeare Company in both Stratford and London. When asked in an interview whether performing in *Rome* assisted in her own performance as Cleopatra, she responded: "To be honest, no . . . I did have a copy of the play with me during filming but it didn't really bear any comparison to Shakespeare's story." Quoted in John (2010).
7 Cleopatra's brief appearance in episode 14 ("Son of Hades") is treated by Daugherty in this volume. Note, however, that Servilia is kidnapped by Atia's henchmen as she makes offering to a sistrum-wielding polychromatic statue of the goddess Isis in episode 16 ("Testudo et Lepus"); such Egyptian cults were popular among elite Roman women of the period.
8 Petrie, Brunton, and Murray (1923: 12–13).
9 Goddio and Clauss (2006: 48–52).
10 Goddio and Clauss (2006: 164–70).
11 Brunton (1920).
12 Edwards (1972), catalogue number 40.
13 See Propertius, *Elegies* III.11.
14 Leca (1982: 59): "These tattoo marks are never seen on ladies of good society in ancient Egypt, either on mummies or in pictures. They always

involve women of dubious morality, which includes the priestess of Amunet, for prostitution was part of her sacred duties."

15 From the XIIth Dynasty: Egyptian Museum Cairo, Inventory Number: JE 44920.

16 Malek (1993: 23–4).

17 In the Royal Museum of Fine Arts, Antwerp.

18 Manniche (1987: 42).

19 Lichtheim (1975: 197).

20 Metropolitan Museum, New York, Accession Number: 07.227.7.

21 Daugherty (2008: 142).

22 Walker and Higgs (2001: 160–1).

16 *Gateways to Vice: Drugs and Sex in* Rome

Alex McAuley

The ancient world as glimpsed by modern eyes has always been a sexy place, and as long as the genre has existed Hollywood has delighted in presenting antiquity as deviantly intriguing, replete with subjects and acts that in any other period would be considered scandalous or taboo.[1] In the dimly sensuous haze of the distant past depictions of such things become somehow permissible, either by virtue of a setting that is seemingly so detached from the present, or in the name of "historical accuracy." Such has always been the case: from the vamptastic and scantily clad Theda Bara as *Cleopatra* (1917) to the milk bath, gold chains, and lesbian dancing of Cecil B. DeMille's *The Sign of the Cross* (1932) to the homoerotic bath of Crassus in Stanley Kubrick's *Spartacus* (1960), antiquity has provided an ambiguously liberated outlet for exploring contemporary fascinations – regardless of their historicity. In the heady years following the post-*Gladiator* (2000) revival of antiquity's popularity on screens big and small we have witnessed this sexuality of the ancients intensify both in the sense of ever-more prevalent and graphic depictions of sexual acts, and the decadence blending into perversion of the acts themselves.[2] Everything, it is safe to say, is getting more racy and risqué with each new film or series, as the cameras have been rolling on antiquity with decidedly unfiltered lenses.

This trend manifests itself in many forms, ranging from the scandalously incestuous tendencies of Commodus toward his sister Lucilla in *Gladiator*, to the controversial depiction of homosexuality of Oliver Stone's *Alexander* (2004), and the digitally enhanced pectorals and six-packs-becoming-twelve-packs of the half-naked cast of *300* (2007).[3] The list goes on, and encompasses television series as well as films: *Rome* raised eyebrows with its moderately racy and fairly numerous depictions of ancient sexuality, while the cable channel STARZ *Spartacus* (2010–13) pushed the envelope further than most thought possible with graphic portrayals of hetero-, homo-, and bisexual relations (both consensual and not), whose frequency led some to brand the series quasi-pornographic.[4] Over the past century, the ancients have not only become more sexual, but more perverse in their pleasures. The tendency has been well noted, and Monica Cyrino's remark in her introduction to *Screening Love and Sex in the Ancient World* provides us with a fitting starting point for the present discussion:[5]

> The process of screening antiquity has . . . allowed filmmakers and television producers to exploit the audience's pervasive and prurient fascination with the unbridled and alluring sexualities of the ancient Greeks and Romans. Modern fascinations about love and sex are thereby projected back vividly onto the ancient world onscreen.

But this tendency does not stop with love and sex. This chapter aims to show that in the second season of *Rome* another modern fascination is projected on to antiquity with increasing prevalence and poignancy: the use of narcotics. The emerging drug culture onscreen goes hand in hand with rampant sexuality, adding another level at which modern fascinations are being grafted on to the ancients along with all the baggage of their contemporary social connotations. That such a drug culture among the Romans is almost completely ahistorical means that these depictions implicitly tell more about us than them, but what precisely? With the prominence of drugs in *Rome*, the culture of sexual decadence is elevated to a culture of vice writ large, rife with all of the prejudices and associations that are cast on to the ancients, as modern narcotics are thrust into hands that never would have held them. To understand this elevation of vice, we must begin with an overview of "drugs" as the ancients would have known and used them, and then compare this to how drug use is depicted in *Rome* to gain some insight into how the viewer is meant to react to such modern echoes. To turn the mirror back toward us, this chapter will then put this into the broader context of drugs in contemporary media to explore how these depictions of ancient drug use relate to our fascination with its modern inspiration.

FOR MEDICINAL USE ONLY: MODERN NARCOTICS IN THE ANCIENT WORLD

Was there a culture of drug use among the ancients? The answer lies somewhere between "no" and "not in the way in which we would understand it," although the historical details of what are now called "narcotic" substances cast these contemporary depictions of ancient drug use in a vastly different light – in particular when it comes to their perceived uses and consequences. Given their explicit appearance in the series *Rome*, two substances must be discussed in turn: opium and cannabis.

Opium (*papaver somniferum*) has a remarkably long history in the ancient world: its archaeological origins can be traced to the Mycenaean period (ca. 1500 BC), and its effervescence tracked during the Classical period in Greece (fifth century BC).[6] The poppy appears in representations of various deities during the Mycenaean period, who are shown to be either wreathed with poppy bulbs or carrying them in their hands. The first literary mention of the substance is from the *Odyssey*, in which Helen gives Telemachus, the son of Odysseus, a drug she had acquired from the Egyptians called *nepenthes* in order to help the young man rest and overcome his grief (Homer, *Odyssey* 4.219–34). In the mythological tradition, the goddess Demeter was associated with opium and its soporific effects: the Greek poet Theocritus (third century BC) describes her as holding poppies in one hand and sheaves of wheat in the other, and the poet Ovid (first century AD) has the goddess using the plant to calm troubled people to sleep.[7] Diodorus Siculus also mentions opium as an antidote to anger and grief, as does Hippocrates, while Pliny the Elder and Celsus later echo this while also discussing the drug's hypnotic and analgesic properties.[8] In small doses, according to the ancients, the poppy could aid sleep, and in large doses it could kill peacefully. From all the authors who mention the substance, the following consensus arises: opium was used primarily as a medicine to aid in sleep and numb pain, grief, or emotional trauma; it was potentially poisonous because of its potency; it was decidedly not an aphrodisiac; and it was almost exclusively mixed with wine or other herbs and taken orally, not smoked. There is no ancient record of it being used recreationally.

Cannabis, in turn, shares many of the same characteristics as opium, but does not seem to have been popular as anything more than a material of everyday convenience. Most ancients would have been readily familiar with it in the form of hemp as an uncontroversial part of daily life by virtue of its use in common domestic objects like nets, shoes, mats, and ropes.[9] In the literary record, cannabis makes its first appearance in the famous passage from Herodotus describing how the Scythians would toss bales of the plant on fires in covered tents as part of a ritual bathing and purification during funeral rites – and thus only in a religious context.[10]

Elsewhere, cannabis lacks the prevalence of opium in medical writing but nonetheless has its uses. According to Pliny, the seeds produce a pleasant warming effect and are specifically useful in treating earaches and preventing flatulence, and more generally for their drying effect. This dessicating property of cannabis led to it being prescribed to young boys because its seeds were thought to extinguish men's semen, and it was therefore useful in treating the much-dreaded nocturnal emissions – thus if anything cannabis has an anti-aphrodisiac effect.[11] Elsewhere, cannabis seeds enjoy brief mention as a snack food to be served while drinking – though only for their dietary rather than narcotic properties. Thus among the ancients cannabis was used occasionally as a medicine, frequently as a basic material for woven goods, and never for recreational purposes – and even when it was consumed it was only by eating or infusing the seeds, not by smoking the buds of the plant. In the historical record, then, both substances are decidedly medicinal and had their specific uses, but there is no mention whatsoever of their use for the purpose of diversion.

PLANTING THE SEEDS: DRUGS IN *ROME*, SEASON ONE

In stark contrast to this intermittently medicinal use of what are now called "narcotic" substances by the ancient Greeks and Romans, the onscreen characters of *Rome* consume them as part of a pleasure-seeking elite culture of diversion that is by no means accidentally similar to our own. While this narcotic culture did not exist among the ancients themselves, such historical technicalities are of less interest to this study than are the consequences for the viewers of this transplantation of a contemporary subculture on to an ancient host that would not have been familiar with it. The connotations, associations, prejudices, and biases – and indeed the stigma – attached to drug use in contemporary society are swept along with such borrowed imagery, and condition us to view these "ancient" characters through a quintessentially modern lens. The questions of how, why, and to what end thus become more pressing than the simple historicity of Romans "using" in their free time.

Although drug use among the characters of *Rome* comes to full and prominent visibility in the show's second season, Season One is nevertheless intermittently laced with references to what seems to be a fairly ubiquitous culture of narcotic consumption. As early as episode 2 ("How Titus Pullo Brought Down the Republic") we hear the first offhand remark that smoking substances was a popular pastime: pausing on the road toward Rome as Mark Antony has his way with a shepherd girl, Vorenus and Pullo chat about their respective plans once they arrive. Vorenus stoically hides his nervousness at seeing his wife again, while Pullo enthusiastically declaims: "Here I come, girls! I'm gonna drink all the wine, smoke all the smoke, and fuck every whore in the city." Smoking easily goes hand in hand with drinking and sex, and thus forms part of the perceived hedonistic pleasure seeking of the Romans that so captivates modern audiences. Also of note is the fact that it is Pullo who mentions indulging in such pleasures: while momentarily well-off, Pullo is by no means a wealthy man, and that such a pastime would be available to a soldier freshly weighted by his coin from campaign suggests an accessibility of drug use among plebeians and patricians alike.

Then in episode 8 ("Caesarion"), along comes Cleopatra. Of all the characters in *Rome* Cleopatra is the one who is most directly and recurrently associated with drug use and dependency, and her substance of choice is opium. Gregory Daugherty has pinpointed the possible Shakespearean inspiration for Cleopatra's drug use in Season One.[12] Cleopatra's first appearance in *Rome* is at the end of a shot that begins by focusing on a very modern-looking opium pipe lying on its side, before the camera pans back to show the Egyptian princess passed out in what the viewer presumes to be an opiate-induced haze. Her handmaiden, Charmian, apparently her trip-sitter, gently strokes her mistress's shoulder as she slowly comes around. The prefiguration of her first onscreen appearance with a shot of a pipe unsubtly leads the viewer to associate her with drug use before she has even spoken a line of dialogue. This intoxicated Cleopatra then decides to try to become pregnant before seducing Caesar and assuring his favor, and immediately thereafter she propositions first Vorenus (who declines) and then Pullo (who enthusiastically accepts). Thus while not explicitly an aphrodisiac, the association between drugs and sex, as in Pullo's planned debauch in episode 2, is again underscored as her opium use becomes a gateway vice, as it were, to sexual promiscuity.

Cut to the next day (in the same episode) as Cleopatra is being borne in her litter, where the connection between the Eastern princess and opium is again reinforced. The Daughter of Isis appears to have had an early start to the day and we see her in a pale, perspiring haze, seeming every bit the addict caught deep in the drug's throes, to her physical and mental detriment. Even Charmian notes "divinity's flesh is turning green." Cleopatra, ever undaunted, demands another hit, and her loyal Charmian obliges. The scene again speaks to dependence and intoxication, and carries with it all of the contemporary prejudices and associations of hard drug addiction as we see Cleopatra fall further into the opiate embrace. The visual blocking of the scene in turn calls to mind the opium dens of the nineteenth century, both in mechanism and association, while Cleopatra's dependence on the substance paints her as the typical well-to-do drug addict, a figure that has graced any number of contemporary films since the 1990s. She is rich, she is privileged, and her station affords the leisure and perhaps arrogance to indulge in such a vice without fear of reproach or consequence. That Cleopatra hails from Egypt may at first associate opium use with oriental opulence, but Pullo's offhand remark earlier in the season hints that such indulgence was accessible to urban Romans as well. Thus with these two depictions of drug use, one explicit and the other inferential, the seeds of a prevalent and accessible drug culture that is as corrupting as it is aphrodisiac are sown.

FAST TIMES AT ROMAN HIGH: THE ELITE PARTAKE

Opium is clearly classified as a hard, destructive drug in the world of *Rome*, but it is not the only narcotic depicted onscreen. Although Cleopatra's drug use is presented with an Eastern exoticism, in Season Two we are shown a drug culture in the city of Rome itself that is at once prevalent and casually recreational. Early in episode 15 ("These Being the Words of Marcus Tullius Cicero") the viewer is treated to a fairly comical interlude in Atia's house that would be equally at home in a contemporary sitcom as it is in this period drama. Octavia is relaxing in her house with her *nouvelle-riche* and somewhat *déclassée* friend Jocasta, a tradesman's daughter, who has just returned to Rome from Macedonia – and she has come bearing gifts. Jocasta produces hemp that is placed on a charcoal brazier and the smoke is inhaled through a narrow brown tube that bears a striking resemblance to a contemporary joint. Jocasta inhales deeply, and exhales a cloud of smoke while proclaiming it "good stuff" – a line that has been heard in films ranging from *The Big Lebowski* (1998) to *Super Troopers* (2001). The rest of the scene unfolds according to the stereotypical "first time getting high" motif that has been prevalent in any number of films and television series in recent years.[13] Octavia, clearly the innocent and sheltered wealthy girl, is coached through her first use of hemp by the more street-savvy

Figure 17 Octavia (Kerry Condon) takes her first puffs of hemp in episode 15 ("These Being the Words of Marcus Tullius Cicero") of *Rome* (2007). HBO BBC.

and experienced Jocasta, who is every bit the enabler (Figure 17). Octavia inhales deeply, and then lapses into a fit of coughing. As she is recovering, suddenly: busted. Atia enters the room, and with irritation – though not furiously – complains that they are making the whole house stink, and admonishes: "In the future, do it outside if you must." Her annoyance fading, Atia then switches to barely masked interest as she asks if it is any good. Once reassured that it is, as if for old times' sake (notice she does not cough), she joins in by taking a puff of the proffered brazier.

The device of a parent walking in on young adults illicitly using drugs has appeared in countless television shows and films, among them everything from *Roseanne* (1988–97) to *That '70s Show* (1998–2006) and even *Homeland* (2011–). When it reappears in the setting of late Republican Rome, the resemblance to contemporary culture is so striking as to be disarming, and it is likely that such was the intent of the creative team. It is a scene that we have seen dozens of times before: the only differences are the costumes and time period. Rather than Atia criticizing the girls or lecturing them on the dangers of drug use, she complains about the moderate inconvenience the smell produces and then proceeds to partake herself – a pattern of parental indulgence that has become more prevalent in television series and films since the 1990s.[14] Unlike the destructive opium use of Cleopatra, in this scene the ancients are shown using drugs for rather more light-hearted ends. Hemp is the purview of the leisured elite, the pastime of young debutantes experimenting with new substances in a manner that is perhaps frowned upon by their parents, but certainly not scandalous or illegal. The impression left by Atia's reaction is one of "teenagers being teenagers," and her own interest in and later consumption of the hemp implies that it was something she herself had done in a wilder period of her youth, but had since put aside.

The irritation, not anger, of Atia speaks volumes: smoking hemp in the world of *Rome* is not illegal or scandalously reprehensible, but rather is treated with the same sort of mild chagrin as marijuana use in contemporary society: not fatal, not life-threatening, but perhaps not praiseworthy either. Such parental acceptance of or resignation to the habit hints at its ubiquity; this idea is further reinforced by Jocasta's assertion that the two sacks of hemp she has brought back from Macedonia are quite good, "far better than the Italian kind." Hemp is a common enough commodity to have regional varieties – and thus another echo of modernity – and a certain reputation for each region, and it is even produced domestically. While opium in the elite culture of *Rome* perhaps bears oriental connotations, in the case of hemp we see that it is neither an exclusively foreign import nor is it perceived as such. The effects of the drug are similarly tame: giddiness, light-heartedness, laughter, and levity, none of which the ancient Romans themselves would have recognized as being inspired by cannabis.

One deleterious effect of hemp use by impressionable young Romans like Octavia is, however, that it acts as a gateway drug. Apparently spurred on by Jocasta, Octavia's stroll down the path of adolescent experimentation seems to lead further into the dark woods of drug use by episode 17 ("Heroes of the Republic"), in which these various strands of narcotic connotation are woven together in the setting of a bacchic orgy. Maecenas and Agrippa first appear on screen, the former smoking some kind of pipe (presumably opium), while Agrippa, the more stoic sober type, looks on with growing discomfort. The sophisticated Maecenas reproaches Agrippa for his severity, encouraging him to "lighten up" and enjoy himself. As the camera pans to Jocasta and Octavia, it is clear that they have progressed from smoking hemp and are now dabbling in something a bit harder. While the drug is never explicitly identified, the positioning of the girls on couches placed at either side of a pipe, which is seen to by an attendant in between them, again clearly suggests an opium den of the nineteenth century. Both come off as being stereotypically high on some sort of psychedelic substance, and Jocasta in particular has the sweaty pallor and glassy eyes of the addict. The dialogue suggests the opium is potent: "The walls are melting," exclaims Jocasta, while Octavia surveys the room with unseeing eyes. The heroic Agrippa chooses his moment to enter and rescue Octavia and her virtue as he spirits her away home, only to be discovered by Atia upon their return. Atia, furious this time, calls Octavia a "little slut" who would have been fellating slaves had Agrippa not rescued her.

Although never fully realized, the implications of Octavia's opium use are clear: while under the potent influence of the drug her virtue and chastity would have been compromised as she was led into sexual promiscuity (with slaves and free men alike) in the decidedly disreputable orgiastic setting. The dim lighting, the background smattering of naked gyrating bodies, and the generally hedonistic haze of the scene squarely place narcotic use in this louche context.[15] Here again the decadent and vice-filled culture of the ancients is shown on screen to be intensified: not only are these Romans portrayed as drinking heavily and preparing for group sex, but they are even smoking mind-altering substances while doing so. Another glimpse of this escalation comes later in the season in episode 20 ("A Necessary Fiction"). Maecenas meets with Posca as he is being borne through the city in his litter, and before discussing more sensitive matters he dismisses the two prostitutes – one female, one male – who are riding along with him. As one of the prostitutes gets up to leave she motions to take an opium pipe with her, but relinquishes it rather reluctantly after a reproaching glance from Maecenas. Here again drug use is shown to go hand-in-hand with sex, in this case a bisexual threesome. That this entire scene takes place in what seems to be the early afternoon only compounds the impression.

For the final appearances of narcotic use in Season Two, the series turns back to the East and to that repeat offender Cleopatra, who presumably was never able to kick her opium habit. Her recurrent drug use is part of a much larger swirl of associations of Eastern decadence that surrounds her character in the series, and which she uses to infect her new Roman lover.[16] After he arrives in Egypt and falls ever further under Cleopatra's spell in episode 21 ("Deus Impeditio Esuritori Nullus"), the change in Mark Antony is striking. The Egyptian princess seems to stoke the worst fires in him, as he is transformed from a robustly Roman figure into an oriental prince in his own right. One vice in particular that Cleopatra has transmitted to her Roman lover is her drug use: the pair are shown lying in bed in broad daylight inhaling deeply from a small opium pipe, and after smoking they promptly have sex in a decadent lust-filled haze. Yet again, the aphrodisiac character of opium is reinforced, as is the viewer's negative perception of Antony as he is shown indulging in his more base motivations instead of attending to pressing political business, all the while betraying his loyalty to Rome. His drug use, along with his adoption of the trappings of a decadent royal lifestyle, lead the viewer to witness just how far he is fallen – and his substance abuse (both alcohol and narcotics) adds yet another level to his degeneracy. All of these connotations and associations of such drug use, along with its perceived effect, stand in stark opposition to what we know of their historical realities.

SEEING THROUGH THE HAZE: CONCLUSIONS

With these various vignettes of conspicuous consumption, *Rome* thus depicts a culture of drug use among the ancients that is equal parts diverse and prevalent. Above all it is perhaps the nonchalance of the characters shown partaking in the use of such illicit substances that is the most striking. Rich and poor Romans alike are aware of the pleasure of smoking substances for recreational diversion. The drugs themselves are grown in the East as they are in the West, and are used in both locations. Except for the sheltered Octavia's momentary shock when trying a substance that she had likely often heard described, the characters of *Rome* are neither stunned nor appalled when they come across narcotics; the implication is that they have seen them before.

Not all the drugs of *Rome* are created equal. Hemp is implicitly coded as equivalent to modern marijuana, and its use brings all of the mellow levity that is associated with the contemporary drug. As a pastime of the idle teenager or twenty-something, the drug is shown to be mostly harmless, part of a phase through which nearly all young well-to-do urbanites pass but from which not all exit at the same time. Although smoking hemp is perhaps not desirable, it is not ruinously destructive either, and thus it can be safely placed into the category of "soft" drugs that are readily accessible to those who would desire them.

Opium use is shown in *Rome* to be a very different story. Far more powerful, far more addictive, and far more corrupting, it casts a dangerous spell on those who use it and holds them unrelentingly in its grip. While hemp made Octavia and Jocasta giggle uncontrollably and seemed to sap them of their productive energy, opium pulls them into in a hallucinogenic haze in which they are prone to sexual deviance and promiscuity. Repeat use brings with it the physical and moral depredations of addiction, best exemplified by the downward spiral Antony enters once he becomes equally hooked on both the drug and

Cleopatra. The use of such a hard drug opens the door to deviant sexuality that compromises standards of class, gender, and propriety. Whether they are hard or soft, drugs make the characters of *Rome* commit acts that they would never otherwise have considered.

The conclusion that the drug culture as depicted by *Rome* is completely ahistorical, while somewhat facile, nonetheless ought to be made. The ancient Greeks and Romans recreationally smoked neither opium nor hemp; neither was held to have had an aphrodisiac effect; neither was viewed as addictive or dangerous. Rather, hemp was a common material used in the construction of everyday objects, and opium was a plant with several medicinal uses thanks to its soporific effect. These were not substances that somehow posed a menace to society, or that stood as gateways to unrestrained deviance.

Although alien to the ancient world, however, the narcotic use shown in *Rome* is strikingly at home in its modern pop-cultural context. The distinction between hard and soft drugs, the relative acceptance and even celebration of the latter and continued vilification of the former, as well as the stereotypes associated with their use are all prevalent in contemporary film and television.[17] On the one hand, the ruinous effects of hard drug use and both the social and sexual deviance it inspires lie at the heart of films such as *The Basketball Diaries* (1995), *Trainspotting* (1996), and *Traffic* (2000); likewise, opium use in *Rome* follows a similar path. On the other hand, films such as *Road Trip* (2000), *The Hangover* (2009), and *This is 40* (2012) all feature light-hearted and entertaining depictions of characters harmlessly smoking marijuana as a means of "lightening up" and freeing themselves of a prudish sense of restraint and propriety: so too with hemp use as depicted in *Rome*. Such films and the cultural milieu with which they interact clearly influence the way narcotics are shown in *Rome*, and the message is very much the same. For better or worse, in the ancient and modern setting drug use makes characters do things that they would not otherwise do.

Rome, for its part, has set a trend of its own among films and television series set in antiquity, as its characters are not the only ancients to be dabbling in modern narcotics. For example, in the recent STARZ prequel series *Spartacus: Gods of the Arena* (2011), the first episode ("Past Transgressions") shows the city-savvy Gaia arriving at the *ludus* of Batiatus and catching up with her old friend Lucretia. As the two remain awake chatting, Gaia suddenly produces a small vial of opium that she has brought with her and offers it to Lucretia, and the two toast their good health. Opium, as it is in *Rome*, is apparently a phenomenally powerful aphrodisiac in

Spartacus, as suddenly the scene cuts to a montage of the two Roman women lying naked together on fur rugs, caressing and kissing each other. The associations are clear: doing such a drug will lead to sexual impropriety and experimentation. Repeat use in later episodes also leads to even more racy sexual encounters, namely a *ménage à trois* with Batiatus, Gaia, and Lucretia. The ever-more creative avenues of indulgence pursued by the onscreen denizens of *Rome* have thus pushed the envelope of ancient deviance yet further.

In the *longue durée* of how ancient vice has been screened, this can indeed be viewed as a new chapter in our fascination with the (real or fictive) decadence of the ancients that continues to intensify. The scandalous content of the early forays into the classical world on film set the standard with the deviance of *Cleopatra* (1917) or *The Sign of the Cross*. The escalating trend was temporarily smothered, or at least made subtler, by the stringent constraints of the Hays Code (1930–68), which attempted to curb onscreen depictions of such ancient excesses.[18] Yet the Code is now a distant memory and the ancient world is back on film and television with a vengeance, and the invitation to enjoy the titillating vices of the ancients has again been issued to audiences. At the start of the new millennium, *Gladiator* picked up where *The Sign of the Cross* left off years ago, as have the numerous films that have followed since. Sexuality and deviance are intensifying, and now *Rome* has upped the ante once more by depicting ancient deviance fuelled by drug use. Ancient sexual excess is thus linked to narcotic excess, and with the bar having been raised yet once more by *Rome*, one wonders what new heights ancient pleasure seeking will attain next.

NOTES

1 I owe my sincerest thanks to Monica Cyrino for her invitation to contribute to this volume, as well as her invaluable guidance and assistance. A preliminary version of this chapter was presented at the *Beauty, Bravery, Blood, and Glory* conference at Ben-Gurion University of the Negev (June 2013), whose organizers and participants provided constructive insights and discussion.

2 For the amplification of deviance in depictions of sexuality in films about the ancient world, see Cyrino (2014).

3 On the problematic portrayal of Alexander's sexuality in Oliver Stone's film, see Pierce (2013).

4 Raucci (2013) provides an excellent discussion of sexuality in STARZ *Spartacus*; on the diverse array of sexual relationships portrayed in the series, see further Augoustakis (2013) and Strong (2013).

5 Cyrino (2013b: 2).
6 The most exhaustive discussion of opium in the Greek world is by Kritikos and Papadaki (1967). See also Rosso (2010) for a more recent discussion of the Egyptian and Greek medical uses of the substance.
7 Theocritus, *Idyll* 7.157; Ovid, *Fasti* 4.544–9.
8 Diodorus Siculus, *Library* 1.97.30; Celsus, *Compositiones Medicamentorum* 21–2; Hippocrates, *On Epidemics* 2.118, and *On Internal Diseases* 12; Pliny, *Natural History* 20.77. See the appendix of Kritikos and Papadaki (1967) for the full listing of ancient references.
9 There is little scholarly discussion of the place of hemp or cannabis in the ancient world, save for Butrica (2002). Although he makes a barely disguised argument for the contemporary legalization of medical marijuana based on its medicinal use by the ancients, his collation of ancient references to the plant is very helpful.
10 Herodotus, *Histories* 4.73–5. Many have claimed that his account of Scythian cannabis use is proof that the ancients were aware of the plant's mind-altering possibilities, but the passage describes a strictly religious context: the cannabis smoke is clearly intended for ritual purification before funerary rites, not recreational or celebratory purposes.
11 Pliny, *Natural History,* 20.259. On cannabis/hemp being used as a material for rope, see Pliny, *Natural History* 19.273–4. Dioscorides, *Materia Medica* 3.149.1 also describes its uses.
12 Daugherty (2008: 141–50) discusses Cleopatra's use of mandragora in Shakespeare's *Antony and Cleopatra* as well as the orientalizing tendencies of her characterization in *Rome*.
13 Axelrod-Contrada (2008: 31–43) provides a concise overview of drug use in contemporary films and television series from the 1990s onwards; however, she paints an overly negative view of drug depictions in pop culture.
14 On drugs and the family in contemporary cinema, see Grist (2007); for drugs in contemporary sitcoms, see Carter (2007).
15 For the disposition of Roman orgies in film, see Raucci (2013).
16 Daugherty (2008: 146–7) discusses this and other depictions of Cleopatra as the seductive oriental princess preying on western men.
17 Manning (2007) contains many articles that discuss the trend toward the "normalization" of some recreational drug use across various facets of popular culture, with the implicit message that marijuana and light drug use have become far more socially acceptable in film and television over the past decade.
18 The Motion Picture Production Code, popularly known as the Hays Code (named for the chief censor in Hollywood in the early 1930s), was a set of industry moral censorship guidelines that governed the production of most American movies released by major studios from 1930 to 1968.

17 *Slashing* Rome: *Season Two Rewritten in Online Fanfiction*

Amanda Potter

Fans of *Rome* used the internet to respond to the series and share their views with other fans by reviewing episodes, responding to polls on favorite characters, and speculating on future plotlines via discussion forums. Fan sites such as the *Rome Fan Club* pages on *Fanpop.com* and the *Rome Fan Wiki* on *Wetpaint.com* make it easy for fans to interact with each other and engage with the text. Creative forms of fan engagement include devising role-playing games based on characters from the series and creating fan art including pictures, icons featuring characters from *Rome* that fans can use to represent themselves, and fan videos or vids, using excerpts from the series set to music.

This chapter explores a specific mode of creative fan production: *Rome* fanfiction. The focus of this study will be on fanfiction written in English and made available online via fanfiction archives on *Fanfiction.net* and *Livejournal* after January 2007, when the first episode of Season Two was first broadcast, and before December 2012. *Rome* fanfiction continued to be produced and posted after this date, but as Matt Hills states, "one can only extract artificially bounded sets of information" from the vast amount of fan-produced material available online.[1] My survey includes all types of creative fiction based on *Rome* from novel-length works to short pieces of less than five hundred words, sometimes referred to by the authors as oneshots, or drabbles, which should be one hundred words exactly in length, but are often slightly longer. Poetry or stories written in languages other than English will not be a part of this study.[2] As most fanfiction is written by female fans, and published under often gender-neutral pseudonyms, authors are referred to by their pseudonyms or preferred first names and the female pronoun will be used throughout.

FANFICTION AND SEX

Fanfiction for *Rome*, as for other films, television series, and novels, can be split into three genres: slash, het, and gen. Slash focuses on same-sex relationships, most frequently male, but femslash is also written by some fans; het focuses on heterosexual relationships; and gen is general, so any other fiction that is not based on romantic or sexual pairings.[3] The majority of fanfiction tends to be relationship-based, and fans often include the pairing or ship (relationship) on which they are focusing in their story as part of the summary for potential readers; so, for example, Pullo/Vorenus will feature the relationship between Pullo and Vorenus, which in *Rome* fanfiction tends to be romantic or sexual in nature. Writers usually include a rating for potential readers on the level of sexual content, adult themes, and language, using terminology based on cinema ratings such as K (suitable for all), T (suitable for teens), and R or NC-17 (which includes adult content, so restricted, or unsuitable for those under the age of 17). Some writers elaborate on this by indicating whether the story includes graphic sex, or includes a scene of non-consensual sex (non con). *Rome* fanfiction includes a mix of stories across all the ratings, with the majority of stories rated R or T. This is hardly surprising when the series itself included many scenes of an adult nature and the DVDs are rated 18. One writer jokingly states that the rating of her slash story is "lower than the show's, anyway."

There are two *Rome* communities on *Livejournal*: *rome_slash*, subtitled "When in Rome do the Romans," and *rome_fic*, subtitled simply "Fan Fiction for HBO's *Rome*." From the community names a reader might expect to find only slash, and potentially sexual content on *rome_slash* and more gen and het stories on *rome_fic*; however, both offer a range of stories, and there is some crossover with stories appearing on the pages of both communities. The *Rome* archive on *Fanfiction.net* includes fanfiction of all genres, and there is very little crossover with stories appearing on *Livejournal*. Some of the fanfiction posted is in response to a challenge or request from fellow fans to write on a specific topic, and fans maintain a dialogue with each other via the comments or reviews that they post relating to specific stories.

Of the 147 stories surveyed for this study, 102 are relationship-based, with 62 of the stories being m/m (male/male) slash, seven femslash, and 33 het. This ratio is not unusual in fanfiction, where female writers often write about relationships between male protagonists like Bodie/Doyle from the television series *The Professionals* (1977–83) or Kirk/Spock from *Star Trek* (1966–69), which is the origin of the term slash fiction.[4] In her essay "Normal Female Interest in Men Bonking," fan critic and fanfiction writer Cat Anestopoulo describes the female fan's wish to write slash as a product of her identification with the male hero over the female "screaming ninny (the romantic interest)."[5] Unlike *Star Trek* and *The Professionals*, *Rome* offers a number of strong female heroines for female fans to write about, including Atia and Servilia, yet writers continue to prefer to write m/m slash. The most popular pairing by far is Pullo/Vorenus, featuring in 26 stories, and the second most popular is Antony/Brutus, featuring in ten stories.

The main screen text of *Rome* offers us many and varied sexual pairings and situations including incest (Octavia/Octavian), lesbian (Servilia/Octavia), Bondage and Discipline, Dominance and Submission (Octavian/Livia), and rape (Servilia). Writers of het and femslash therefore can, and often do, base their fiction on pairings included in the series. The most popular pairings for het stories are Antony/Atia and Octavia/Agrippa, each with five stories posted, and the most popular femslash pairing is Octavia/Servilia, also with five stories. In addition there are two Atia/Servilia femslash stories, and the writer of one of these refers to this relationship as an "underused pairing." In contrast to the abundance of heterosexual activity in the series, there are no male homosexual relationships between free men depicted in *Rome*.[6] The nearest the series gets to open male homosexuality between primary characters is Atia's suggestion of the possibility that Caesar is bisexual when she erroneously congratulates Octavian for "seducing" Caesar in episode 4 ("Stealing from Saturn"). Atia shows no displeasure at this, and is only unsure whether it is "decent" because Caesar is Octavian's great-uncle. *Rome* m/m slash writers therefore have to focus on sexual relationships that are not present in the series, transforming the Pullo/Vorenus homosocial relationship into a homoerotic romance, and the Antony/Brutus rivalry to a sexual relationship based on power and control. This follows in the tradition of earlier slash fiction, where two male protaginists in a homosocial relationship on screen are given a sexual relationship by fan writers, for example Kirk/Spock in *Star Trek*. In his early work on fanfiction, Henry Jenkins suggested that fan writers "often want to explore the erotic dimensions of characters' lives" by creating stories that "transform the relatively chaste, though often suggestive, world of popular television into an erogenous zone of sexual experimentation."[7] Where the unchaste *Rome* is concerned, writers continue to push the boundaries by creating new sexual pairings and situations.

Slash writers draw on a "perceived homoerotic subtext" in the series as the genesis for their slash stories.[8] Outside of the realm of fanfiction, fans have perceived the relationship between Pullo and Vorenus as a romantic one: for example, the "ROMEance Bromance" page on *Romewiki.wetpaint.com* includes a number of stills from the series featuring Pullo and Vorenus together with the subtitle "Never mess with this Bromance . . . they represent for the 13th Legion!!! Brotherly love for life!!!"[9] Pullo/Vorenus is the pairing or ship of choice for this and many other fans, and fan writers often concentrate on one pairing, so that in *Rome* fanfiction Sarah has only posted Octavia/Agrippa stories and yunitsa has only posted Pullo/Vorenus stories. One specific scene that a fanfiction writer drew on for a story focusing on the Pullo/Vorenus relationship is a conversation between Eirene and Pullo about Pullo's potential lack of love for Eirene in episode 17 ("Heroes of the Republic"). In the scene, Eirene's words are ambiguous as she does not directly accuse Pullo of loving Vorenus more than her, but seems to imply this when she asks Pullo first: "Why do you leave me here for Vorenus?" Then she states: "Vorenus, him you love, me no." Pullo's answer is also ambiguous, as he replies with a joke; he would save Eirene before Vorenus if they were both drowning not because he loves her the most, but because she is "half his weight, not so heavy, easier to save." In her story "Drowning in the Tiber" mcicioni adds a new "missing scene" so that Vorenus overhears this exchange between Pullo and Eirene and is jealous, until the two men share an intimate moment after Pullo explains that he has seen Vorenus swim. The story is rated by the writer as "gen(ish)," but the homoerotic undertones are clear.

As the "primary sex symbol of the series" it is unsurprising that along with Pullo and Vorenus, Antony features in a number of slash and het stories.[10] The fanfictional Antony, like his historical and televisual counterparts, is the most promiscuous of *Rome* fanfiction characters, included in more pairings than any other character. Antony is paired with Brutus, Cicero, Caesar, Octavian, Vorenus, Atia, Cleopatra, and Octavia; in one story, "In Expectation," he initiates a threesome with Brutus and Cicero. Antony is a useful character for writers of slash fiction as he was slashed long before the term existed.[11] In the second season of the series he is feminized in his relationship with Cleopatra in Egypt, or to use Elizabeth Woledge's term for male characters in slash fiction, he is presented as a "gender-bending" man, with eye make-up and androgynous clothing (Figure 18).[12] Antony's shaved chest in Egypt is even commented on by fans in an online discussion entitled "Why do you love Mark

Figure 18 Antony (James Purefoy) and Cleopatra (Lyndsey Marshal) enjoy their final days in Alexandria in episode 22 ("De Patre Vostro") of *Rome* (2007). HBO BBC.

Antony?" but the fans ultimately decide that they prefer the earlier "furry" Antony.[13] The image of a feminized Antony and a masculine Cleopatra comes to us from Plutarch and then Shakespeare. In Plutarch, Antony is described as "an appendage of the woman,"[14] and Shakespeare expands on this, when he has Octavian say that Antony[15]

> is not more manlike
> Than Cleopatra, nor the queen of Ptolemy
> More womanly than he.

Slash fiction allows fanfiction writers to play with the sexuality of their characters, and presenting Antony in m/m slash is a logical next step for a character who is both eroticized and feminized in *Rome*.

Although some pairings are preferred by fan writers, writers are free to pair any characters whether or not the relationship is suggested in the series, and so Octavian muses on the convenience of his proximity to Antony in "My Lover is my Sister's Husband," and Octavia indulges in a threesome with her previous lovers from the series Octavian and Agrippa in "Inspiration." Most *Rome* fanfiction with sexual content features consensual sex, but some slash and het stories do include scenes of rape and sexual violence. In fanfiction non-consensual sex can be used as a means to achieve revenge, for example by Brutus on Octavia for her relationship with his mother in "Each Thorns," or to seal a victory, by Antony in his defeat of Brutus in the short piece "To the Victor." This story does not describe graphic sex, but the reader is left under no illusion as to how Brutus becomes "the trophy" and what will fill Antony's mouth. As with the story "First," about the first sexual encounter between Pullo and Vorenus, these stories featuring non-consensual sex are not simply porn, but, as Cynthia Jenkins states of "harder edged slash" stories generally: "The point of these stories is to situate these practices in the context of a relationship and examine how they function as part of that relationship."[16] The use of non-consensual sex by fan writers mirrors the use of sexual violence in *Rome*, where Servilia is raped on the orders of Atia as an act of revenge in the context of the relationship between the two women.

CLASSIFICATION, CONTINUATION, AND NEW ENDINGS

Fanfiction communities and archives allow writers to classify their own work, and this classification is more descriptive than the three main genres. Stories posted to *Fanfiction.net* can be described as Angst, Adventure, Romance, or Friendship, or a mixture of these and more story types. Writers sometimes feel that the classifications available to them do not necessarily correctly describe their work. For example Beth, whose story, "Love Will Change a Man" comprises an alternative ending for Season One in which Vorenus forgives Niobe and she does not kill herself, is classified as "Romance/Friendship," but the writer states in her notes to readers: "In my mind, the genre for this fic is 'Love' which is different from 'Romance' these days." Some specific subgenres work well for *Rome* stories, so Pullo/Vorenus slash can be a "campfire scene," where Pullo and Vorenus declare their love for each other while alone at night by the campfire. This situation is used in slash stories based on other texts, for example *Star Trek* stories, as two men alone at night by a campfire provides a good opportunity for male bonding.

Another popular Pullo/Vorenus subgenre is the post-series futurefic "on the farm story," where Pullo and Vorenus have retired together and live on a farm. Fanfiction can also be PWP (Plot? What Plot?) focusing on sex rather than story; and *Rome*, a series including plenty of sex scenes, unsurprisingly generates plenty of this type of writing. This can be het, for example Antony and Cleopatra having sex in a bath house in "Shades of Gold," or slash, as in Moth's "First" where Pullo and Vorenus start by fighting and end by having sex, in her only *Rome* story, described as "PWP . . . but history and the BBC provide more plot than anyone could possibly want." However, as Catherine Driscoll states in her comparison of erotic fanfiction with pornography: "PWP stories are never just any utilitarian sex scene as they must still be fan fiction," featuring characters and context from the original show.[17] In "First," the fight between Pullo and Vorenus that precipitates the sex starts with the accusation that Pullo and Niobe have been lovers. Niobe's unfaithfulness to Vorenus is perhaps the most important plot point in the first season of *Rome*, and in the early episodes of Season Two Vorenus accuses Pullo of cuckolding him, so Moth uses a plot point as the basis for a story she identifies as PWP.

Some readers see the main purpose of fanfiction as to continue where the story left off in the main screen text, so a reviewer of "De Patre Vostro," the final episode of *Rome*, on fan site *TV.Com* states: "I guess it's up to the fanfiction writers to continue with the story of how things turned out for Pullo and Caesarion."[18] The cancellation of *Rome* with some questions unanswered has made the series into an "endlessly deferred narrative," a term proposed by Matt Hills relating to cult series posing questions "which will never *officially* be answered or closed down, remaining open to multiple fan productions, speculations and recreations."[19] Many fan writers choose to rewrite the ending of the series to bring it to a more satisfying conclusion, in which favorite characters do not die, or relationships from the series come to happier conclusions. In the farm stories of mcicioni and yunitsa, Vorenus has been nursed back to health by Pullo, and in Sarah's stories "All is Never Lost" and "Let's Start Again," Octavia and Agrippa resume their relationship as lovers after Octavian's triumph, and Agrippa is revealed to be the father of Antonia, Octavia's daughter. Readers commenting on these stories found them to be "fitting" endings and like the fan writers prefer the happier endings for the characters. One reviewer of an early farm story from yunitsa, posted before the final episode was broadcast, commented: "We can only hope that they get an ending as beautiful as this." The strategy of changing a series ending is common in fanfiction for series that have ended through early cancellation or without the fan's preferred resolution being achieved. Examples include the BBC science fiction series *Blake's 7* (1978–81), which ended with the apparent deaths of the majority of the characters, and the CBS fantasy series *Beauty and the Beast* (1987–90), which ended without the consummation of the protagonists' romantic relationship.[20]

Much fanfiction is written while a series is still being broadcast, with writers speculating on how plotlines could potentially be brought to a conclusion, or adding missing scenes. For example yunitsa's "Wheel of Fortune," in which Pullo and Vorenus are reunited in Egypt and consummate their relationship, was written in March 2007. Yunitsa states in her notes that she is "posting this short bit of self-indulgence before it's inevitably jossed [disproved] by the finale." She has also written "But in the Suburbs" as a commentary on the Vorenus/Pullo/Eirene love triangle as a missing scene from episode 15 ("These Being the Words of Marcus Tullius Cicero"); then, after watching further episodes, she writes: "Okay, wow, really sort of redundant now. Sorry!" This fanfiction writing is an example of "just in time fandom," as fans use the creative medium of story writing to comment on episodes as they are broadcast, and share their immediate views with other fans.[21]

FANFICTION AND HISTORY

With science fiction and fantasy an infinite number of alternative endings to a series can be proposed by a fan writer, as fanfiction operates in a world of "work in progress" that never ends despite the originating series being long finished.[22] However, when writing fanfiction based on *Rome*, and therefore bound to some extent by historical narratives, fan writers need to make a choice about whether or not to follow history where historical characters are concerned. Most writers of *Rome* futurefic and *Rome* fanfiction generally do choose to follow a historically plausible plot. For example, none of the *Rome* stories surveyed in my study included fanfiction in which Antony survived beyond his historical and series-specific suicide, even though he is a popular character for fan writers, appearing in 22 slash stories and 11 het stories with various sexual partners. However, fictional characters within the series have no historical time boundaries. In "Love Will Change a Man" Beth changes the ending of the first season of *Rome* by having Niobe survive, but Vorenus still arrives at the Senate too late to save Caesar, thus adhering to the historical fact of Caesar's death. Beth offers as a subtitle to her story: "An alternative ending to *Rome* Season 1 without messing with the actual history." Futurefic writers can also offer historical plausibility by returning historical characters to the future stories of fictional characters. In one of her farm stories, "Not Unbecoming Men that Strove with Gods," yunitsa has Augustus travel to the farm to visit Vorenus, having found out he is alive via "the great census," only to arrive too late as Vorenus' body is awaiting burial. Greeted by Pullo, Augustus is introduced to Pullo's son Aeneas, not realizing that he is in fact Caesarion. In her writer's notes yunitsa advises readers that she "did some research for this," so along with depicting a happy life for the fictional characters Vorenus and Pullo, yunitsa adds the historical detail that Augustus conducted a census in 8 BC, and that the Roman month of Sextilis was renamed after him in the same year, when Augustus is in his fifties. This date would also make sense from the perspective of the Pullo/Vorenus timeline, as by 8 BC both Vorenus and Pullo would be old men, having been last seen in the series in 29 BC, the year of Octavian's triumph.

Writers of historical fanfiction are often fans of both the historical period the series depicts and the media text itself. For example, one fan writer states on her profile page that she is a "Romaniac meaning one who is obsessed with ancient Rome," who started writing fanfiction after she "got hooked on *Rome*" and decided to include "the historical character Porcia" in her novel-length work "Strictly Patrician." Her shorter story "Faded Dreams" also focuses on a historical character, Julia, daughter of Augustus, as seen from her aunt Octavia's point of view. In this story Julia grows up under the watchful eyes of Octavia, until she and Maecenas collude to have Julia marry Agrippa, to save her from marriage to Tiberius, even though Octavia still loves Agrippa herself. This story successfully weaves together the fictional relationship between Octavia and Agrippa from *Rome* with the historical marriage between the young Julia and the older Agrippa, shedding light on the character of Julia as a girl who, as the emperor's daughter, is faced with limited choices. Historical research can therefore provide fanfiction writers with material in addition to the media source text, and the use of well-researched historical detail is often applauded by online reviewers, who may even be encouraged to do further research themselves.[23]

The inclusion of a historical character such as Porcia, daughter of Cato, in a narrative featuring characters from *Rome* can serve the same purpose as the insertion of a "Mary Sue," an idealized invented figure, as an original character into fanfiction. This character may be "all too often an avatar of the author herself,"[24] but can also be a useful point-of-view character with whom the readers can identify. Some *Rome* fanfiction does include an original character, and a story of this type that is particularly enjoyable is mcicioni's "Laundry," which introduces Silvia as the woman who takes in laundry from Pullo; she follows his story through the blood-stained and torn clothing he leaves with her to launder. Fan writers can also insert a character from another media text or genre into their writing to add another dimension to the story, producing crossover fiction. In the sample surveyed for this study, one *Rome* fanfiction writer who posts her stories to *Livejournal* has created *Battlestar Galactica*/

Rome crossover fiction, including a long piece of fiction entitled "To the Slave With Dark Eyes," as well as fanfiction based on *Rome* only, while another writer includes an original vampire character in her story "Sparkling Angel," which she classifies as "Romance/ Supernatural."

In an unusual approach, fan writer Dan Sickles chooses consciously to play with history in her fanfiction. In "Brutus the Rise to Power" she overturns the expectations of readers familiar with Caesar's funeral speech from Shakespeare by making Brutus' speech the one that rouses the crowd to action, in this version against Antony. In a speech worthy of a great politician, Brutus explains to the populace that he killed Caesar for "what he did to my mother," and they shout and cry for their own mothers, before shouting for Antony to be brought out to face them. Caesar's prominent abandonment of Servilia in *Rome* would seem to be a starting off point for this interesting rewriting of history. In "Felix Natalis Ad Vos" Hamato Talia also uses a historical fact present in episode 18 ("Philippi"), that the battle of Philippi is fought on Cassius' birthday, as the basis for her story with a humorous twist. In the *Rome* episode Cassius dies in Brutus' arms with the words "hell of a birthday," but in the fan story as he dies in the arms of his friend, Cassius asks Brutus to sing "Happy Birthday" to him, or "Felix Natalis Ad Vos." Both of these stories play with the readers' expectations based on the series and earlier texts.

A reader could ask the question whether writing based on a fictional historical series supplemented by additional historical research should be described as fanfiction at all, or whether instead it could be classified as historical fiction. Some fan researchers, including Catherine Driscoll and Elizabeth Woledge, would have us question the boundaries between fanfiction and other forms such as romance and pornography.[25] If we analyze fanfiction and other writing side by side, the 2012 Orange prizewinning novel *The Song of Achilles* by Madeline Miller could be described as *Iliad* fanfiction, and with its focus on the Achilles/Patroclus sexual relationship this novel bears many similarities with slash. Perhaps Miller would not call herself an Achilles fan, but her novel reveals her to be one. However, fan writers who post their stories based on *Rome* on *Livejournal* and *Fanfiction.net* do describe their work as fanfiction, and produce their writing within a community of fanfiction writers. If their work needs further classification then perhaps this should be a new subgenre, historical fanfiction, not yet described by fan researchers such as Jenkins and Hills who have focused primarily on fan activity relating to science fiction and fantasy.

The prevalence of historical fanfiction based on television series, films, and novels set in the ancient world offers researchers the opportunity to understand how fans creatively engage with ancient history via a fictionalized medium. Long after the final episode of the series was first broadcast in 2007 fan writers continue to use *Rome* as a source of inspiration for their creative work. *Rome* is a particularly slashable text, offering fan writers a range of sexual relationships to build on and invert. Following *Rome*, and attracting a similar fan base, the STARZ series *Spartacus* (2010–13) offers fanfiction writers an even larger range of onscreen relationships, including male homosexual relationships between primary characters. This new *Spartacus* could be read as a slashed version of *Rome*, one that was precipitated by the fan writers' interest in the sexual relationships between characters, and this series has in turn generated a new collection of fanfiction.

In his seminal work on fans and fanfiction, *Textual Poachers*, Henry Jenkins states:

> The cumulative effect of reading [fanfiction] is to alter one's perception of the series. Readers return to it with alternative conceptions of their characters and motivations, repositioning the events into a greatly expanded narrative and a more fully elaborated world.[26]

This argument is similar to the purpose of classical reception studies put forward by Lorna Hardwick, who argues that studying new texts based on classical sources can "focus critical attention back towards the ancient source and sometimes frame new questions."[27] However, this two-way relationship between the media text and the reader, or ancient source text and modern producer, becomes more complex when the media text itself is mediated history, and the fanfiction writer uses both the media text and additional historical sources as the basis for their work. Therefore, if we read or write historical fanfiction for *Rome* – or *Spartacus* or *Gladiator* (2000) – we are engaging in classical reception and its multiple layers *par excellence*. It is also quite fun, and includes plenty of sex.

NOTES

1 Hills (2002: 174).

2 The vast majority of fanfiction based on *Rome*, as with fanfiction based on other English-language series, is written in English. Of the sources used in this study, *Livejournal* contained only English-language fiction, and *Fanfiction.net* contained only five non-English stories out of the 63 stories that met my criteria, three in Spanish and two in French.

3 For a summary of fanfiction genres and subgenres, see Busse and Hellekson (2006: 9–12).
4 On Kirk/Spock and other early slash, see Jenkins (1992: 185–222).
5 In Green, Jenkins, and Jenkins (2006: 66–8).
6 One scene of homosexual sex occurs in the series when Castor, Atia's chief male slave, is shown penetrating the slave boy, Duro, in episode 16 ("Testudo et Lepus").
7 Jenkins (1992: 175).
8 Busse and Hellekson (2006: 10).
9 *Romewiki.wetpaint.com*, "ROMEance Bromance" page.
10 For Antony as sex symbol, see Raucci (2008: 208–11).
11 For an analysis of Spike as a similarly slashed male character in *Buffy the Vampire Slayer* (1997–2003), see Williamson (2005: 168–74).
12 Woledge (2005: 50–65).
13 *Romewiki.wetpaint.com*, "Why do you love Mark Antony" thread.
14 Plutarch, *Life of Antony* 62.1.
15 Shakespeare, *Antony and Cleopatra* 1.4.5–7.
16 Green, Jenkins, and Jenkins (2006: 83–4).
17 Driscoll (2006: 86).
18 *TV.com*, "*Rome*: De Patre Vostro (About Your Father)," fan review by Ting13 (April 13, 2007).
19 Hills (2002: 137).
20 See Stasi (2006: 126) on *Blake's 7*, and Jenkins (1992: 146–9) on *Beauty and the Beast*.
21 Hills (2002: 178).
22 On the concept of "work in progress," see Busse and Hellekson (2006: 6–7).
23 For example, one reviewer of "Faded Dreams" on *Fanfiction.net* is researching Scribonia, while another compares Julia and Agrippa with Caesar's daughter Julia and Pompey Magnus.
24 Busse and Hellekson (2006: 11).
25 Driscoll (2006: 79–96); Woledge (2006: 97–114).
26 Jenkins (1992: 177).
27 Hardwick (2003: 4).

Filmography

FEATURE FILMS

300 (2007). Directed by Zack Snyder. Legendary Pictures, Warner Bros.

Alexander (2004). Directed by Oliver Stone. Intermedia Films, Warner Bros.

Apocalypse Now (1979). Directed by Francis Ford Coppola. Zoetrope Studios, United Artists.

Asterix et Obelix: Mission Cleopatre (2002). Directed by Alain Chabat. Miramax Films.

The Basketball Diaries (1995). Directed by Scott Kalvert. New Line Cinema.

Ben-Hur (1959). Directed by William Wyler. Metro-Goldwyn-Mayer.

The Big Lebowski (1998). Directed by Joel Coen. Working Title Films, Gramercy Pictures.

The Birth of a Nation (1915). Directed by D. W. Griffith. David W. Griffith Corp.

Born Losers (1967). Directed by T. C. Frank. American International Pictures.

The Brave One (2007). Directed by Neil Jordan. Warner Bros. Pictures.

Caesar and Cleopatra (1945). Directed by Gabriel Pascal. Eagle-Lion Films.

Cleopatra (1917). Directed by J. Gordon Edwards. Fox Film Corporation.

Cleopatra (1934). Directed by Cecil B. DeMille. Paramount Pictures.

Cleopatra (1963). Directed by Joseph L. Mankiewicz. 20th Century Fox.

The Eagle (2011). Directed by Kevin Macdonald. Toledo Productions, Focus Features.

The Egyptian (1954). Directed by Michael Curtiz. 20th Century Fox.

Fiddler on the Roof (1971). Directed by Norman Jewison. The Mirisch Production Company, United Artists.

First Blood (1982). Directed by Ted Kotcheff. Orion Pictures.

Gangs of New York (2002). Directed by Martin Scorsese. Miramax Film Corp.

Gladiator (2000). Directed by Ridley Scott. DreamWorks Pictures, Universal Pictures.

The Godfather I–III (1972, 1974, 1990). Directed by Francis Ford Coppola. Paramount Pictures.

The Hangover (2009). Directed by Todd Phillips. Legendary Pictures, Warner Bros.

Jawbreaker (1999). Directed by Darren Stein. TriStar Pictures.

Kill Bill vol. I (2003). Directed by Quentin Tarantino. Miramax Films.

King Arthur (2004). Directed by Antoine Fuqua. Touchstone Pictures.

King of Kings (1961). Directed by Nicholas Ray. Samuel Bronston Productions, Metro-Goldwyn-Mayer.

Last Days of Pompeii (1935). Directed by Ernest B. Schoedsack. RKO Radio Pictures.

The Last Legion (2007). Directed by Doug Lefler. Dino de Laurentiis Company.

Little Caesar (1930). Directed by Mervyn LeRoy. First National Pictures.

Lock, Stock, and Two Smoking Barrels (1998). Directed by Guy Ritchie. SKA Films, The Steve Tisch Company, Summit Entertainment, Handmade Films.

The Long Good Friday (1980). Directed by John Mackenzie. Black Lion Films, Handmade Films.

The Lord of the Rings (2001, 2002, 2003). Directed by Peter Jackson. WingNut Films, New Line Cinema.

Mean Girls (2004). Directed by Mark Waters. Paramount Pictures.

The Mummy (1932). Directed by Karl Freund. Universal Studios.

Once Upon a Time in America (1984). Directed by Sergio Leone. The Ladd Company.

The Outlaw Josey Wales (1982). Directed by Clint Eastwood. Warner Bros. Pictures.

Party Girl (1958). Directed by Nicholas Ray. Euterpe, Metro-Goldwyn-Mayer.

Public Enemy (1931). Directed by William A. Wellman. Warner Bros. Pictures.

Road Trip (2000). Directed by Todd Phillips. DreamWorks Pictures.

Robin Hood: Men in Tights (1993). Directed by Mel Brooks. 20th Century Fox.

Scarface (1932). Directed by Howard Hawks. The Caddo Company, United Artists.

Scarface (1983). Directed by Brian De Palma. Universal Pictures.

Serpent of the Nile (1953). Directed by William Castle. Columbia Pictures.

The Sign of the Cross (1932). Directed by Cecil B. DeMille. Paramount Pictures.

Spartacus (1960). Directed by Stanley Kubrick. Bryna Productions, Universal Pictures.

Stop Loss (2008). Directed by Kimberly Peirce. MTV Films, Paramount Pictures.

Super Troopers (2001). Directed by Jay Chandrasekhar. Fox Searchlight.

The Ten Commandments (1956). Directed by Cecil B. DeMille. Paramount Pictures.

Thelma and Louise (1991). Directed by Ridley Scott. Metro-Goldwyn-Mayer.

This is 40 (2012). Directed by Judd Apatow. Universal Pictures.
Traffic (2000). Directed by Steven Soderbergh. Universal Pictures.
Trainspotting (1996). Directed by Danny Boyle. Channel Four Films.
Two Nights with Cleopatra (1953). Directed by Mario Mattoli. Excelsa Film.
The Untouchables (1987). Directed by Brian De Palma. Paramount Pictures.
Who's Afraid of Virginia Woolf? (1966). Directed by Mike Nichols. Warner Bros. Pictures.

TELEVISION SERIES AND FILMS

Battlestar Galactica (2004–9). Developed by Ronald D. Moore. Sci-Fi Channel.
Beauty and the Beast (1987–90). Created by Ron Koslow. CBS.
Blake's 7 (1978–81). Created by Terry Nation. BBC.
Cleopatra (1999). Directed by Franc Roddam. Hallmark Entertainment.
Desperate Housewives (2004–12). Created by Marc Cherry. ABC.
Dynasty (1981–9). Created by Esther and Richard Shapiro. ABC.
Gossip Girl (2007–12). Created by Josh Schwartz and Stephanie Savage. CW.
Homeland (2011–current). Developed by Howard Gordon and Alex Gansa. Showtime.
I, Claudius (1976). Produced by Martin Lisemore. BBC.
Imperium: Augustus (2003). Directed by Roger Young. EOS Entertainment.
Julius Caesar (2002). Directed by Uli Edel. De Angelis Group, TNT.
Masada (1981). Directed by Boris Sagal. ABC.
The Professionals (1977–83). Created by Brian Clemens. ITV
The Real Housewives (2006–12). Created by Scott Dunlop. Bravo.
Rome, Season One (2005). Created by Bruno Heller, William J. MacDonald, and John Milius. HBO BBC.
Rome, Season Two (2007). Created by Bruno Heller, William J. MacDonald, and John Milius. HBO BBC.
Roseanne (1988–97). Created by Matt Williams. ABC.
Sex and the City (1998–2004). Created by Darren Star. HBO.
The Sopranos (1999–2007). Created by David Chase. HBO.
Spartacus: Blood and Sand (2010). Created by Steven S. DeKnight. STARZ.
Spartacus: Gods of the Arena (2011). Created by Steven S. DeKnight. STARZ.
Spartacus: Vengeance (2012). Created by Steven S. DeKnight. STARZ.
Spartacus: War of the Damned (2013). Created by Steven S. DeKnight. STARZ.
Star Trek (The Original Series) (1966–9). Created by Gene Roddenberry. NBC.
That '70s Show (1998–2006). Created by Bonnie Turner, Terry Turner, and Mark Brazill. Fox.

Bibliography

Alföldy, G. (1985). *The Social History of Rome*. Trans. D. Braund and F. Pollock. London: Croom Helm.

Allen, A. (2008). "Staging Interiors in *Rome*'s Villas," in M. S. Cyrino (ed.), *Rome Season One: History Makes Television*. Oxford: Blackwell Publishing, 179–92.

Anbinder, T. (2001). *Five Points*. New York: Free Press.

Ando, C. (2011). "From Republic to Empire," in M. Peachin (ed.), *The Oxford Handbook of Social Relations in the Roman World*. Oxford: Oxford University Press, 37–66.

Augoustakis, A. (2008). "Women's Politics in the Streets of *Rome*," in M. S. Cyrino (ed.), *Rome Season One: History Makes Television*. Oxford: Blackwell Publishing, 117–29.

Augoustakis, A. (2013). "Partnership and Love in *Spartacus: Blood and Sand* (2010)," in M. S. Cyrino (ed.), *Screening Love and Sex in the Ancient World*. New York: Palgrave Macmillan, 157–66.

Austin, R. G. (ed.) (1971). *P. Vergili Maronis Aeneidos Liber Primus*. Oxford: Clarendon Press.

Axelrod-Contrada, J. (2008). *The Facts about Drugs and Society*. Tarrytown, NY: Marshall Cavendish Benchmark.

Babington, B. and P. Evans (1993). *Biblical Epics: Sacred Narrative in the Hollywood Cinema*. Manchester: Manchester University Press.

Baldwin, T. W. (1944). *William Shakspere's Small Latine & Lesse Greeke*. Urbana: University of Illinois Press.

Barnes, J. (2010). "Cinematical Seven: When Good Girls Get Revenge," *Moviefone.com*, October 7.

Barnes, J. (2011). "Vengeance, Thy Name Is Woman! So Says *The Brave One* and *Kill Bill*." *AMC Blog/amctv.com*.

Barrett, A. A. (2002). *Livia: First Lady of Imperial Rome*. New Haven, CT, and London: Yale University Press.

Bate, J. (1993). *Shakespeare and Ovid*. Oxford: Clarendon Press.

Baum, D. (2010). *The Non-Orthodox Jew's Guide to Orthodox Jews*. New York: Veracity Press.

Bial, H. (2005). *Acting Jewish: Negotiating Ethnicity on the*

American Stage and Screen. Ann Arbor: University of Michigan Press.

Bianco, R. (2007). "*Rome* goes into decline." *USATODAY.com*, January 11.

Blanshard, A. and K. Shahabudin (2011). *Classics on Screen: Ancient Greece and Rome on Film*. London: Duckworth.

Bowman, A. (1998). *Life and Letters on the Roman Frontier: Vindolanda and its People*. New York and London: Routledge.

Boyd, B. W. (2008). "Becoming Augustus: The Education of Octavian," in M. S. Cyrino (ed.), *Rome Season One: History Makes Television*. Oxford: Blackwell Publishing, 87–99.

Braden, G. (2004). "Plutarch, Shakespeare, and the Alpha Males," in C. Martindale and A. B. Taylor (eds), *Shakespeare and the Classics*. Cambridge: Cambridge University Press, 188–205.

Brice, L. L. (2008). "The Fog of War: The Army in *Rome*," in M. S. Cyrino (ed.), *Rome Season One: History Makes Television*. Oxford: Blackwell Publishing, 61–77.

Brice, L. L. (2011). "Disciplining Octavian: An Aspect of Roman Military Culture during the Triumviral Wars 44–30 BCE," in W. E. Lee (ed.), *Warfare and Culture in World History*. New York: New York University Press, 35–60.

Brink, C. O. (1971). *Horace on Poetry. The Ars Poetica*. Cambridge: Cambridge University Press.

Brunt, P. A. (1988 [1962]). "The Army and the Land in the Roman Revolution," *Journal of Roman Studies* 52: 69–86. Reprinted and revised in P. A. Brunt (ed.), *The Fall of the Roman Republic and Related Essays*. Oxford: Clarendon Press, 240–75.

Brunton, G. (1920). *Lahun I: The Treasure*. London: British School of Archaeology in Egypt.

Burrow, C. (2013). *Shakespeare and Classical Antiquity*. Oxford: Oxford University Press.

Busse, K. and K. Hellekson (2006). "Work in Progress," in K. Hellekson and K. Busse (eds), *Fan Fiction and Fan Communities in the Age of the Internet*. Jefferson, NC, and London: McFarland, 5–32.

Butrica, J. L. (2002). "The Medical Use of Cannabis Among the Greeks and Romans," *Journal of Cannabis Therapeutics* 2: 51–70.

Caluori, S. (2007). "HBO's Other Italian Drama," *imediaconnection.com*, January 9.

Carney, E. D. (2010). "Olympias and Oliver: Sex, Sexual Stereotyping, and Women in Oliver Stone's *Alexander*," in P. Cartledge and F. R. Greenland (eds), *Responses to Oliver Stone's Alexander*. Madison: University of Wisconsin Press, 135–67.

Carroll, B. E. (2003). *American Masculinities: A Historical Encyclopedia*. New York: The Moschovitis Group.

Carson, R. A. G. (1978). *Principal Coins of the Romans*. London: British Museum Press.

Carter, J. M. (1970). *The Battle of Actium: The Rise and Triumph of Augustus Caesar.* London: Hamish Hamilton.

Carter, P. (2007). "Drug Dealers as Folk Heroes? Drugs and Television Situation Comedy," in P. Manning (ed.), *Drugs and Popular Culture: Drugs, Media, and Identity in Contemporary Society*. Devon: Willan Publishing, 168–75.

Chocano, C. (2011). "'Housewives,' Rebranded." *The New York Times/ nytimes.com*, November 20.

Christensen, T. and P. J. Haas (2005). *Projecting Politics: Political Messages in American Film.* New York: M. E. Sharpe.

Clark, M. (1986). "Remembering Vietnam," *Cultural Critique* 3: 46–78.

Clatterbaugh, K. (1997). *Contemporary Perspectives on Masculinity: Men, Women and Politics in Modern Society.* 2nd edition. Boulder: Westview Press.

Cohen, B. (1972). *Sociocultural Changes in American Jewish Life as Reflected in Selected Jewish Literature.* Cranbury, NJ: Associated University Presses.

Connell, R. W. (2005). *Masculinities.* 2nd edition. Berkeley and Los Angeles: University of California Press.

Cook, A. (1996). "The Transmutation of Heroic Complexity: Plutarch and Shakespeare," *Classical and Modern Literature* 17.1: 31–43.

Cooke, B. (2008). "Caesar's Soldiers: The *Pietas* of Vorenus and Pullo," in M. S. Cyrino (ed.), *Rome Season One: History Makes Television.* Oxford: Blackwell Publishing, 78–86.

Crawford, J. (1984). *Marcus Tullius Cicero: The Lost and Unpublished Orations.* Göttingen: Vandenhoeck and Ruprecht.

Cyrino, M. S. (2005). *Big Screen Rome.* Oxford: Blackwell Publishing.

Cyrino, M. S. (ed.) (2008a). *Rome Season One: History Makes Television.* Oxford: Blackwell Publishing.

Cyrino, M. S. (2008b). "Introduction," in M. S. Cyrino (ed.), *Rome Season One: History Makes Television.* Oxford: Blackwell Publishing, 1–10.

Cyrino, M. S. (2008c). "Atia and the Erotics of Authority," in M. S. Cyrino (ed.), *Rome Season One: History Makes Television.* Oxford: Blackwell Publishing, 130–40.

Cyrino, M. S. (ed.) (2013a). *Screening Love and Sex in the Ancient World.* New York: Palgrave Macmillan.

Cyrino, M. S. (2013b). "Introduction: Screening Love and Sex in the Ancient World," in M. S. Cyrino (ed.), *Screening Love and Sex in the Ancient World.* New York: Palgrave Macmillan, 1–10.

Cyrino, M. S. (2014). "Ancient Sexuality on Screen," in T. K. Hubbard (ed.), *A Companion to Greek and Roman Sexualities.* Malden, MA, and Oxford: Blackwell Publishing, 613–28.

Daugherty, G. N. (2008). "Her First Roman: A Cleopatra for *Rome*," in M. S. Cyrino (ed.), *Rome Season One: History Makes Television.* Oxford: Blackwell Publishing, 141–52.

Daugherty, G. N. (2009). "The Greatest Story Ever Drawn: Cleopatra in American Comics," *International Journal of Comic Art* 11.2: 208–30.

Daugherty, G. N. (2013). "Glenn Close in *Maxie* (1985): A Chapter in the Social History of the Snake Bra," in M. S. Cyrino (ed.), *Screening Love and Sex in the Ancient World*. New York: Palgrave Macmillan, 183–94.

Del Sapio Garbero, M. (2009). *Identity, Otherness and Empire in Shakespeare's Rome*. Farnham: Ashgate Publishing.

Dessau, H. (1892–1916). *Inscriptiones Latinae Selectae*, three vols. Berlin: Weidmann.

Donaldson, M. (1993). "What is Hegemonic Masculinity?" *Theory and Society* 22.5: 643–57.

Driscoll, C. (2006). "One True Pairing: The Romance of Pornography and the Pornography of Romance," in K. Hellekson and K. Busse (eds), *Fan Fiction and Fan Communities in the Age of the Internet*. Jefferson, NC, and London: McFarland, 79–96.

Duff, T. (1999). *Plutarch's Lives: Exploring Virtue and Vice*. Oxford: Oxford University Press.

Edwards, C. (1993). *The Politics of Immorality in Ancient Rome*. Cambridge: Cambridge University Press.

Edwards, I. E. S. (1972). *The Treasures of Tutankhamun*. London: British Museum Press.

Edwards, T. (2006). *Cultures of Masculinity*. London and New York: Routledge.

Eichholz, D. E. (ed.) (1962). *Pliny: Natural History, Volume X*. Cambridge, MA: Harvard University Press.

Erens, P. (1984). *The Jew in American Cinema*. Bloomington: Indiana University Press.

Fairweather, J. (1984). "The Elder Seneca and Declamation," *Aufstieg und Niedergang der romischen Welt* II 32.1: 514–56.

Fien, A. (2009). "Postfeminism in Popular Culture: A Potential for Critical Resistance?" *Politics and Culture* 4, *politicsandculture.org*, November 9.

Fisher, C. D. (ed.) (1922). *Tacitus. Annales*. Oxford: Oxford University Press.

Flory, M. B. (1984). "*Sic exempla parantur*: Livia's Shrine to Concordia and the Porticus Liviae," *Historia* 33: 309–30.

Flory, M. B. (1988). "*Abducta Neroni Uxor*: The Historiographical Tradition on the Marriage of Octavian and Livia," *Transactions of the American Philological Association* 118: 343–59.

Fordham, G. (2004). "A Study in Ambiguity: *The Godfather* and the American Gangster Movie Tradition," *Crimeculture.com*. Reprinted in A. Silver and J. Ursini (eds), *Gangster Film Reader*. Pompton Plains, NJ: Limelight Editions, 2007, 165–82.

Friend, T. (2007). "Power Play: *Rome* Returns to HBO." *The New Yorker/ newyorker.com*, January 15.

Fuzier, J. (1974). "Rhetoric *Versus* Rhetoric: A Study of Shakespeare's *Julius Caesar*, Act III, Scene 2," *Cahiers Elisabethains* 5: 25–65.

Gabba, E. (1956). *Appiano e la storia delle guerre civili*. Florence: La Nuova Italia.

Gager, J. G. (1992). *Curse Tablets and Binding Spells from the Ancient World*. Oxford: Oxford University Press.

Gallman, J. M. (2003). "Review of 'Gangs of New York,'" *Journal of American History* 90: 1124–6.

Gantz, T. (1993). *Early Greek Myth*. Baltimore: Johns Hopkins University Press.

Garofalo, A. (2014). "*Game Of Thrones* Big Budgets Bring Huge Success: How HBO Series Makes Money With High Cost Per Episode," *International Business Times/ibtimes.com*, August 26.

Genz, S. and B. A. Brabon (2009). *Postfeminism: Cultural Texts and Theories*. Edinburgh: Edinburgh University Press.

Goddio, F. and M. Clauss (eds) (2006). *Egypt's Sunken Treasures*. Berlin: Prestel Publishing.

Gold, D. L. (1985). "Jewish English," in J. A. Fishman (ed.), *Readings in the Sociology of Jewish Languages*. Leiden: Brill, 280–98.

Grace, P. (2009). *The Religious Film: Christianity and the Hagiopic*. Malden, MA, and Oxford: Wiley Blackwell.

Graves, R. (1934). *I, Claudius*. New York: Vintage Books.

Green, S., C. Jenkins, and H. Jenkins (2006). "'Normal Female Interest in Men Bonking': Selections from the Terra Nostra Underground and Strange Bedfellows," in H. Jenkins (ed.), *Fans, Bloggers and Gamers: Exploring Participatory Culture*. New York and London: New York University Press, 61–88.

Greene, D. (2011). *The Jewish Origins of Cultural Pluralism: The Menorah Association and American Diversity (The Modern Jewish Experience)*. Bloomington: Indiana University Press.

Grist, L. (2007). "Drugs, the Family, and Recent American Cinema," in P. Manning (ed.), *Drugs and Popular Culture: Drugs, Media, and Identity in Contemporary Society*. Devon: Willan Publishing, 117–33.

Gudeman, A. (1902). *The Sources of Plutarch's Life of Cicero*. Philadelphia: University of Pennsylvania Press.

Halberstam, J. (1997). *Schmoozing: The Private Conversations of American Jews*. New York: Perigree Trade.

Hardwick, L. (2003). *Reception Studies. Greece and Rome New Surveys in the Classics no. 33*. Oxford: Oxford University Press.

Hark, I. R. (1993). "Animals or Romans: Looking at Masculinity in *Spartacus*," in S. Cohan and I. R. Hark (eds), *Screening the Male: Exploring Masculinities in Hollywood Cinema*. London and New York: Routledge, 151–72.

Haynes, H. (2008). "*Rome*'s Opening Titles: Triumph, Spectacle, and Desire," in M. S. Cyrino (ed.), *Rome Season One: History Makes Television*. Oxford: Blackwell Publishing, 49–60.

Heidenreich, S. and Roth, J. (2015). "Neurophysiology of Panic on the Ancient Battlefield," in L. L. Brice (ed.), *New Approaches to Greco-Roman Warfare*. Malden, MA, and Oxford: Wiley Blackwell, 129–43.

Heilman, S. C. (1995). *Portrait of American Jews: The Last Half of the Twentieth Century*. Seattle: University of Washington Press.

Helmling, S. (1992). "The Bitch Goddess Failure," *The Sewanee Review* 100.3: lxxix–lxxxi.

Henkin, D. (2003). "Review of 'Gangs of New York,'" *American Historical Review* 108: 620–1.

Hervé, H. (2007). "Psychopathy Through The Ages: A History of the Hare Psychopath," in H. Hervé and J. C. Yuille (eds), *The Psychopath: Theory, Research and Practice*. Mahwah, NJ: Lawrence Erlbaum Associates, 31–56.

Hibberd, J. (2008). "*Rome* Might Not be History, Series Creator Says," *The Hollywood Reporter*, December 1.

Hilliard, R. L. (2009). *Hollywood Speaks Out: Pictures That Dared To Protest Real World Issues*. Malden, MA, and Oxford: Wiley Blackwell.

Hills, M. (2002). *Fan Cultures*. London and New York: Routledge.

Holderness, G., B. Loughrey, and A. Murphy (eds) (1996). *Shakespeare: the Roman Plays*. London and New York: Longman.

Homeyer, H. (1977 [1964]). *Die antiken Berichte über den Tod Ciceros und ihre Quellen*. Baden-Baden: Bruno Grimm. Republished as "Die Quellen zu Cicero's Tod," *Helikon* 17: 56–96.

Hope, V. (2003). "Trophies and Tombstones: Commemorating the Roman Soldier," *World Archaeology* 35.1: 79–97.

Humphries-Brooks, S. (2006). *Cinematic Savior: Hollywood's Making of the American Christ*. Westport, CT: Praeger Publishers.

Jaffe, A. (2005). *What Do You Mean, You Can't Eat In My Home? A Guide To How Newly Observant Jews And Their Less-Observant Relatives Can Still Get Along*. New York: Schocken Books.

Jenkins, H. (1992). *Textual Poachers: Television Fans and Participatory Culture*. New York and London: Routledge.

John, E. (2010). "Cleopatra? She's All Woman," *The Guardian.com*, April 3.

Jones, P. J. (2006). *Cleopatra: A Sourcebook*. Norman: University of Oklahoma.

Joshel, S. R. (2001). "*I, Claudius*: Projection and Imperial Soap Opera," in S. R. Joshel, M. Malamud, and D. T. McGuire, Jr. (eds), *Imperial Projections: Ancient Rome in Modern Popular Culture*. Baltimore: Johns Hopkins University Press, 119–61.

Jospe, R., T. G. Madsen, and S. Ward (2001). *Covenant and Chosenness in Judaism and Mormonism*. Denver: University of Denver Press.

Kahn, C. (1997). *Roman Shakespeare: Warriors, Wounds, and Women*. London and New York: Routledge.

Kamiya, G. (2007). "Fueled by Obscenity, HBO's series *Rome* Shocks Us Back 2,000 Years – and Reflects the Horror Show in Iraq Today," *Salon.com*, February 13.
Keaveney, A. (2007). *The Army in the Roman Revolution*. London and New York: Routledge.
Kelly, R. (2009). "The Iconography of Mark Antony," *Networking Knowledge: Journal of the MeCCSA Postgraduate Network* 2.1: 1–16.
Kelly, R. (2010). "Th' Abstract of All Faults: Antony vs. The Hegemonic Man," *Networking Knowledge: Journal of the MeCCSA Postgraduate Network* 3.1: 1–16.
Kelly, R. (2013). "Virility and Licentiousness in *Rome*'s Mark Antony (2005–7)," in M. S. Cyrino (ed.), *Screening Love and Sex in the Ancient World*. New York: Palgrave Macmillan, 195–209.
Kelly, R. (2014). *Mark Antony and Popular Culture: Masculinity and the Construction of an Icon*. London: I. B. Tauris.
Kennedy, G. A. (1994). *A New History of Classical Rhetoric*. Princeton: Princeton University Press.
Keppie, L. (1983). *Colonisation and Veteran Settlement in Italy, 47–14 B.C.* London: British School at Rome.
Kirk, G. S. (1974). *The Nature of Greek Myths*. Harmondsworth: Penguin Books.
Kleiner, D. E. E. (1996). "Imperial Women as Patrons of the Arts in the Early Empire," in D. E. E. Kleiner and S. B. Matheson (eds), *I, Claudia: Women in Ancient Rome*. New Haven, CT: Yale University Art Gallery, and Austin: University of Texas Press, 28–41.
Kleiner, D. E. E. (2005). *Cleopatra and Rome*. Cambridge, MA: Harvard University Press.
Knapp, R. (2005). *The American Musical and the Formation of National Identity*. Princeton: Princeton University Press.
Kofman, L. (2007). "On Becoming a Jew," *Griffithreview.com*, Edition 15.
Kolnai, A. (2005). *Sexual Ethics: The Meaning and Foundations of Sexual Morality*. Trans. and ed. F. Dunlop. Aldershot: Ashgate Publishing.
Kritikos, P. G. and S. P. Papadaki (1967). "The History of the Poppy and of Opium and their Expansion in Antiquity in the Eastern Mediterranean Area," *Bulletin of Narcotics* 19: 17–38.
Lacey, W. K. (1974). "Octavian in the Senate, January 27 BC," *Journal of Roman Studies* 64: 176–84.
Lacey, W. K. (1978). *Cicero and the End of the Roman Republic*. London: Hodder and Stoughton.
Laurence, R. (1997). "History and Female Power at Rome," in T. Cornell and K. Lomas (eds), *Gender and Ethnicity in Ancient Italy*. London: Accordia, 129–39.
Leca, A.-P. (1982). *The Cult of the Immortal: Mummies and the Ancient Egyptian Way of Death*. London: Paladin Books.
Leitch, T. (2002). *Crime Films*. Cambridge: Cambridge University Press.

Lehman, P. (1993). "Don't Blame This on a Girl: Female Rape-Revenge Films," in S. Cohan and I. R. Hark (eds), *Screening the Male: Exploring Masculinities in the Hollywood Cinema*. New York and London: Routledge, 103–17.

Levine, L. (2005). *The Ancient Synagogue*. New Haven, CT: Yale University Press.

Lichtheim, M. (1975). *Ancient Egyptian Literature: Volume I: The Old and Middle Kingdoms*. Berkeley: University of California Press.

Lindemann, D. J. (2012). *Dominatrix: Gender, Eroticism, and Control in the Dungeon*. Chicago: University of Chicago Press.

Lott, J. B. (2004). *The Neighbourhoods of Augustan Rome*. Cambridge: Cambridge University Press.

Lotz, A. D. (2001). "Postfeminist Television Criticism: Rehabilitating Critical Terms and Identifying Postfeminist Attributes," *Feminist Media Studies* 1.1: 105–21.

Lowry, B. (2007). "Review: 'Rome,'" *Variety.com*, January 11.

MacInnes, J. (1998). *The End of Masculinity*. Buckingham: Open University Press.

MacMullen, R. (1990 [1984]). "The Legion as Society," *Historia* 33: 440–56. Reprinted in *Changes in the Roman Empire*. Princeton: Princeton University Press, 225–35.

Malek, J. (1993). *The Cat in Ancient Egypt*. London: British Museum Press.

Manniche, L. (1987). *Sexual Life in Ancient Egypt*. London: Kegan Paul International.

Manning, P. (ed.) (2007). *Drug Use in Popular Culture: Drugs, Media, and Identity in Contemporary Society*. Devon: Willan Publishing.

Martindale, C. and M. Martindale (1994). *Shakespeare and the Uses of Antiquity*. London and New York: Routledge.

Martindale, C. and A. B. Taylor (2004). *Shakespeare and the Classics*. Cambridge: Cambridge University Press.

McDermott, W. (1972). "M. Cicero and M. Tiro," *Historia* 21: 259–86.

McFarland, M. (2007). "On TV: Hail to the Return of HBO's 'Rome,'" *Seattle Post-Intelligencer/seattlepi.com*, January 10.

McRobbie, A. (2008). *The Aftermath of Feminism: Gender, Culture and Social Change*. London: Sage Publications.

Miles, G. B. (1989). "How Roman are Shakespeare's 'Romans'?" *Shakespeare Quarterly* 40.3: 257–83.

Millar, F. (1964). *A Study of Cassius Dio*. Oxford: Clarendon Press.

Miller, M. (2012). *The Song of Achilles*. London: Bloomsbury.

Miola, R. S. (1983). *Shakespeare's Rome*. Cambridge: Cambridge University Press.

Moles, J. (1988). *Plutarch. The Life of Cicero*. Warminster: Aris and Phillips.

Monfette, C. and J. Vejvoda (2009). "Rome – The Complete Series Review: Et Tu HBO? Another Amazing Series Release?" *IGN Entertainment/ign.com*, November 17.

Morgan, L. (1998). "Assimilation and Civil War: Hercules and Cacus (*Aen.* 8.185–267)," in H.-P. Stahl (ed.), *Vergil's Aeneid: Augustan Epic and Political Context*. London: Duckworth, 175–97.

Mossman, J. (ed.) (1997). *Plutarch and His Intellectual World: Essays on Plutarch*. London: Duckworth.

Mowat, B. A. and P. Werstine (eds) (1992). *Folger Shakespeare Library: Julius Caesar*. New York: Simon and Schuster.

Mozley, J. H. and G. P. Goold (eds) (1979 [1929]). *Ovid. The Art of Love and Other Poems*. 2nd edition. Cambridge, MA: Harvard University Press.

Mulvey, L. (1975). "Visual Pleasure and Narrative Cinema," *Screen* 16.3: 6–18.

Mynors, R. A. B. (ed.) (1969). *P. Vergili Maronis Opera*. Oxford: Clarendon Press.

Ogilvie, R. M. (ed.) (1965). *A Commentary on Livy, Books 1–5*. Oxford: Oxford University Press.

Opelt, I. (1965). *Die lateinischen Schimpfwörter und verwandte sprachliche Erscheinungen*. Heidelberg: Carl Winter.

Peachin, M. (ed.) (2011). *The Oxford Handbook of Social Relations in the Roman World*. Oxford: Oxford University Press.

Peers, P. M. (2009). "Brothers Are Better Than Sisters: A Semiotic, Feminist Analysis of HBO's *Rome*," MA thesis, University of Nevada, Las Vegas.

Pelling, C. B. R. (ed.) (1988). *Plutarch: Life of Antony*. Cambridge: Cambridge University Press.

Pelling, C. B. R. (1997). "Plutarch on Caesar's Fall," in J. Mossman (ed.), *Plutarch and His Intellectual World: Essays on Plutarch*. London: Duckworth, 215–32.

Pelling, C. B. R. (2002). *Plutarch and History*. Swansea: Classical Press of Wales.

Perrin, B. (ed. and trans.) (1918–20). *Plutarch: Parallel Lives, Volumes 6, 7, and 9*. Cambridge, MA: Harvard University Press.

Perry, J. S. (2011). "Organized Societies: *Collegia*," in M. Peachin (ed.), *The Oxford Handbook of Social Relations in the Roman World*. Oxford: Oxford University Press, 499–515.

Petersson, T. (1920). *Cicero: A Biography*. Berkeley: University of California Press.

Petrie, W. M. F., G. Brunton, and M. A. Murray (eds) (1923). *Lahun II*. London: British School of Archaeology in Egypt.

Pierce, J. B. (2013). "Oliver Stone's Unmanning of Alexander the Great in *Alexander* (2004)," in M. S. Cyrino (ed.), *Screening Love and Sex in the Ancient World*. New York: Palgrave Macmillan, 127–42.

Press, A. L. (1991). *Women Watching Television: Gender, Class, and Generation in the American Television Experience*. Philadelphia: University of Pennsylvania Press.

Projansky, S. (2001). *Watching Rape: Film and Television in Postfeminist Culture*. New York: New York University Press.

Purcell, N. (1985). "Livia and the Womanhood of Rome," *Proceedings of the Cambridge Philological Society* 211 [31]: 78–105.

Rankov, B. (2007). "Military Forces," in P. Sabin, M. Whitby, and H. van Wees (eds), *The Cambridge History of Greek and Roman Warfare*, vol. 2. Cambridge: Cambridge University Press, 30–75.

Raucci, S. (2008). "Spectacle of Sex: Bodies on Display in *Rome*," in M. S. Cyrino (ed.), *Rome Season One: History Makes Television*. Oxford: Blackwell Publishing, 207–18.

Raucci, S. (2013). "The Order of Orgies: Sex and the Cinematic Roman," in M. S. Cyrino (ed.), *Screening Love and Sex in the Ancient World*. New York: Palgrave Macmillan, 143–56.

Rausch, M. (ed.) (1998). *La Gloire d'Alexandrie*. Paris: Musée du Petit Palais.

Rawson, E. (1975). *Cicero, A Portrait*. London: Allen Lane.

Reiss, W. (2011). "The Roman Bandit (*latro*) as Criminal and Outsider," in M. Peachin (ed.), *The Oxford Handbook of Social Relations in the Roman World*. Oxford: Oxford University Press, 693–714.

Renger, A.-B. and J. Solomon (eds) (2013). *Ancient Worlds in Film and Television: Gender and Politics*. Leiden: Brill.

Rice, L. (2007). "Winter TV Preview: *Rome*," *Entertainment Weekly* 915: 35, January 12.

Richardson, L. (1992). *A New Topographical Dictionary of Ancient Rome*. Baltimore: Johns Hopkins University Press.

Riehle, W. (1990). *Shakespeare, Plautus and the Humanist Tradition*. Cambridge: D. S. Brewer.

Ritterband, P. (1995). "Modern Times and Jewish Assimilation," in R. M. Seltzer and N. J. Cohen (eds), *The Americanization of the Jews*. New York: New York University Press, 377–94.

Rodgers, Z. (2006). "HBO Promotes 'Rome' in Catfight Style," *clickz.com*, December 7.

Roe, J. (2004) "'Character' in Plutarch and Shakespeare: Brutus, Julius Caesar, and Mark Antony," in C. Martindale and A. B. Taylor (eds), *Shakespeare and the Classics*. Cambridge: Cambridge University Press, 173–87.

Rolfe, J. C. (ed.) (1914). *Suetonius. Lives of the Caesars, Volume I*. Cambridge, MA: Harvard University Press.

Roller, D. W. (2010). *Cleopatra: A Biography*. Oxford: Oxford University Press.

Roller, M. B. (1997). "Color-blindness: Cicero's Death, Declamation, and the Production of History," *Classical Philology* 92: 109–30.

Rosso, A. M. (2010). "Poppy and Opium in Ancient Times: Remedy or Narcotic?" *Biomedicine International* 1: 81–7.

Rothwell, K. S. (2004). *A History of Shakespeare on Screen: A Century of Film and Television*. 2nd edition. New York and Cambridge: Cambridge University Press.

Russell, D. A. F. M. (1983). *Greek Declamation*. Cambridge: Cambridge University Press.

Sante, L. (1991). *Low Life: Lures and Snares of Old New York*. New York: Vintage.

Saylor, S. (2005). "Quo Vadis, HBO?" *Stevensaylor.com*.

Schoonhoven, H. (ed.) (1992). *The Pseudo-Ovidian* Ad Liviam De Morte Drusi*: A Critical Text with Introduction and Commentary*. Groningen: Egbert Forsten.

Schwarzbaum, L. (2007). "Empire's State," *Entertainment Weekly* 917: 63, January 26.

Seo, J. M. (2008). "The Gender Gap: Religious Spaces in *Rome*," in M. S. Cyrino (ed.), *Rome Season One: History Makes Television*. Oxford: Blackwell Publishing, 168–78.

Severy, B. (2003). *Augustus and the Family at the Birth of the Roman Empire*. New York and London: Routledge.

Shay, J. (2002). *Odysseus in America: Combat Trauma and the Trials of Homecoming*. New York: Scribners.

Shelton, J. (1998). *As the Romans Did: A Sourcebook in Roman Social History*, 2nd edition. Oxford and New York: Oxford University Press.

Shields, S. A. (2002). *Speaking from the Heart: Gender and the Social Meaning of Emotion*. Cambridge: Cambridge University Press.

Silver, A. and J. Ursini (eds) (2007). *Gangster Film Reader*. Pompton Plains, NJ: Limelight Editions.

Skinner, M. B. (2010). "*Alexander* and Ancient Greek Sexuality: Some Theoretical Considerations," in P. Cartledge and F. R. Greenland (eds), *Responses to Oliver Stone's Alexander*. Madison: University of Wisconsin Press, 119–34.

Stamp, J. (2007). *Rome*. London: DK ADULT.

Stanley, A. (2005). "HBO's Roman Holiday," *The New York Times/nytimes.com*, August 21.

Stanley, A. (2007). "Television Review: Friends, Romans, Countrymen, Lovers, Haters, Murderers, Barbarians," *The New York Times/nytimes.com*, January 12.

Stasi, M. (2006). "The Toy Soldiers from Leeds: The Slash Palimpsest," in K. Hellekson and K. Busse (eds), *Fan Fiction and Fan Communities in the Age of the Internet*. Jefferson, NC, and London: McFarland, 115–33.

Stevens, D. (2005). "Toga Party: HBO's *Rome* is an Expensively Mounted, Lovingly Researched Snore," *Slate.com*, August 26.

Stransky, T. (2007). "DVD: *Rome*, Season 2," *Entertainment Weekly* 948: 59, August 17.

Stringer, R. (2011). "From Victim to Vigilante: Gender, Violence, and Revenge in *The Brave One* and *Hard Candy*," in R. Stringer and H. Radner (eds), *Feminism at the Movies: Understanding Gender in Contemporary Popular Cinema*. New York and London: Routledge, 268–82.

Strong, A. K. (2008). "Vice is Nice: *Rome* and Deviant Sexuality," in

M. S. Cyrino (ed.), *Rome Season One: History Makes Television*. Oxford: Blackwell Publishing, 219–31.

Strong, A. K. (2013). "Objects of Desire: Female Gazes and Male Bodies in *Spartacus: Blood and Sand* (2010)," in M. S. Cyrino (ed.), *Screening Love and Sex in the Ancient World*. New York: Palgrave Macmillan, 167–82.

Tarpin, M. (2002). Vici *et* pagi *dans l'Occident romain*. Rome: École française de Rome.

Tasker, Y. and D. Negra (2005). "In Focus: Postfeminism and Contemporary Media Studies," *Cinema Journal* 44.2: 107–10.

Tatum, W. J. (2008). "Making History in *Rome*: Ancient vs. Modern Perspectives," in M. S. Cyrino (ed.), *Rome Season One: History Makes Television*. Oxford: Blackwell Publishing, 29–41.

Taylor, A. B. (ed.) (2000). *Shakespeare's Ovid: The Metamorphoses in the Plays and Poems*. New York and Cambridge: Cambridge University Press.

Thomas, R. F. T. (ed.) (1988). *Virgil: Georgics, Volume 1: Books I–II*. Cambridge: Cambridge University Press.

Thompson, S. (1946). *The Folktale*. Berkeley and Los Angeles: University of California Press.

Torok, L. (1995). *Hellenistic and Roman Terracottas from Egypt*. Rome: L'erma di Bretschneider.

Toscano, M. M. (2008). "Gowns and Gossip: Gender and Class Struggle in *Rome*," in M. S. Cyrino (ed.), *Rome, Season One: History Makes Television*. Oxford: Blackwell Publishing, 153–67.

Toscano, M. M. (2013). "The Womanizing of Mark Antony: Virile Ruthlessness and Redemptive Cross-Dressing in *Rome*, Season Two," in A.-B. Renger and J. Solomon (eds), *Ancient Worlds in Film and Television: Gender and Politics*. Leiden: Brill, 123–35.

Tritle, L. A. (2000). *From Melos to My Lai: War and Survival*. London and New York: Routledge.

Tritle, L. A. (2015). "Soldiers Home: Life After Battle," in L. L. Brice (ed.), *New Approaches to Greco-Roman Warfare*. Malden, MA, and Oxford: Wiley Blackwell, 34–46.

Trope, B. T., S. Quirke, and P. Lacovara (eds) (2005). *Excavating Egypt: Great Discoveries from the Petrie Museum of Egyptian Archaeology*. Atlanta: Michael C. Carlos Museum, Emory University.

Vaznetti (2007). "Whip Hand," *LiveJournal.com*, March 12.

Walbank, F. W. (1960). "History and Tragedy," *Historia* 9: 216–34.

Walker, S. and P. Higgs (eds) (2001). *Cleopatra of Egypt: From History to Myth*. London: British Museum Press.

Walkowitz, D. J. (2003). "'The Gangs of New York': the Mean Streets in History," *History Workshop Journal* 56: 204–9.

Warshow, R. (2007 [1948]). "The Gangster as Tragic Hero," *Partisan Review* 15.2. Reprinted in A. Silver and J. Ursini (eds), *Gangster Film Reader*. Pompton Plains, NJ: Limelight Editions, 11–18.

Wenzel, D. (2005). *Kleopatra im Film: Eine Koenigen Aegyptens als Sinnbild fuer orientalischee Kultur. Filmstudien* 33. Remscheid: Gardez! Verlag.

Whitehead, S. M. and F. J. Barrett (2001). "The Sociology of Masculinity," in S. M. Whitehead and F. J. Barrett (eds), *The Masculinities Reader*. Cambridge: Polity Press, 1–26.

Williamson, M. (2005). *The Lure of the Vampire: Gender, Fiction and Fandom from Bram Stoker to Buffy*. London and New York: Wallflower Press.

Wills, G. (2011). *Rome and Rhetoric: Shakespeare's Julius Caesar*. New Haven, CT, and London: Yale University Press.

Winkler, M. M. (1985). "Classical Mythology and the Western Film," *Comparative Literature Studies* 22.4: 516–40.

Winkler, M. M. (ed.) (2004). *Gladiator: Film and History*. Oxford: Blackwell Publishing.

Winkler, M. M. (ed.) (2006). *Spartacus: Film and History*. Oxford: Blackwell Publishing.

Wiseman, T. P. (1993). "Lying Historians: Seven Types of Mendacity," in C. Gill and T. P. Wiseman (eds), *Lies and Fiction in the Ancient World*. Austin: University of Texas Press, 122–46.

Witt, R. E. (1971). *Isis in the Ancient World*. Baltimore: Johns Hopkins University Press.

Woledge, E. (2005). "From Slash to the Mainstream: Female Writers and Gender Blending Men," *Extrapolation* 46: 50–65.

Woledge, E. (2006). "Intimatopia: Genre Intersections Between Slash and the Mainstream," in K. Hellekson and K. Busse (eds), *Fan Fiction and Fan Communities in the Age of the Internet*. Jefferson, NC, and London: McFarland, 97–114.

Wood, R. (2007 [1968]). *Howard Hawks*. Garden City, NY: Doubleday, 52–8. Reprinted as "Scarface," in A. Silver and J. Ursini (eds), *Gangster Film Reader*. Pompton Plains, NJ: Limelight Editions, 19–28.

Woodworth, D. C. (1935). "Review: *I, Claudius* by Robert Graves," *Classical Journal* 30.6: 366–9.

Wright, A. (2001). "The Death of Cicero. Forming a Tradition: the Contamination of History," *Historia* 50: 436–52.

Wyke, M. (1994). "Woman in the Mirror: The Rhetoric of Adornment in the Roman World," in L. J. Archer, S. Fischler, and M. Wyke (eds), *Women in Ancient Societies: An Illusion of the Night*. New York: MacMillan, 134–51.

Wyke, M. (1997). *Projecting the Past: Ancient Rome, Cinema and History*. New York and London: Routledge.

Wyke, M. (2007). *Julius Caesar: A Life in Western Culture*. London: Granta Books.

Zanker, P. (1988). *The Power of Images in the Age of Augustus*. Trans. A. Shapiro. Ann Arbor: University of Michigan Press.

Index

EU Authorised Representative:
Easy Access System Europe Mustamäe tee 50, 10621 Tallinn, Estonia
gpsr.requests@easproject.com

Printed and bound by CPI Group (UK) Ltd, Croydon, CR0 4YY
29/09/2026
02224986-0010